**Architectural Design** 55 5/6-1985

Editorial Offices: 42 Leinster Gardens, London W2 ☎01-402 2141  Subscriptions: 7/8 Holland Street London W8 ☎01-402 2141

EDITOR
**Dr Andreas C Papadakis**
HOUSE EDITOR: Frank Russell
CONSULTANTS: Catherine Cooke, Dennis Crompton,
Kenneth Frampton, Charles Jencks, Leon Krier, Robert Maxwell, Demetri Porphyrios, Colin Rowe, Derek Walker

## Architectural Design Profile 59

# SCHOOL OF VENICE

### Guest-edited by Luciano Semerani

MASSIMO SCOLARI, 'ACROPOLI', 1985

Venice is one of the oldest schools of architecture in Europe and, in 1936, with the arrival of Giuseppe Samonà, it once again became a centre for innovative thinking, a 'city of exile' in Luciano Semerani's words, for restless, non-academic intellectuals from Samonà and Bruno Zevi to Carlo Aymonino and Manfredo Tafuri. The progressive teaching of the School of Venice has, in recent years, contributed to a major re-evaluation of the Modern Movement and especially to our understanding of typology and figuration. This issue is presented in six major sections – the City, the Territory, Type, Figuration, Architectural History and Representation – and features essays and projects by outstanding architects including Carlo Aymonino, Augusto Romano Burelli, Vittorio Gregotti, Gianugo Polesello, Aldo Rossi and Giuseppe Samonà among others, all of whose work derives from and contributes to the *genius loci* of Venice. For a full list of contents, see page 3.

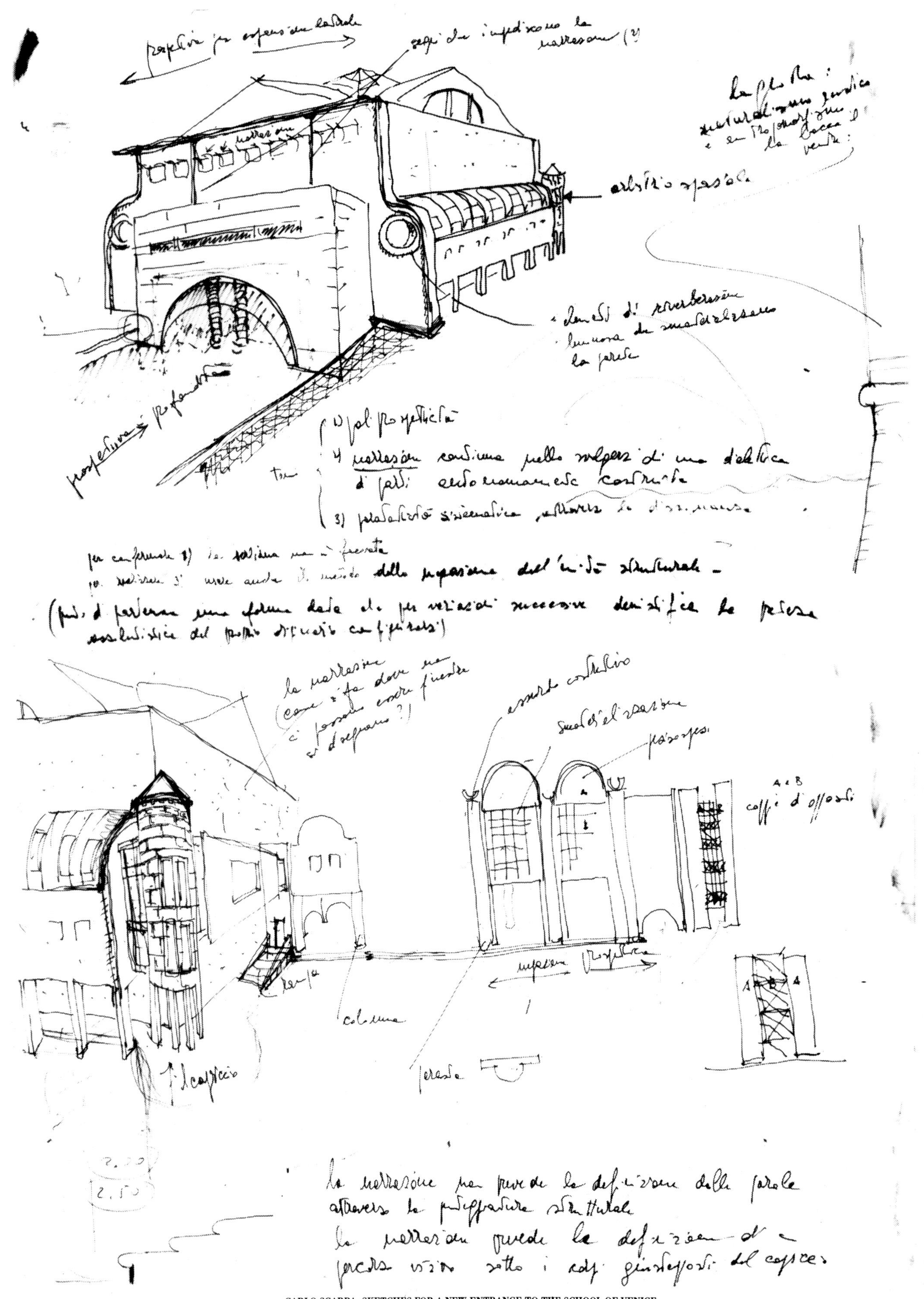

CARLO SCARPA, SKETCHES FOR A NEW ENTRANCE TO THE SCHOOL OF VENICE

# THE SCHOOL OF

# VENICE

## Guest-edited by Luciano Semerani


**INTRODUCTION**
Luciano Semerani *Why Not?* 4

**THE CITY**
Giuseppe Samonà *An Assessment of the Future of the City* 16
Aldo Rossi *What is to be Done with Old Cities?* 19
Luciano Semerani *Hypothesis for the Restructuring of the Town of Mestre Altobello* 24

**THE TERRITORY**
Vittorio Gregotti *Territory and Architecture* 28
Vittorio Gregotti *Project for the Venice Lagoon: A Student Thesis* 35

**THE TYPE**
Gianugo Polesello *Typology and Composition in Architecture* 40
Augusto Romano Burelli *Unearthing the Type* 45
Carlo Aymonino *Type and Typology* 49
Aldo Rossi *The Architecture of the Squares in the Veneto: A Student Thesis* 52

**FIGURATION**
Giuseppe Samonà *Architectural Traditionalism and Internationalism* 57
Luciano Semerani and Gigetta Tamaro *The New Town Hall at Osoppo* 60
Oswald Zoeggeler *Competition for the Conversion of the Old Cotton Mill in Venice* 63
Gino Valle *New Housing on Giudecca Island, Venice* 67

**THE DEPARTMENT OF ARCHITECTURAL HISTORY**
Paolo Morachiello *The Department of Architectural History* 70

**REPRESENTATION**
Massimo Scolari *Elements for a History of Axonometry* 73
Massimo Scolari *Suggestions for an Exercise on Palladio* 79



The Guest-Editor thanks Giovanni Fraziano, a researcher at the School,
for his conceptual contribution to this issue.

# LUCIANO SEMERANI
## Why Not?

BÖCKLIN, SKETCH FOR 'THE ASSAULT OF THE PIRATES' (HESSISCHES LANDESMUSEUM)

*Ever since humanity has known the greatness of classical antiquity, the great masters have had but one thought: am I teaching as Socrates would have taught?*

**T**HERE ARE OTHER MODELS FOR SCHOOLS IN THE world. Our profession has two: the Ecole des Beaux-Arts, and the Ecole des Ponts et Chaussées. Together they make an antinomic pair. These two types of school still exist, in fragmented alternatives, within many of our institutions throughout the world. Not only do they survive: they are in perpetual competition with one another. But the fact that these models are still being kept alive in Philadelphia or Berlin does not prove that the cultural or scientific grounds on which they were founded in the eighteenth or nineteenth century are still topical and vital today.

In 1936 a barbarian came to Venice. He was Giuseppe Samonà: an engineer, a Sicilian aristocrat, a provincial. In the long period of transition commonly known as the Decline of the Roman Empire, the barbarians were the only ones who could maintain security and keep power in their hands. Samonà became emperor. Slowly, but tenaciously and intelligently, he destroyed the legacy of Venice's Accademia delle Belle Arti; conventions that were also rules, techniques, that constituted a profession.

To do this, he turned to the Modern Movement, the formalism of Rietveld, to Frank Lloyd Wright and the prophecies of Le Corbusier and he used the suggestions they offered without espousing their causes. Samonà played a cunning game with the Modern Movement, setting against it not architecture but economics, sociology and anthropology, mixed with a large dose of philosophical idealism. He thus gave the ingenuous avant-garde its due, countering its detachment of words from things, quite simply, with material reality. In this way he overcame storms, fashions and switches in taste to create a safe climate for the formation of a school of architecture within the university.

Exile is the tradition of our school; from its founding, it has taken in refugees from the polytechnics in Milan and Turin, ill-suited or unruly intellectuals, or possibly those who were not academic enough for Rome. Samonà and Zevi, and Aymonino and Tafuri have come here. The history of the IUAV (*Instituto Universitario di Architettura di Venezia*) from 1926 to 1984 could be summed up with just three images: enforced co-existence, a tormented passion for architecture (the object and also the cause of imprisonment) and betrayal interwoven with tradition.

It seems we have to choose between building and knowing. We might lament, with Paul Valery's Socrates: *Within me there was an architect whom circumstances did not fulfil.*

In choosing building, Samonà locked the philospher inside the architect, but tried to make the two souls co-exist. His originality lay in his reinterpretation of the origins of the modern city. He attacked the ingenuous disurbanism of historians and sociologists and so-called urbanists, whether rationalist or organic, put the schematism of the Athens Charter in doubt and ridiculed the 'urbanist as demiurge' who was then, as now, a product of the Ecole des Beaux-Arts.

The enormous breadth and depth of architectural and urban phenomena throughout the ages thus crushed the prophecies of the 'machine architects' in a triumph of facts over ideologies. For Samonà, the architect needed an awareness of the richness of life, the complexity of behavioural sciences, the pluridisciplinality of analyses and the materialism of data. This of course made the architect's profession almost impossible, but it meant that the architect could not camouflage himself as a political co-ordinator or designer or territorialist. On the contrary, he had to fit himself into a strong and traditional discipline where architecture and town-planning were brought together in a single unity.

The next step was to unravel the history of the city with the eyes of the architect and put architecture at the centre of relations with the past and future. Three productive contradictions are immediately obvious.
a) No single universal *treatise* can resolve the relationship between the theory (or theories) of architecture and the inventive process, so we must retain individual theoretical principles in the border area. This requires a true intellectual 're-founding'.
b) When historians and architects in Italy reconsidered the theories of architecture, they divided themselves into two groups; those who put forward *composition* as the centre of architecture, and those who believed in the practice of *design* completely independent of the historical theories of architecture.
c) Because it is impossible to resolve the relationship between architecture and planning and management there is a breach between the planner's techniques and the architect's practices; autobiographical, literary passions for the city are pitted against the reliable management practices of the planners.

Samonà's 'open' reading finds more or less naive, more or less enlightened, more or less faithful followers to carry it on.

Aymonino talks of architecture as a strictly urban *phenomenon*, the antithesis of the term used by those who construct urban and architectural history ideologically, outside the *experience of the real city*. Morphology must provide us with answers that do not depend so much upon an ideal and universal interpretation of things as a pragmatic attitude which sees the *reasons* of architecture in the material conditions of development, in particular the material conditions which make the building of the city possible.

Polesello talks not of phenomena—a complex interweaving of forms and functions—but of *urban facts*, a term which encompasses some urban manifestations which may once have been, or are still to become, *buildings* (architecture). The material data of the city, as *urban facts*, may be denatured by being essentially accidental or physical, and thus comparable to natural phenomena. In this case, they undergo a normative standardisation into homogeneous classes and abstract schemes.

At the IUAV, under the heading *urban analysis*, the themes of *city* and *territory*, and *type* and *figuration* have been reconsidered and developed. In Samonà's theories, these pairs co-existed, but now they are seen to be in positive opposition to each other. City, territory, type and figuration are the conceptual figures of the 're-founding' of the theory of architecture, an operation made possible because the school is a monastery.

At this point, it is necessary to provide an answer to the questions: Does the re-evaluation of a disciplinary *corpus*, the attempt at some return to conceptual unity, coincide with genuine restoration? How does a plan for 're-founding' differ from an attempt at restoration?

*Que' cittadin che poi la rifondarono*
*Sovra'l cener che d'Attila rimase*—Dante
(Those citizens then refounded it
On the ashes left by Attila)

Anyone involved in 're-founding' *knows* that the previous founding is always an heroic and ideal action that cannot be repeated; the 're-founder' does not identify with the founder, he knows the reason for the ashes and that they can never be completely forgotten. Restoration was the tool used by the Nazis and the Fascists, who pretended to ignore (out of bad faith) or actually did ignore (out of stupidity) revolution and the reason for revolution, merely imitating heroes and ideals. On the other hand, 're-founding' belongs to the post-modernists. What belongs to the post-modern condition is the necessity to go beyond the 'silence' and return to using words ironically, not innocently. The answer is not in a post-modern style; far from it. The necessity of a style derives from two classic, contrasting definitions:
a) Style is recognisable through the repetition of elements (phonetic, morphological, syntactical, linguistic) which are common to the works of a particular era, nation, genre (tragi-comic, lyric). In this way style is recognisable as the implicit or explicit observance of a body of rules.

*It is the unity of multiplicity*—Goethe. *It lies in the nobility of the form*—Viollet-le-Duc. It is also the exact, rational adaptation of one's own strengths to the difficulties created by the disciplinary conventions of an exercise, whether the exercise is the playing of piano music or acrobatics on parallel bars.
b) Alternatively style is an individual's ability to give himself a style (like Saba, or the Beatles). In this case, style can be based on either internal bodies of rules or (as in Petrarchan formulae and oriental sonorities) on references to external bodies of rules which have been adapted to compositional abilities, individual wisdom and the individual's

GUIDO CIRILLI, COMPETITION FOR THE WAR MEMORIAL AT CHIARAVALLE 1927
(VENICE ACADEMY OF FINE ARTS)

way of being and feeling. Rational self-critical adaptation and striving towards the essential ensures that this individual style does not become a vain seeking after originality. The style of an era and personal style will co-exist or contrast, but one will only dominate the other when the artist resolves the internal tension caused by a real search for style as necessity. We may see Ernesto Nathan Rogers' maxim in this light: 'Coherence is the quality which the artist needs to establish his own relations with the moral world on a balanced level so that every action he takes is heightened; tendency is the deliberate translation of those acts within a clearly defined intellectual furrow; style is the formal expression of coherence and tendency.'

VITTORIO ZECCHIN, 'THE PRINCESS AND THE WARRIORS' 1914
(CA'PESARO MUSEUM OF CONTEMPORARY ART, VENICE)

space-making is the free giving over of places where the destinies of the people who inhabit them are accomplished in the happiness of possessing a country or the unhappiness of being deprived of one or the indifference of either of these possibilities. Space-making is the free giving over of the place where a god has revealed himself, the place where the gods have fled, the place where the manifestation of the divine is long in coming. Space-making allows the place to prepare itself to become a dwelling place. Profane spaces are profane in all cases insofar as they are referred to sacred places which lie in the background. Space-making is the free giving over of places. In space-making an occurrence speaks out and is hidden at the same time.' And Aristotle was surely the first to say 'The Topos seems to be a thing that is very important and difficult to grasp...' *Topos* meaning space-as-place.

The roots of the Venice school lie midway between a 'vision of the world' which places the action, and hence the project, in the subjective balance between inner space and outer space, and a 'praxis of the world' which is metaheroic but unsuited to concerning itself with 'baggage': it is a school which up till now, as far as conceptual reasons, themes and figures are concerned, has appeared to be a *rear-guard school*.

The teaching of our masters Giuseppe Samonà and Ernesto N Rogers re-proposed the salvaging of history, of *all* lived history, emphasising heterodoxy rather than orthodoxy, the *orthodoxy of heterodoxy*. It is therefore still important to reconsider the work of Karl Friedrich Schinkel, Gottfried Semper, Christopher Wren, Nicholas Hawksmoor and John Soane, Joźe Plećnik, Josef Frank and Otto Wagner, as well as Adolf Loos and Peter Speeth.

In fact the architect is less concerned with the exact semiological or structural definition of the morpheme or the basic syntagma of a composition than he is with the autonomy of an element or a rule of proportion in classic heterodox formulations. Knowing, for instance, whether the architectural expedient is expressed more correctly with the term 'round arch' or 'Serlian arch' is of little interest to us. What we are interested in is the expedient's autonomy and adaptability in the hands of Plećnik and Semper, as well as its passage from classical-romantic to post-Wagnerian tragic.

In arranging so many similar or identical architectural elements in sequence, romantics and eclectics came to replace assonances with dissonances, isolated words blotting out the flow of the line, monodies without counterpart, as in late Beethoven or Hölderlin. We admire the Mahlerian use of the architectural expedient by Schinkel, Semper and Plećnik. They were astute administrators of memory, using the expedient *before* the dissolution of institutionalised language. They were on the threshold, but well this side, of detaching words from things, in the place where paradox, irony, narration and tragedy still occurred.

The concepts, instruments and figures of post-modern 're-founding' are necessarily inscribed within a *tekne*—a project for the world—which starts from the project for our life. Emmanuel Lévinas said: '*We must succeed in seeing that one can go ahead only by proceeding inwards.*' In typological terms, Lévinas made the coinciding of *going inwards* and the desire for *possession of the place* even more explicit than Webern. 'Inhabiting is...the spirit of being, not like the famous snake which takes possession of itself by devouring its own tail, but like the body which exists on the earth and is external to it. My "own house" is not a place of containment, but a place in which I can do things, a place in which, though I am still dependent on another reality, I exist and am free, despite this dependence or perhaps because of it. I need only walk and act in order to take possession of, to seize, everything. Everything, in a certain sense, is in the place, however few reckonings I make and however little I calculate intermediaries and means. The place, the environment, offer means. Everything is here, everything belongs to me; everything is seized, right from the beginning, with the original grasp, everything is included.'

Heidegger wrote of the appropriation of space as a project for the world: 'Space-making causes what is free and open to become suitable for the settlement and dwelling of man. When considered in its essence,

For this reason we act *as if* the progression and predominance of architectural expedients are the counterproof of the importance of metaphor, metonymy, symbol, hyperbole and allegory in the continual unveiling and concealment of reality by means of architecture. The eloquence of any project rests on the knowledge and logic of the architect. He must create rich rhetorical figures, images and words with evocative strength.

The task of the rear-guard is to *hold the field*. This is also the main task of a school of architecture today. In military usage the rear-guard is the body of troops which protects a column on the march against attack from behind, while the vanguard, or avant-garde, is the group which attempts sallies in war (and in art), falling on the field but falling for victory, heroic in the eyes of the public. It is however the rear-guard which protects the retreat of an operational unit, slowing down the enemy advance by acts of resistance. A few well-placed machine guns can save a whole retreating army from defeat. Compared to the main European cities—London, Paris, Munich, Milan—which are being massacared in the noisy and victorious spread of the enemies of Architecture and the City, Venice is in a good defensive position for the moment. The role of the rear-guard is especially important now that historical conditions are making it necessary to retreat, serry the ranks, and salvage what can be saved on the run.

The rear-guard has always been important in my culture, which is the culture of Central Europe. There is a story about two Jews from Trieste—one wrote poetry and sold old books, the other painted and squandered his inheritance. The poet was called Umberto Saba and the painter was called Vittorio Bolaffio. The poet didn't think highly of Bolaffio, but after the painter's death, recalled him with respect: one evening in the cafe a young man came up to Bolaffio, called him master and told him that his painting was avant-garde. (Young painters have always had an obsession with the avant-garde, as though art were a battle and its exclusive aim was to scandalise and annoy.) Bolaffio drew himself up to his full height and began to shriek that his place was in the rear-guard, in the last conceivable rear-guard of painting.

The intellectual's reasons lie neither in success nor in moralism, but in deep, innermost morality. He must try to give shape to being, he must attempt civic construction. In the writings of Denis Diderot, *tekne* is an impediment, but *tekne* is the project for the world, the project of my life.

A rear-guard school must of course study the visible elements of architecture because they have a primal value and give building practice the character of a ritual to be spelled out like the words of a chant: wall, column, threshold, door, step, staircase, room, window, fireplace, place for sleeping, place for love, for celebrations, place for leisure, roof, entrance hall, front, back, garden, orchard. However, it must also study the invisible structure of architecture: the plan (the importance to the Romans of the large plan, which takes on the same dimensions as the opening in chess for the houses of Adolf Loos); the type (the stamp and character of the building); the proportions.

We are quite aware that there are as many techniques of composition as there are tonalities and genres. The use of quotation, the explanatory and literary value of decoration, the search for the sublime, the hermeticism necessary in an age when those in power have nothing to say to the citizen, the return to myth, the transference of the banality of everyday existence to the level of myth; these are the motifs of a rear-guard school. We know quite well that these questions and attitudes may produce serious distortions and illusions that will be frustrated. We know that they will draw attention to the repression of the twenties and thirties.

We are led to a conception of the rhythm of architecture that is much closer to the idea of being than to that of existing if we pursue the sublime, the mythical—architecture as the magnificent product of a resplendent functionality, the real fruit of a *Zweckmässigkeit*, where the building is conceived for its utility value and not for its exchange value.

The present panic. Pan appears in the glitter of midday. It is the moment when my shadow and I are one. What matters is the mysterious, imminent fact, the instantaneous, unrelated, unexpected, unrepeatable event which cuts through the chronological succession of time. The present dominates the past and future, the *synchronic* prevails.

Furthermore, the layman Jean-François Lyotard points out the incompatibility of Modernism and occurrence: 'The occurrence, the *Ereignis*, has nothing to do with the *petit frisson*, the rentable pathos, that accompanies innovation. Hidden in the cynicism of innovation is surely the despair that nothing further will happen. But to innovate means to behave as though any number of things could happen, and it means taking action to make them happen. In affirming itself, it will affirm its hegemony over time.'

## The territory

At the beginning of the twentieth century Marcel Mauss, in a study of social morphology, gave a well-known and very clear definition of the notion of territoriality. In his 'Essay on seasonal variations in Eskimo society' he shows how man's *identity*, once the thresholds of individuality have been crossed, is not merely a question of belonging to the tribe. The indissoluble relation between social grouping and territorial unity consititutes the principle of identification of the group, accounting for a linguistic, moral and religious unity which has 'clearly fixed boun-

GIUSEPPE TORRES, STUDY FOR KEYS, VENICE 1905

GIUSEPPE TORRES' HOUSE, VENICE 1905

daries'. Attachment to a territory is not easily separable from a complex of habits, social relations and rituals.

The 'territorial' wars currently being waged between the peoples who belong to theoretical African and Asian states, by urban guerrillas in big cities, and even by the ETA and IRA and the Corsican and Sardinian separatists, inevitably derives from the single ideological matrix in which habitat (lands occupied or possibly only passed through) coincides with culture.

Every return to regionalism in the history of our ideas, even in Kenneth Frampton's theory, contrasts the following concepts: mobility of industrial society and rootedness; unmanageability of the dynamics of social relations in the metropolis and collective control; crisis of institutions of the production-oriented enlightened State and the behavioural patterns and feelings of a civilisation that give the transformations of the territory a symbolic representation. It makes no difference whether the region is Jože Plečnik's Slovenia or the San Francisco Bay; a return to regionalism is part of a 'project for the world' which contrasts, to some degree, with the culture of the city.

During the sixties Italian town-planning gave free rein to this ideology. It was at this time that Giuseppe Samonà wrote his own book on town-planning and the future of the city, tore apart Mumford's 'disurbanism' with his reassessment of Haussmann and then put himself at the head of a new cultural and political battle over the *compensorio* (district).

The IUAV has examined the district economy, district sociology and even district justice with reference to the large-scale works of land reclamation and colonisation in the Veneto and the diversion of rivers and construction of lakes and deltas by the Magistrati of the Most Serene Republic of Venice. Samonà, however, set himself the task of evoking the meaning of the layout and measurements of the fields, the figurative nature of the rows of mulberry trees, the density of the banks and the slowness of the raised rivers—the Piave, the Brenta, the Sile, the Adige—which curve between high-water beds, old Roman *castra*, *centuriationes*, medieval monasteries and eighteenth-century villas, then run into the Lagoon and from there into the Adriatic. He states: 'The idea of presence built by man cannot be explained as an object in itself, but as part of the space in which it is immersed. Its formal configuration is perceptible as a unity of relations between the parts which make it up and link it to the surrounding space.'

However, this idea of presence has artificial characteristics and corresponds to one or more objects articulated among themselves as expressively determinable representations. The idea of presence may emerge from the natural characteristics of a place when it makes its morphological influence felt in the space which shapes its elements. The idea of presence does not necessarily refer to material objects, but can also mean actions carried out by individuals or groups whose personalities bring about large-scale transformations in culture and taste as well as transformations in the pattern of settlement. Material presence always has to be a built fact, or a material object or fact that has been formally subordinated to the conceptual positions assigned by the categories of physical space which illuminate the history of the present.

The mainstay of Samonà's discourse is the figurative, but structuralism also plays a very important role in view of the need to determine a metahistorical structure of the region, district and territory. He continues: 'For this reason, when one says that the idea of structure is ahistorical, one is giving a partial and possibly incorrect definition. If we are referring to the present, the structure which is a part of it in a synchronic way manifests itself objectively and subjectively. In this

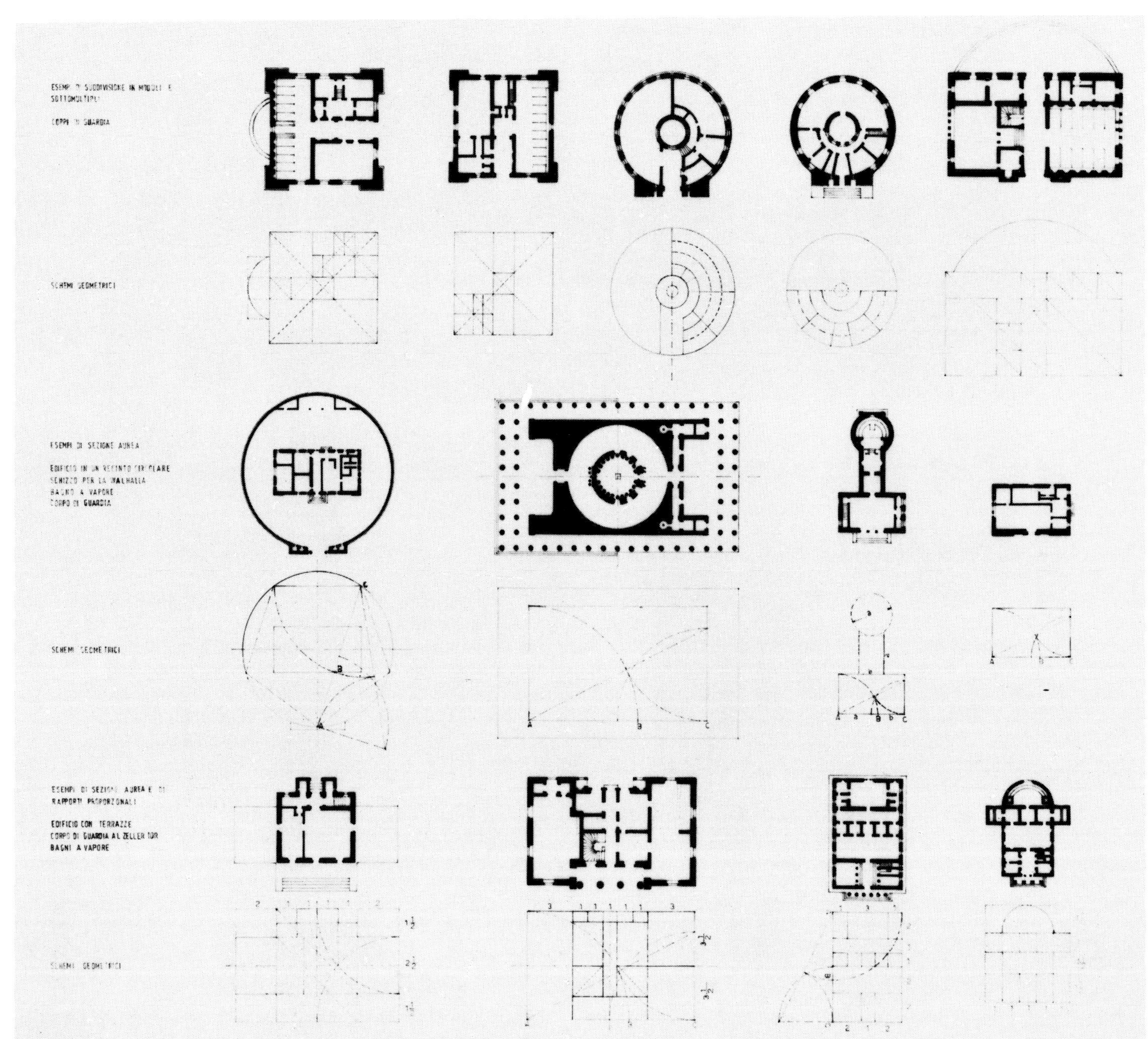

PETER SPEETH, COMPOSITIONAL PRINCIPLES (STUDENT THESIS 1984)

sense structuralism is an essential element of our time, clearing the way for highly productive dialectical experiments, particularly in the sphere of historical materialism.'

It was through the concept of *presence* that Samonà tied together the logical method and the historical method of knowledge, finding a point of juncture between the morphological-structural analysis of the constants of settled space and the identification of its historical essence.

The courses on a variety of themes concerning the district closed with Ludovici Quaroni delivering an apotheosis of the new liberating territorial dimension of architecture. There is no point in pretending that this rediscovery of territoriality is not the hope of the promised land for architects who want to abandon the unitary nineteenth-century State and reinterpret the place and its boundaries with large-scale designs. At the same time it is a political battle, for the theme was in fact appropriated for a few years by a large section of the Left.

Through the National Institute for Urban Studies Samonà tirelessly promoted debates and seminars on the theme of territory. However, the discourse gradually moved away from his initial utopian ideals: Samonà had given structural constants the meaning of 'unchanging values'. Referring both analyses and projects to a synchronic approach, we subverted the terms of the discourse and tried to lead the subject back into a neutral sphere free of ideology.

Meanwhile 1968 arrived in Italy. Architects tried to salvage what they could of their profession. Those who tried at the time to experiment with a process of joint research and self-planning that would grow with the culture and the political action of the minorities later paid dearly when the bold union of Marxist culture and Catholic tradition broke down in crisis. Of those who carried the theme of territory to safety through the breakers and tempests of its political exhaustion, Vittorio Gregotti was the calmest. With antihistoricist logic, the new *Casabella* systematically proposed territorial modulation and layout as a middle way between unvarying settlement space and large-scale infrastructures which, like the great Roman aqueducts, express however little or much of our civilisation is left to us. Others, like ourselves, took the synchronic and metahistorial approach to the heart of the problems of urban re-use and worked to produce a gradual reduction in scale from 1968 to

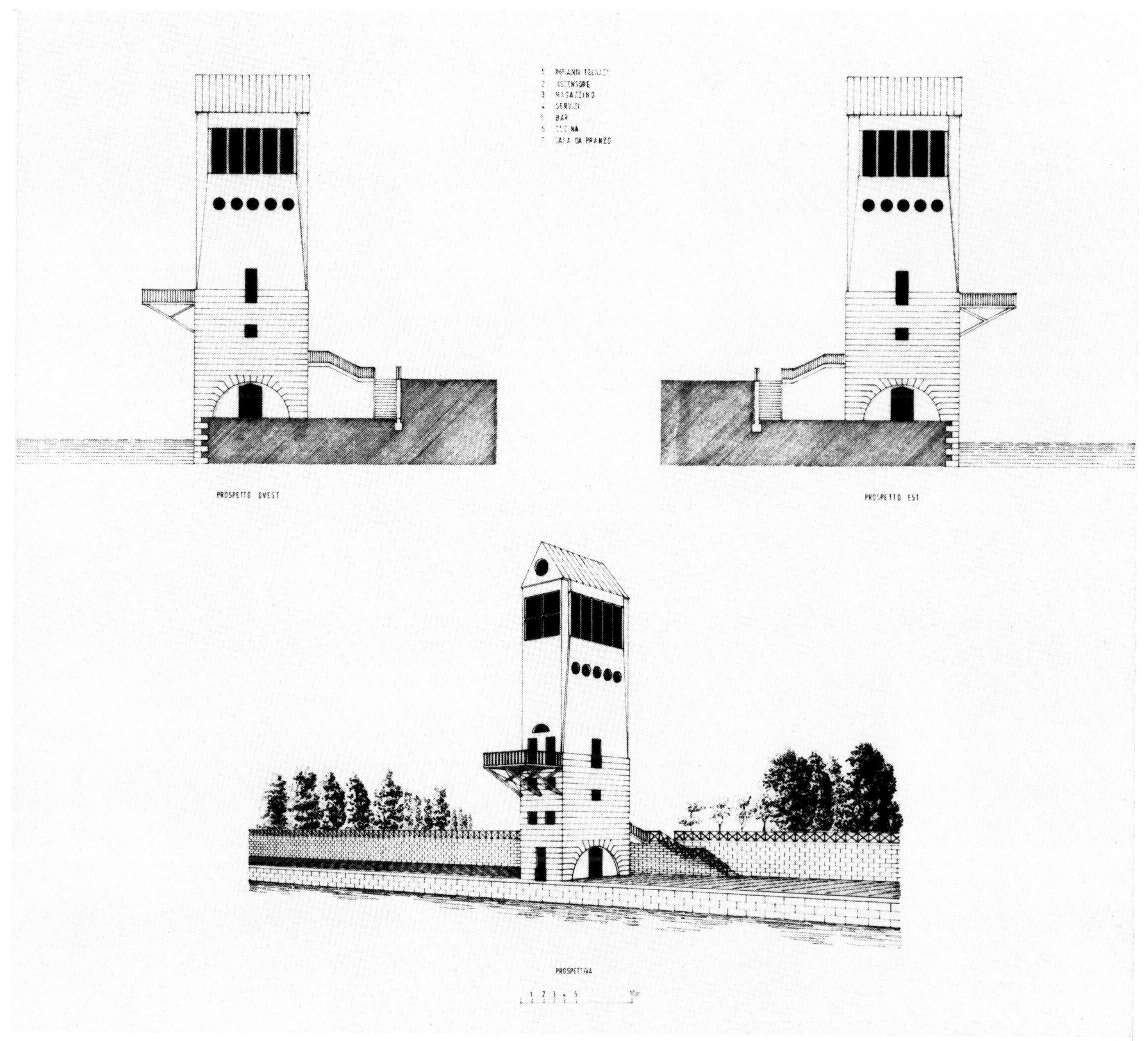


PETER SPEETH, THE TOWER, SPREEBOGEN, BERLIN (STUDENT THESIS 1984)

today. It was like a child at the zoo, unable to grasp the reasons and existential dimensions of an elephant (which in the zoo are indeed paradoxical), suddenly taking an interest in a sparrow at the elephant's feet, seeing something small but familiar. But now we are moving onto a different theme: the city and its characters.

## The city—civic architecture

While still a voluntary assistant in Rome, Aymonino obtained financing from the National Centre for Research for work on the relations between building regulations and urban morphology in old Venice. While still a student, Aldo Rossi wrote an article for *Società* on the concept of tradition in neoclassical Milanese architecture and as soon as he graduated, he concerned himself with the relationship between land, building typology and urban morphology in the development of the region of Milan around Corso di Porta Romana. These and other works form the basis of *Gruppo Architettura's* international analysis of the relations between building typology and urban morphology.

In researching a language of architecture, it is very important to see the old city as though time had stood still. Designing a city is rewriting it, redescribing it. Ours is above all a syntactic exercise. In general the cities in the Veneto have recurrent themes such as the square, the circle of walls and the river. The territory of the Veneto has the Roman settlement, the sixteenth-century villa and the enlightened agricultural town. These things occupy us wholly. They are in the left hemisphere of our brain because they are history, categories, ways of inhabiting, and they are in the right hemisphere because they are images, memories, signs. Building, following this path, becomes *monument*.

To sum up: the city is viewed synchronically, as a morphological fact; study and project, analysis and proposal are then no longer separate— 'there is no jump in logic, but unity,' as Aldo Rossi wrote in 1964; architectural composition becomes the *description* of precise choices— architecture as history, architecture as an element in the city, architecture as construction; this description requires *eloquence*, so there is a *monumental*, *museum-like*, *sombre* and *desperate* intensification of the discourse.

However, the question of tone slips into the discourse alongside the epic, comedy and farce. Together they blunt the awareness felt by the architect in the field. To quote Renato Nicolini in *Controspazio*: 'We may well talk of volumes, of skylines, of maximum outlines when architecture is entirely contained in an idea; it inevitably translates into a style.'

On several occasions Aldo Rossi has battled those who want to commit the future of the city to conservation alone. He has called for'...(an) alternative city, an analogous city which uses its own history not for a museum but for a project. The meaning of this project rather than its form (if the two things can be separated) may be the object of a new understanding beyond the narrowness of the disciplines in Italian culture.'

The city has a double nature. On the one hand, it is a place moulded by manifestations which were once historical but are now aspatial and metahistorical; on the other, it is *the place of Epiphanies*. The last place where this order of ideas occurred was the magnificent project for the Carlo Felice Theatre in Genoa by Ignazio Gardella and Aldo Rossi. Today it is the last 'inevitable' manifestation of the laws of the building in the place and a necessary and simple interpretation of the theatre as Theatre.

All forms of theatrical auditorium designed by Gardella from 1934 to the present day are summed up in this 'city interior'. The great masonry tower above the stage is connected with other powerful out-of-scale objects. (Gardella has said, 'The great Doric column will be built, if not in Chicago, then in some other city, if not for the Chicago Tribune, then for someone else, if not by me, then by some other architect.')

This theatre is laden with power, the fruit of great experience. At the very moment when it seems to soar above the condition of prototype, it is suddenly transformed into the theatre of *that* city, because *that* tower can only be placed as a pivot between the sloping system of the streets, squares and galleries in the centre of Genoa and the arcades designed by the architect Barabino. The monumental transversal pronaos is the approach to a paratactical composition of which the tower and perforating cone are only the most striking figures, the most acute dissonances. The themes of the great public building and the city merge because the building has been raised to the level of an experimental metahistorical city.

## The type

What is clear for the philosopher is not always clear for the artist. Anyone who studies a cultural product follows a method and it is impossible, for a variety of reasons, to confuse the method used to study culture with the method of producing culture.

The architecture of the past and the built city are classified by types. When the architect refers to the type, he is pursuing the idea, but once the idea is evoked it gives itself up. Giulio Carlo Argan claims that

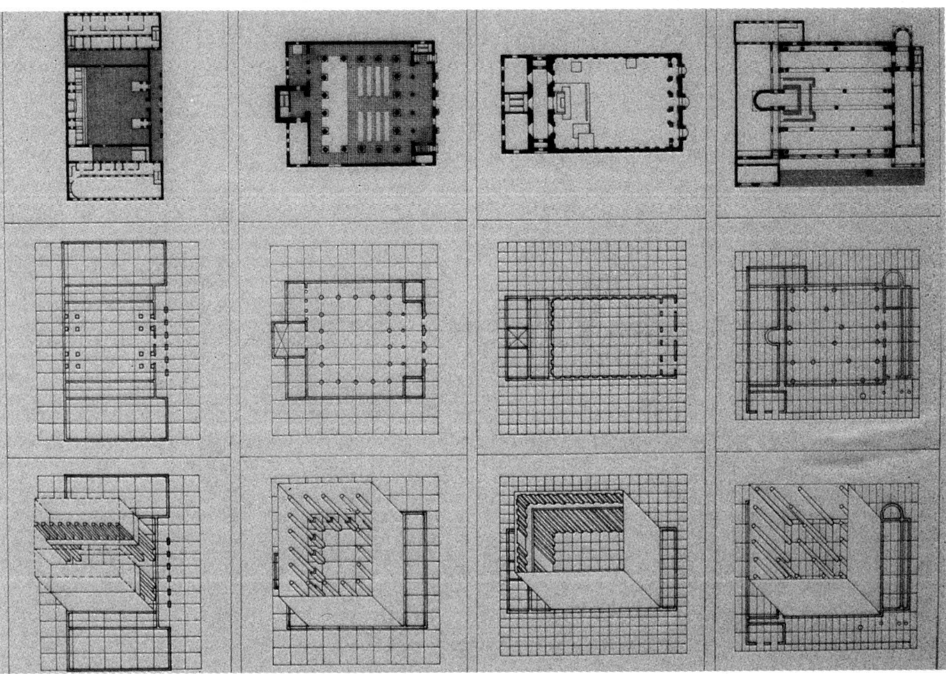

LEFT: PROJECT FOR AN ANCIENT CITY WITH REFERENCE TO JOZE PLECNIK. RIGHT: JOZE PLECNIK, COMPOSITIONAL PRINCIPLES (BOTH STUDENT THESES)

typological reference started with neoclassicism because imagination became blocked and allegory became conceptualised in symbols. However, we can see from Raphael's painting *Galatea* that the ideal of femininity existed before that. '*Since beauties among women are so rare, I use a certain idea which I have formed in my mind.*' Raphael's classicism antedates Winckelmann's by several centuries.

It may be true that the idea of the *type* as an imaginative model assumed clarity with Quatremère de Quincy and lost it with Jean-Nicolas Louis Durand, but the proposal of 'image as idea' is as old as the world. Winckelmann wrote of the Greeks: 'They began to form certain general ideas of beauty, both of the single parts and of the whole proportions of bodies, ideas which transcended nature herself; their image referred to a spiritual nature, conceived purely intellectually.'

In Italian architectural culture it was one of the IUAV's professors, Saverio Muratori (influenced by Asplund and Tessenow), who reassessed the notion of *type* in a course on distributive features that was subsequently published under the title 'Studies for a Working Urban History of Venice'. He saw in the building type 'a unified vision of reality and a continuity of development which can be perceived in its every moment and which is characterised by a selective and consequently historical orientation.' In designating urban history a conditioning and (insofar as it brings sense) irreversible element, Muratori removed the study of the distributive character of buildings from the positivist tradition and, like Quatremère, rejected any confusion with the model or the archetype-prototype, making the type coincide with the idea.

Every day, in every project, we find ourselves wondering about the effectiveness of this idea. Every graphic representation of the type, every diagram of urban building types takes *from the mould* its characteristic of being the internal structure and deep geometry of the architectural object and the matrix of various possible architectures. However, this brings it down from the level of an idea to that of an interpretative diagram, little more than a model for deciphering morphological complexity. It is only possible to visualise the type when all three invisible structures of the architectural object—proportions, plan and type—are superimposed in a unity.

Man and building have a perfect relationship in scale; all is united, classic, eternal. The architecture of the temple is the image of the temple, and because of our faith and the proportions which God has given us, each one of us is—in his body—a temple.

Palladio's Rotunda is set, like a glider, on a universal site, to which its appearance is indissolubly linked by *symmetry* and *numbers*. There is a description of it in Isaac Ware's version of *The Four Books of Palladio's Architecture*: 'The site is pleasant and delightful as can be found, because it is on a small hill of very easy access, and is watered on one side by the Bacchiglione, a navigable river; and on the other it is encompassed about with most pleasant risings which look like a very great theatre and are all cultivated about with most excellent fruits and most exquisite wines; and therefore as it enjoys from every part most beautiful views, some of which are limited, some more extended, and others which terminate with the horizon, there are loggias in all four fronts...The ancient sages commonly used to retire to such places, where being oftentimes visited by their virtuous friends and relations,

UMBERTO SABA 'PORTRAIT OF VITTORIO BOLAFFIO'

having houses, gardens, fountains and such like pleasant places, and above all their virtue, they could easily attain to as much happiness as can be attained here below.'

Colin Rowe observes: 'Perhaps these were the dreams of Virgil; and, freely interpreted, they have gathered around themselves in the course of time all those ideas of Roman virtue, excellence, imperial splendour and decay which make up the imaginative reconstruction of the ancient world. It would have been, perhaps, in the landscapes of Poussin—with their portentous apparitions of the antique—that Palladio would have felt at home...'

The strength within the type is also obvious in Karl Friedrich Schinkel's project to rebuild the Villa Laurentina according to Pliny the Younger's description or in his project for a classical villa in Potsdam.

It is clear in fact that yet another definition of the term is not of great interest: we know that typological research is topical not so much because it enables us to understand tradition or provides us with a statistical summary of the most technically advanced planning experiments relating to a type of building (theatre, prison, hospital) but rather because it investigates the constituent laws of the ordinary building in their *Zweckmässigkeit*.

The requirement that *the construction* should correspond to its rational aim brings in all the sensory and emotional facts of man, the complete sphere of his desires. In the house, the *tectonics* of the architectural object act as a *metaphor for the creative process itself* (contained form, arrangement of the places and *bildung* are all one). The house is the theme which makes it possible to develop a magnificent, resplendent (though not of course petit-bourgeois) functionality. The house is destined to give enjoyment and pleasure, it does not anticipate bio-engineering robots; if anything, it offers illusions of warmth and light.

VITTORIO BOLAFFIO, 'THE PORT'

However, the symbolic functionality of the public building replaces the invention of new institutions with a more ambiguous and more general research into a *new* functionality of the city; the functionality of the *new city*. The celebration through architecture of the collective civic monument is thus matched by a desire for an architectural language which is neither private nor personal, but rational and classical.

**The figuration**

The characters of the modern city, which developed during the second half of the nineteenth century, are to be found along the monumental axes of Paris, Vienna and Berlin, or set in the heart of Florence, Milan and Prague, or planted like hinges in the urban development of Dresden, London and Turin. They are now exchanging masks and roles, starting the last battle against repetitiveness.

The agreed, conventional sense of both the building and the historic city can be subverted by an architectural expedient (figure), or a scenographic effect (arcade, urban park, horse on a base) or quotation (the Loggia in Munich, Palazzo Pandolfini in Dresden, Napoleonic pavilion in Charlottenburg). This subversion is an indicator of the transformation taking place, the direction in which history is moving.

Historicism and eclecticism vindicate the right to the image and the right to eloquence which both stem from the *topos*, from agreed meanings. The new figuration and the demand for the narrative are an essential feature of *rear-guard* architecture (as it was defined earlier). Both have matured at the same time as a reassessment of the *theatre* or urban space, of the ephemeral, and dialectically, of representation.

Radical art and avant-garde architecture live in the empty space between the *spirit* and its *expression*, described by Adorno as follows: 'As the coherence and intransigence with which they pursue their spiritualisation grows, so does the distance between them and that which should be spiritualised. Their spirit hovers above and empty space opens up between it and its expression. The pre-eminence of the spirit becomes the loss of the spirit, the loss of a sense of the imminent. From then onwards all art suffers from this difficulty; the more serious the art the more painfully it suffers. Spiritualisation...seems to drive out the spirit of the thing itself. The thing intended to spiritualise the material (cf Kandinsky, Schoenberg—author's note) ends up as bare material, mere existence...'

In Venice, as elsewhere, a final battle is currently being waged. The fight regarding the primacy of *composition over planning* has replaced the previous diatribes which pitted architecture and planning or architecture and design against each other. The *compositional* demand is not an abstract refinement, just as the narrative in architecture is not a simple return to mannerism and the use of metaphor and metonymy and return to a discontinuous and paratactical composition are not merely modish.

We are well aware that architectural discourse is not literary discourse and that compositions of architectural signs cannot be interpreted in the same way as poetic or musical compositions. And yet, every time we want to spell out the relationship of necessity that exists between the parts and the whole of a poetic or philosophical discourse, we speak of architecture. Even De Saussure turned to architecture when he needed an example to clarify a general discourse on language. He referred to the existence of two axes; the syntagmatic, operating *in praesentia*; and the systematic, operating *in absentia*. Every linguistic unit is like a column in an ancient building. This column is in a relationship of contiguity with other parts of the building, for instance the architrave (syntagmatic relationship). However, if the column is Doric it arouses a desire for comparison with other intellectual orders, such as the Ionic or the Corinthian, and this is a virtual relationship of substitution (associative relationship).

In its boundless silence the avant-garde has led architecture to become 'bare material, mere existence'. It could do this because it gave precedence to the project of the single object, the *outil*, according to the standpoint of industrial design, and suppressed the paradigmatic axis of language, often reducing the building to a single syntagm, a single figure, a single form for the whole city.

GIANCARLO LEONCILLI MASSI, PORTICO FOR SPOLETO CATHEDRAL

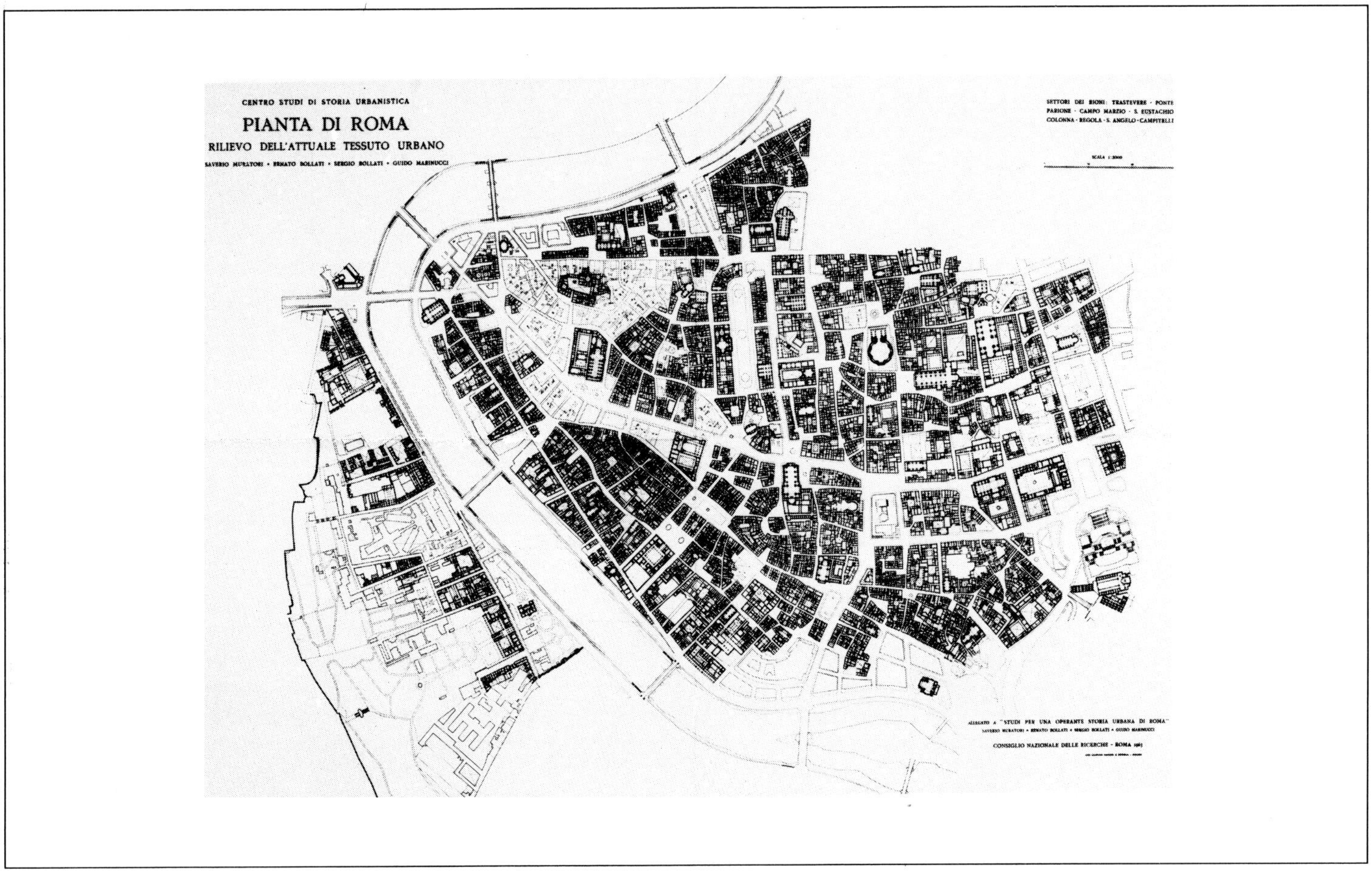

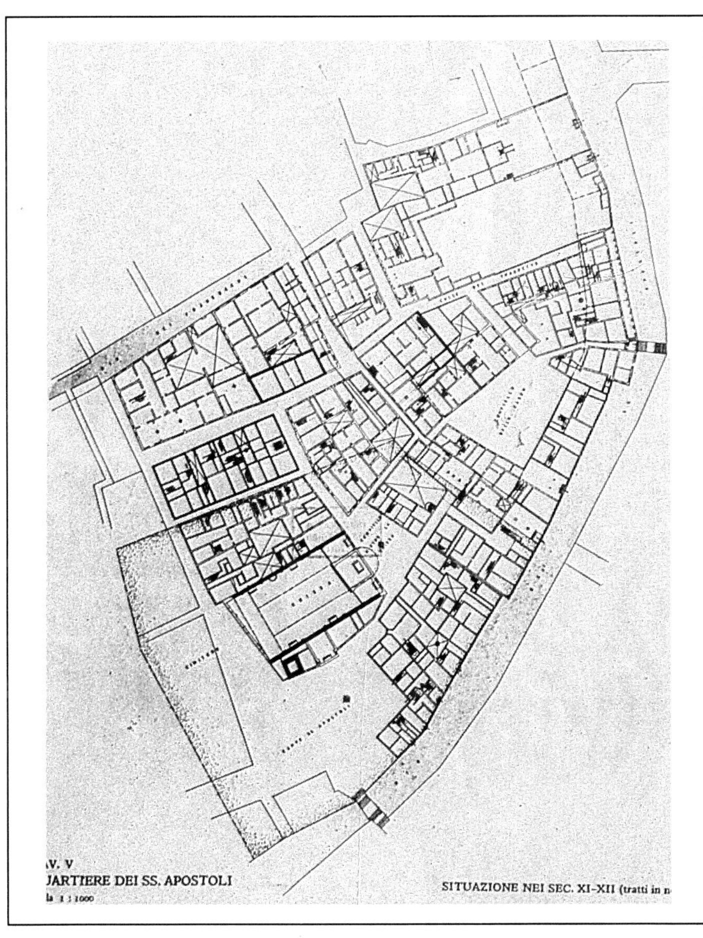


SAVERIO MURATORI, PLAN OF ROME

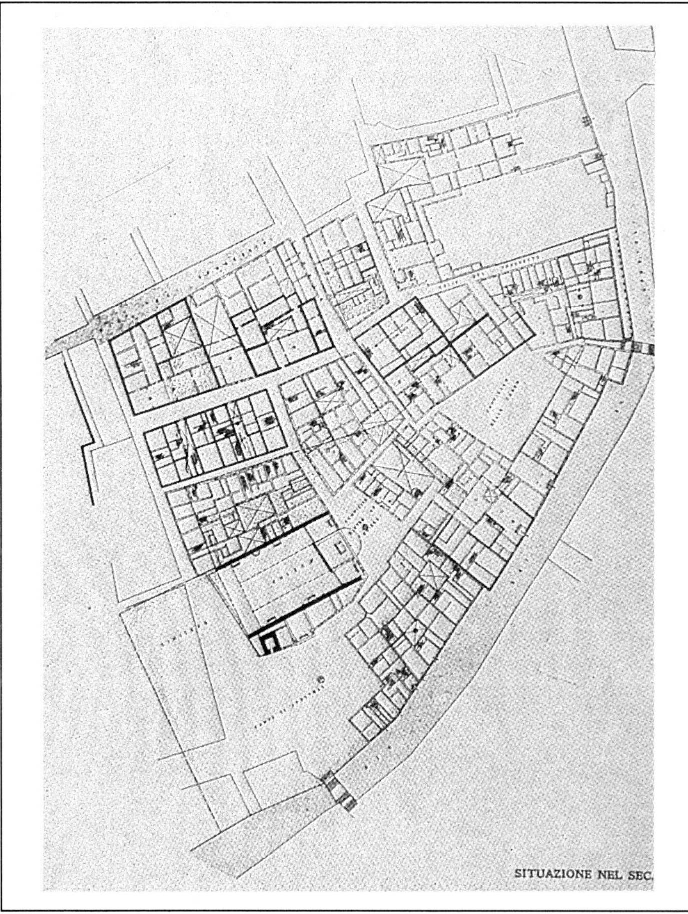

SAVERIO MURATORI, THE APOSTLES' QUARTER IN VENICE, (LEFT) IN THE 11-12TH CENTURY, (RIGHT) IN THE 11TH CENTURY

It is no longer a question of going back to the old architectural orders, but of assembling and re-assembling the various facades within the urban street and the different architectural expedients of the same building type by substituting the canonised language of the associative relationship and exalting it. Metonymy, metaphor and allegory have returned to architecture as logical procedures which are more complex and functional in their description and narration of the architectures of Architecture (and hence of the City). A feeling for context, urban analysis, territory and type are at the heart of a reinstatement of polysemy and figuration into building.

The theme of decoration has also been revived. For a long time, the Semperian notion of *type* as a vehicle for the meaning of architecture was reassessed in isolation, independently of the *theory of applied styles* where ornament, through the intervention of decorative form, gives the building architectural qualities, that is, aesthetic qualities. In one of the IUAV's seminars on decoration, Giancarlo Leoncilli Massi said: 'The problem of creating form is something more than just *matter and form*. It is, as Benjamin has claimed, *imagination*, the capacity for interpolation in the smallest thing, and thus an ability to realise precisely that it is *variation* which avoids the accusation of sameness.'

Thus we come back to Adorno who, in agreeing with Adolf Loos, stated that the artistic materials of industrial design have lost any air of essentiality and that is is impossible to love them because they no longer allow the age-old faith in their beauty, the magic residue of the virtues of the precious stones. Poor Klimt, setting the last gems, variegated marbles and gold leaf in Mr Stocklet's drawing room! Poor Loos. The bourgeois morality of his Moravian clientele forced him to temper his pleasure, which resulted in wasted energy, withdrawal from work. By vindicating an objective and rational formal order, he was contributing, in his public polemic on the Viennese life-style, to a general principle of repression of pleasure, embodied by the emperor himself. We take the side of the emperor's wife Sisi—that of insatiability over repression, anxiety over certainty.

Finally, Ernesto Rogers said: 'Many of the uses which decoration has assumed over the centuries find their justification and origin in the desire to make the building talk and give it a soul.'

**Conclusions**

To assert the primacy of architectural composition is not just a poetic matter. In a school of architecture the main matter is teaching. To reason about and discuss the principles and rules of composition constitutes not only the defence (from rear-guard positions) of Architecture but also the replacement of speechlessness with the mastery of the techniques of a specific language. The teaching of architecture is not a pedagogical problem; in his time, Giuseppe Samonà was able to keep the whole range of matters broadly open. His sons have given partial answers, taking the discipline back to a degree of transmissibility. How can one avoid the retreat, rearticulation and reorganisation of technical responses which would put the School of Venice into the same rut as the Ecole des Beaux-Arts or the Ecole Polytechnique? How can one protect the orthodoxy of heterodoxy?

Plato relates that Socrates once arrived late, almost half-way through a symposium. After dining Eriximachus spoke and, repeating the words of Phaedrus, proposed to discuss why no man had ever dared to celebrate Eros with poetic hymns and paeans. And he asked each of those present to praise him in the best way possible. Phaedrus, Pausanias, Eriximachus, Aristophanes and Agathon spoke on the power of the god, some attributing it to his original primacy (for he was the oldest god), some to his universality, some to his sweetness and beauty. When his turn came Socrates praised but did not pass judgement on the reasonings of those who had preceded him. He had no theory to expound but could only repeat a conversation, in the form of questions and answers, with an outsider, Diotima of Mantinea, who was an initiator into amorous mysteries and hence equipped to speak thusly of Eros: 'Not only as a *daimon* but also as an *idea*, the divine equilibrium in the life of men and cities.'

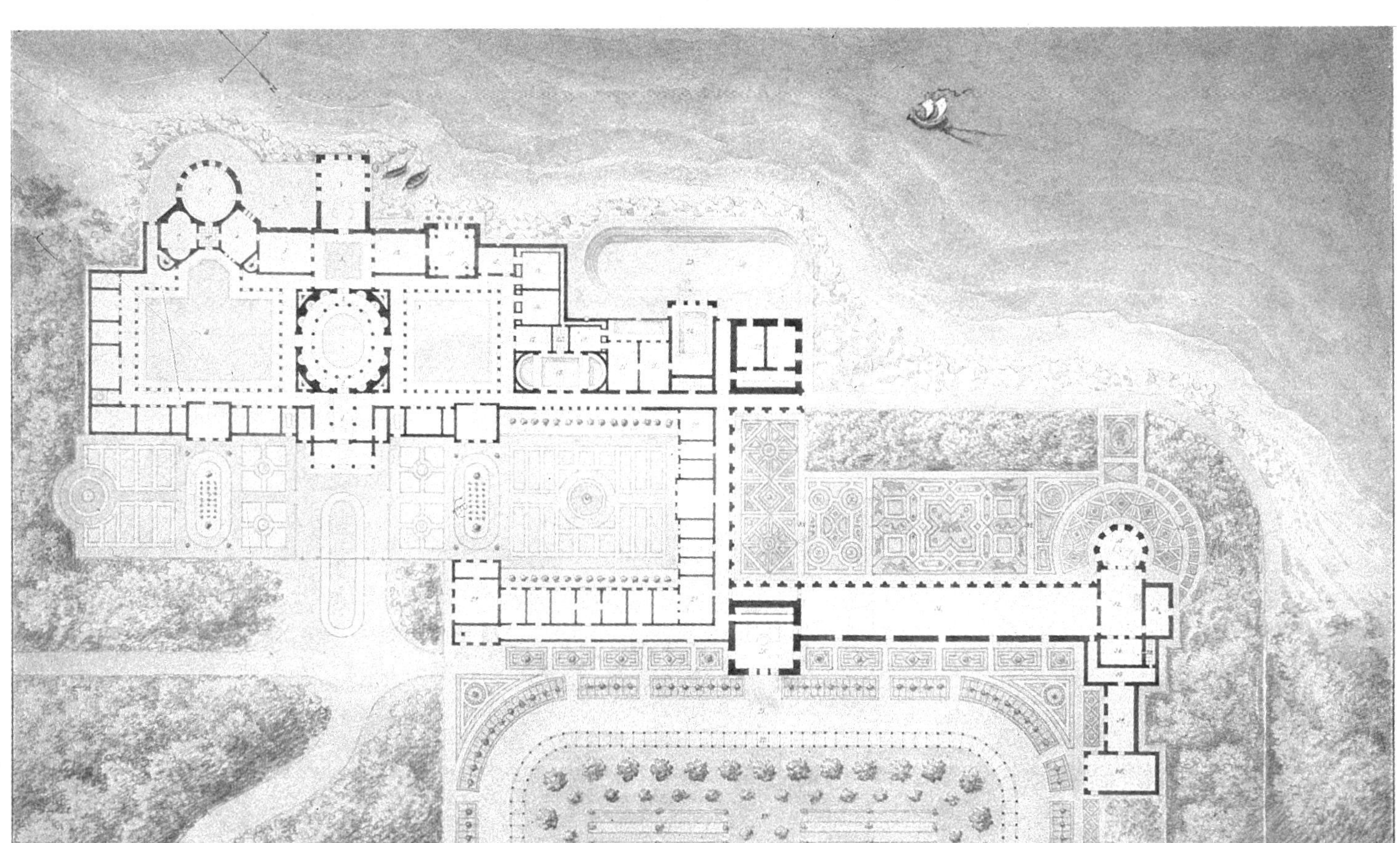

K F SCHINKEL, PLAN FOR THE VILLA LAURENTINA

A ROSSI, E CONSOLACIO, B REICHLIN AND F REINHART, THE ANALOGOUS CITY, 1976

# THE CITY

# GIUSEPPE SAMONA
## An Assessment of the Future of the City as a Problem
## of its Relationship with Architecture

**T**HE RELATIONSHIP BETWEEN ARCHITECTURE AND **the city is very topical and problematical. It therefore seems to me important to sound out its values, posing the** question: is the relationship which once existed between architecture and the city still valid? This question seems to presuppose that, prior to our own time, the relationship between architecture and the city was constant throughout the history of human settlement. If for the moment we accept this notion, the previous question may be posed more clearly in these terms: is the relationship which once existed between the human being and urban architecture still valid? With this second question the social demands connected to the idea of settlement (which the community refers to in every expression of its urban activity) once again make the relationship between architecture and the city more concrete and graspable; it is in fact this relationship which impinges upon the development of social demands. Having defined this condition, one may accept that the profound changes in social demands of community life after the Industrial Revolution and the triumph of the bourgeoisie affected and transformed this relationship. One can see the increasing radicality of this transformation in the events of the last fifty years, when the contrasting blocks of capitalist and Marxist societies were consolidated and a middle-cultural and parapolitical term was born, brought into being by the theoretical interpretations of historical materialism.

But for this discourse to continue in a less schematic and more constructive form it must be referred to our own discipline, that of architecture and town planning. Let us begin, therefore, from some indispensable definitions: commonly accepted as a premise to all considerations about architecture and town planning is the claim that the totality of the two spheres, typological and morphological, constitutes the essence of the motivations inspiring these activities. In the broadest and most general sense, these motivations refer above all to the need to base an appreciable technical experience on methods of typifying the processes of formation of the things which serve the common, and in many ways homogeneous, customs of society regarding matters of settlement. These motivations give rise to all considerations regarding the formal-functional sense which is to be understood as typological.

The typology of the city can therefore be imagined as corresponding

G SAMONÀ WITH C DARDI, V PASTOR, G POLESELLO, A SAMONÀ, L SEMERANI, G TAMARO, E TRINCANATO, INTERNATIONAL COMPETITION FOR THE SACCA DEL
TRONCHETTO IN VENICE, 1965

to a model in which regulations, criteria of development, limits of dimension and techniques of formation are summed up and integrated with one another, making it possible to represent everything which, in the urban context, may be identified as a function from which architecture in the city is formed. Within this sphere, typology is therefore that form of knowledge, partly factual, partly creative, which expresses the method of giving physical space its urban structure.

Typology can be understood as a phenomenon of culture which, in the interests of the community, generalises technical and technological elements and contributes to norms, regulations and modes of conduct; typology is also an indispensable contribution to the social definition of physical space, from which an assortment of public and private behaviour derives; typology guarantees the recognition and organisation of space in specific geographical and urban areas.

This organising or layering of space generates an historical reality, as indicated by the features of the place, the size and mutual position assumed by the things which are modified there or those which fit with existing dimensions but create new relations of volume; this layering is subject to a formal-functional behaviour which every place tends to impose.

In every place, therefore, a relationship is created between the formal-functional sedimentation or layering of the typological activities carried out there throughout time, and the physical configuration and changes of the place itself from its natural to its modified or built state. This relationship constitutes the essence of architectural and urban morphology: it stands beyond the abstraction of typology and recognises the form in its context.

If we refer these concepts to one of the most exceptional cases in the history of human settlement, that is, to Greek architecture, we see that the actual site must have fascinated the Greeks to an extraordinary

degree and even contributed to their most significant buildings: we sense a most singular example of *place* conceived as a protagonist in an already very precisely typological architecture. Even today one is struck by the intense completeness which unifies the things themselves, the works of architecture sited within a context of relationships whose harmony and coherence is truly exceptional. This particular world of perfect architecture is so integrated with typology as to give it a crucial pre-eminence in building. For this reason the morphological sphere, while on the one hand important for situating works in appointed places, has on the other hand an appreciable effect only in the vibrations of the architectural elements which, in their entirety, are broadly ready-made.

In these examples from Greek architecture, and indeed in those from Roman architecture where the typological element still has exceptional importance, the physical configuration of the architectural systems determines fairly simple relations in the transition from function to form in the architecture of the city. The medieval city, on the other hand, emerges in an almost exclusively morphological form; typological facts are reduced to a minimum, sewn together by boundaries of ownership. In the morphology of the medieval city we recognise a system of associative links where there are great variations in the moulding of physical space to the relatively simple requirements of the group.

These examples prove the importance of the role of typology and morphology, understood in the sense we have explained. We see that typological propositions reveal a series of new facts which are outside architecture. In this context we may also observe that the bourgeois revolution shifted the focus of production from the countryside to the city, making it the centre of production, consumption and distribution.

In the city, this situation was aggravated by the conflict over relations of production; this in turn contributed to struggles concerning legitimacy and authority which were to spread throughout the sphere of relations between capital and labour. This phenomenon placed new ideological and political demands on the workers; an ordering occurred which gradually determined a divorce between architecture and the city and between the city and the countryside. Finally, the social definition of space in Western cities moved to guide and limit the very considerable range of activities linked to private property.

Originally an extremely flexible element constituting the parameters of the city, typology later became a demanding cultural instrument: through a series of plans, from the most general to the most particular, typology imposed dominant values of a non-spatial nature, assigning architecture the task of last pawn in the game of political interests.

Western Europe and the Soviet Union have tried all sorts of ways to find satisfactory solutions in the form of districts and satellite-units—organisations which make a single architecture out of a group of activities. These attempts have proved unable to resolve the problems of the new relationship between city and architecture. It should therefore be said that neither the greatness of daring structures nor other traditional means have managed to find a new architecture.

In general this revolution gives the advantage to the proletariat in certain highly debated conditions, but it is still incapable of transforming the traditional urban structure into a new physical space which might express the sense of a new relationship between architecture and the city. It is irrelevant that the definition of space can be achieved with a highly perfected, highly technological typology. This method is not capable of providing architecture with the terms of its own typology which might express a new mode of being in morphological form. There are things beyond the limits of the urban operator with increasingly highly perfected methods. These things create an unknown base, which is one of the main reasons why certain problems of future civic life are completely avoided and urban development is falling headlong into crisis.

The complexity of current typologies in the overall typology of the city is not matched by morphological expressions capable of stabilising the relationship between architecture and the city. History cannot be expressed by urban structures, even if the history of the society living within them is extremely rich. We therefore cannot manage fully to live

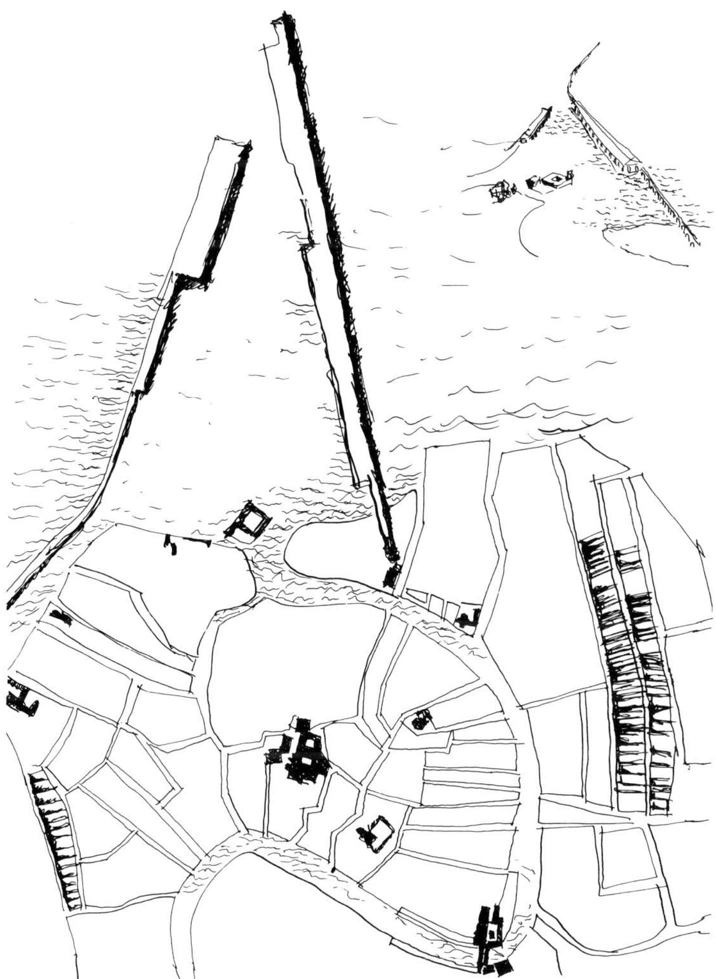

SKETCH PLAN OF TRONCHETTO PROJECT

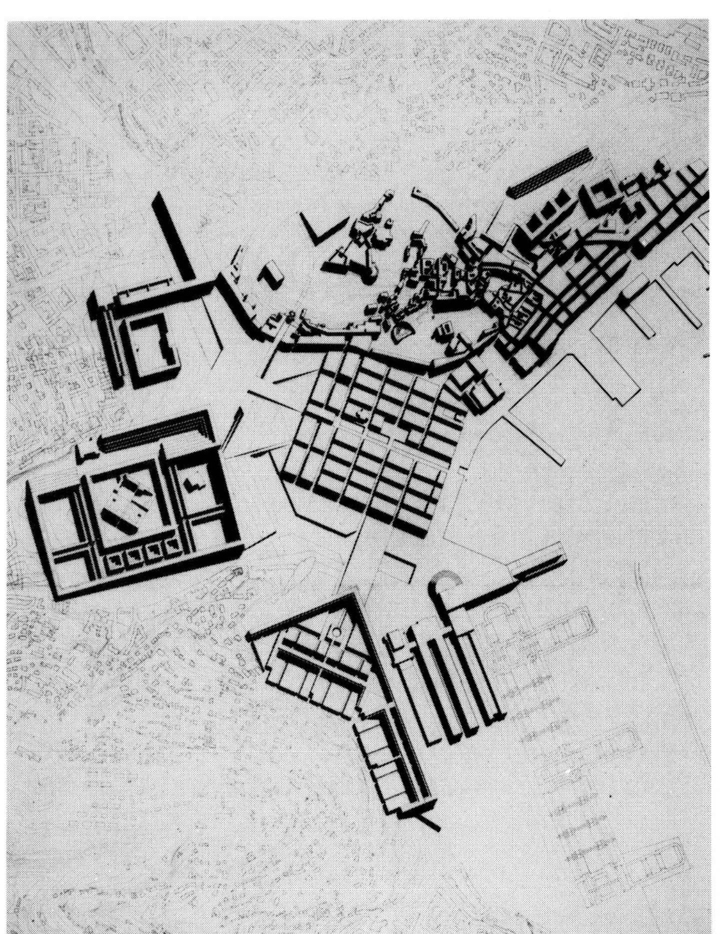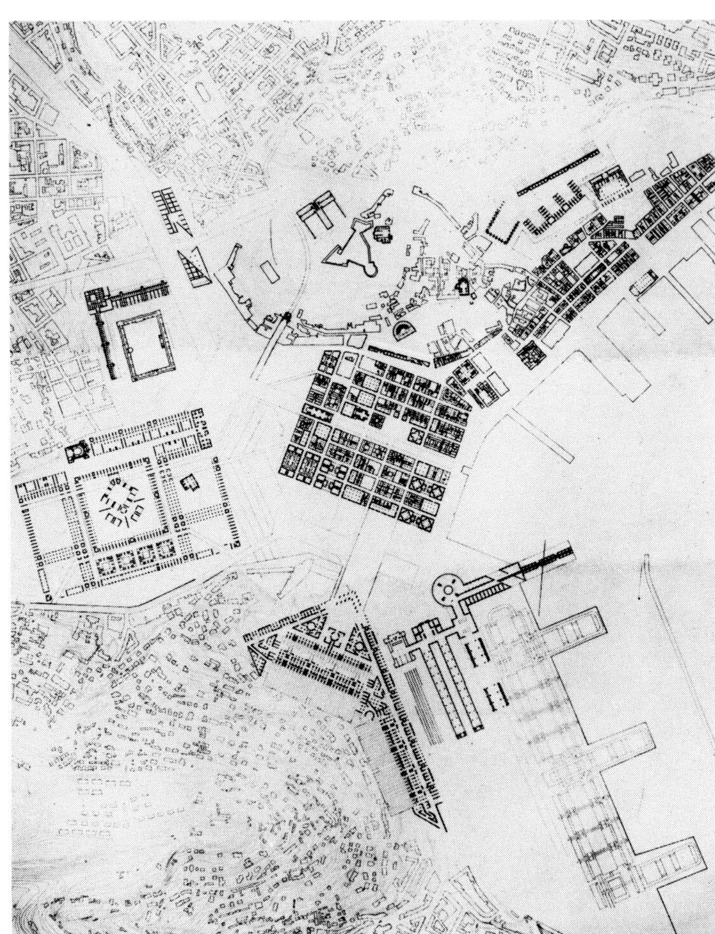

L SEMERANI, G TAMARO, A BURELLI, A ROSSI, E SAVONIZZO, V TRARONTIN, COMPETITION FOR THE HISTORIC CENTRE OF TRIESTE, 1969

in the new districts of the city; we merely adapt ourselves to their failed consistency.

Both in the East and West, those who concern themselves with architecture and town planning—geographers, sociologists, town planners—approach territory and the people who live in it as if their historical situation did not exist. They omit the liveliest, most culturally crucial material from their scientific and technical enquiries. They exclude the most concrete and creative data and images, making their projects abstract exercises outside real history.

The choices regarding the development of future social organisations have roots which go deep into current world history. The architects and town-planners must translate their choices for the future into scientific and technical forms which will help unite the structural relations between architecture and the city with the current historical situation. Furthermore, we must completely renew the instruments of morphology and typology if we are to define a relationship between architecture and the city that has been profoundly altered by the new meanings of current history, and restore to architecture the role it once had in the city.

Today the human dimension has changed, but architecture will always remain the dimension measuring how much or how little has been done for man. Architecture must therefore become the basic element of the city once more, even if the city currently tends to cut it off with its huge and complex organisation.

The direction of studies in this area is therefore determined by the attempt to define a systematic foundation of methodological criteria (in morphological and typological terms) for the great syntheses of the current forms of the urban context. On the one hand, the aim is to demystify current official town-planning; on the other, it is to question the generally piecemeal nature of civic design. This must start out from the strengths of the city as a significant centre of the new political panorama, for us,

on the European level.

In the context of these studies, there is a new direction of morphological research based on the association of systematic contexts of basic signs—points, lines and surfaces—which are linked by relations of interdependence and connected by groups of associability or continuity. In any one given place, these signs would replace the reductive prescriptions synthesising the morphological elements characteristic of the place itself. Here we have a new system of signs which can ideally translate the morphological significance of real space into the conventional space of a drawing which then rejects all reference to reality and signifies instead the phenomena of the morphological relationship.

*First published in* Il Mulino, *no 218, November/December 1971.*

# ALDO ROSSI
## What is to be Done with the Old Cities?

PERSPECTIVE VIEW OF THE CARLO FELICE THEATRE

**T**HE DEBATE ON OLD CITIES HAS NOW GONE BEYOND **the traditional problem of their historic centres to concern specific architectural questions; modern architecture's** dream of introducing the new into the old by a process of rational and gradual replacement has been checked in the face of the pressing need to preserve or destroy entire portions of towns. The objective process of urban dynamics has threatened the very survival of the old city in all its continuity and at the same time has revealed the pettiness of much of modern architecture, providing fuel for the arguments of those who want to conserve the old environment.

Thus our society now seems to accept the idea that it is necessary to save an Italy or a Europe and to respect the environment absolutely. But everyone knows and can see how far this programme is possible and how far it answers the truth. Continually and fatally the environment that is made up of the small buildings, the old fabric and the much-loved houses of the past with their colours and peeling plaster is collapsing, changing, becoming something else. In Italy, part of this change is attributable to the well-intentioned activities of the Sovrintendenze, a government body concerned with monuments and fine arts whose presence is necessary because, as everyone knows, even minor replastering in a setting which we care about very deeply often means an unwelcome alteration. Thus cities change before our very eyes.

Furthermore, if we get out of practice, we shall forget how to justify this old environment because often it is merely a reminder of old poverty and it is dear to us as evidence of a people's pain; thus the canalside houses of the washerwomen of Lodi or Milan can be preserved as a museum of this pain, along with the farmyards and the densely-packed housing of the south, the Neapolitan basement slums and the Genoese alleyways. Whatever we do with them, we still need time for their old and gloomy images to disappear. Think of what Kafka said about the old ghetto in Prague: 'Today we walk through the broad streets of the rebuilt city, but our feet and eyes are unsure. Still we tremble inwardly as if we were in the wretched old streets. Our hearts have not yet registered any of the improvements. The old unhealthy Jewish district within us is more real than the new hygienic city around us.'

I believe that when the image of the wretched old streets has disappeared completely from within us, we shall also lose the sense of the beauty of these places. Don't we already see the Venice ghetto only in this way, as a desolate place, an embarrassing place to direct tourists to? But even when we leave this tragic urban setting, we come up against a thousand cultural—not to mention practical—difficulties in every work of conservation. For example, the tourist-oriented conservation of Asolo, Portofino and Carcassone is acceptable only insofar as it is an architectural invention, romantically suited to a setting frozen in time. It is the plaster cast of the last expression of a genius, a statue in its turn.

The process of urban dynamics destroys the old buildings. Habits, customs, social groups, functions and interests inexorably change the use and form of the old city. The dwelling place, which is renewed according to new cultural standards and altered in accordance with new technologies, has a relatively faster cycle of consumption; under the present conditions, the renewal of old houses has no sense and can only be viewed as an elite operation. But in fact houses largely form what we call the environment and so we must inevitably abandon this environment to its fate, knowing that whatever sentimental reason binds us to it is just a fragment of personal or group experience and not the collective memory of the town, its events and its history. On the contrary, we know that the characteristic elements which have a primary function in the structure of the cities remain immobile and persist in the urban dynamic.

These are, for the most part, monuments.

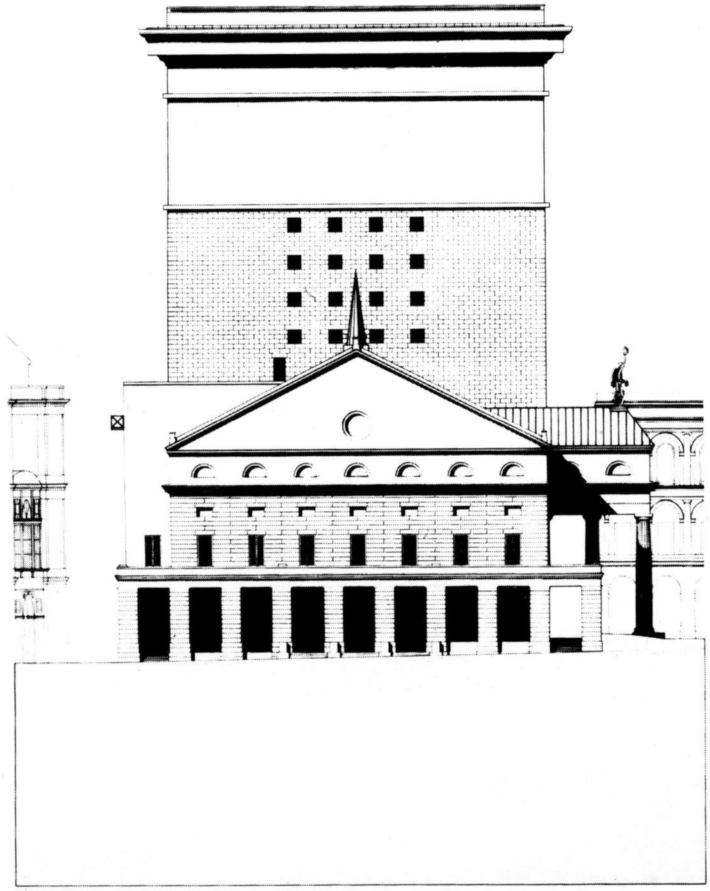

FRONT ELEVATION

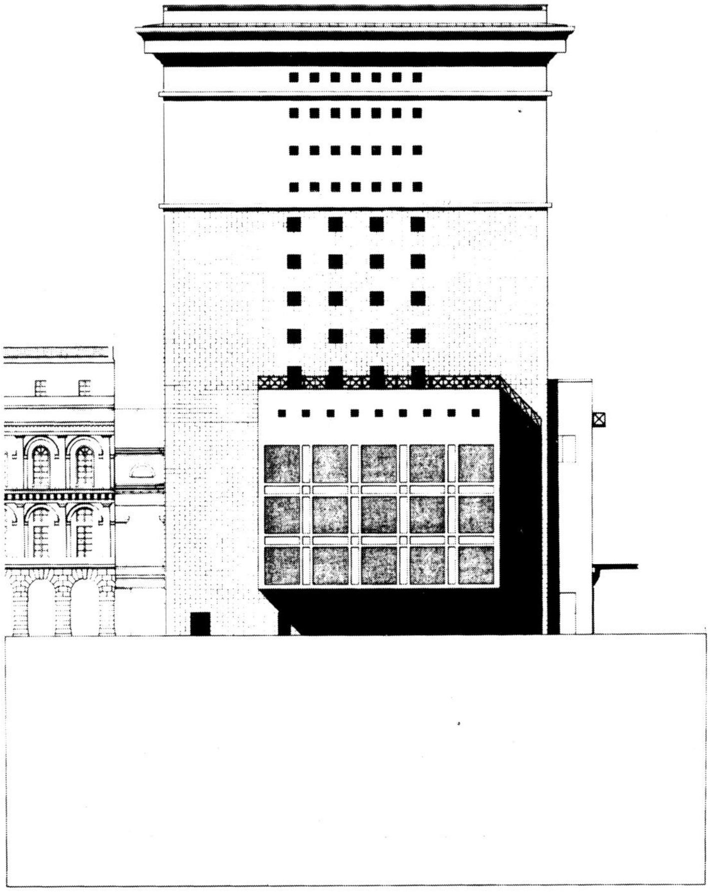

NORTH ELEVATION

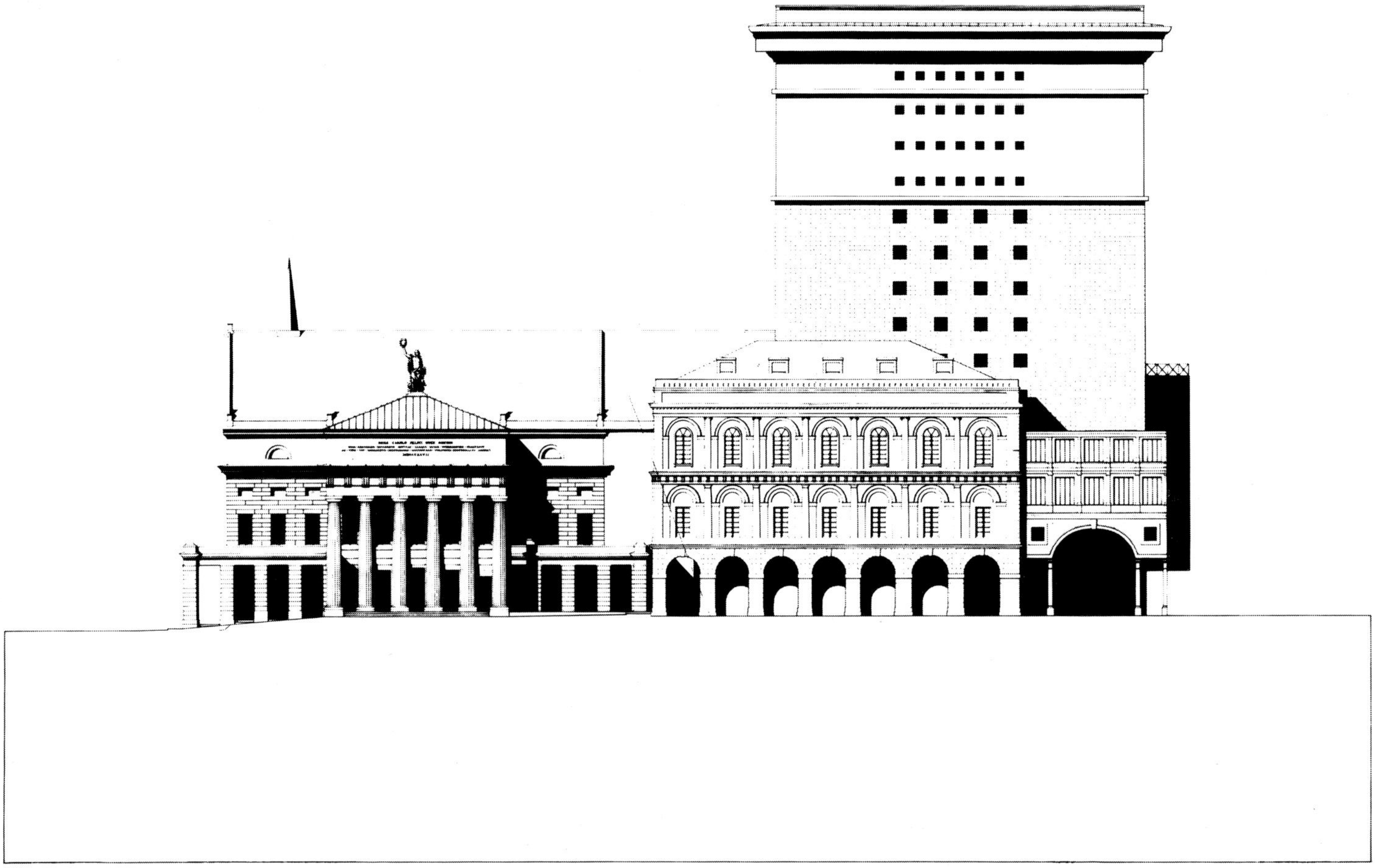

SOUTH ELEVATION

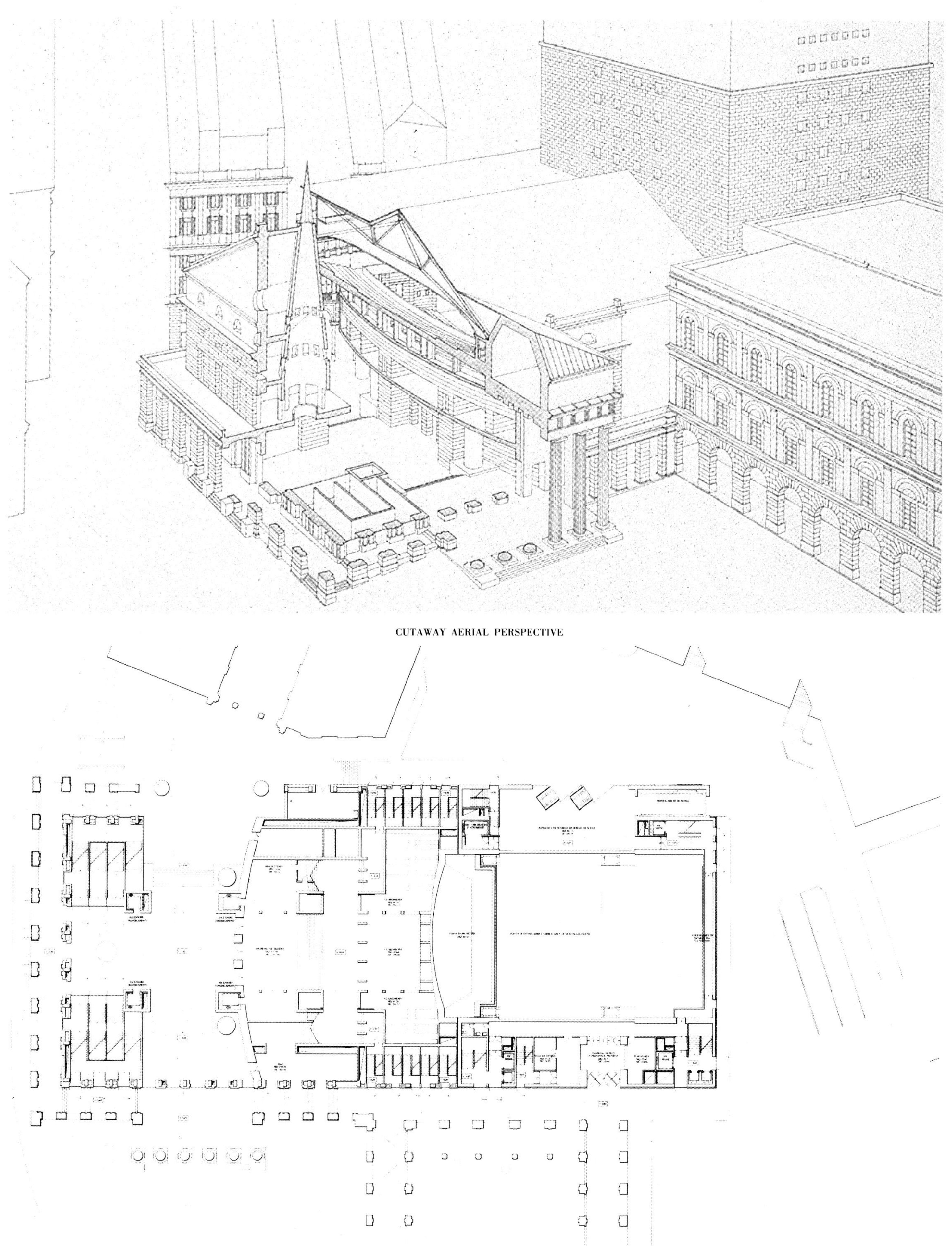

CUTAWAY AERIAL PERSPECTIVE

GROUND FLOOR PLAN

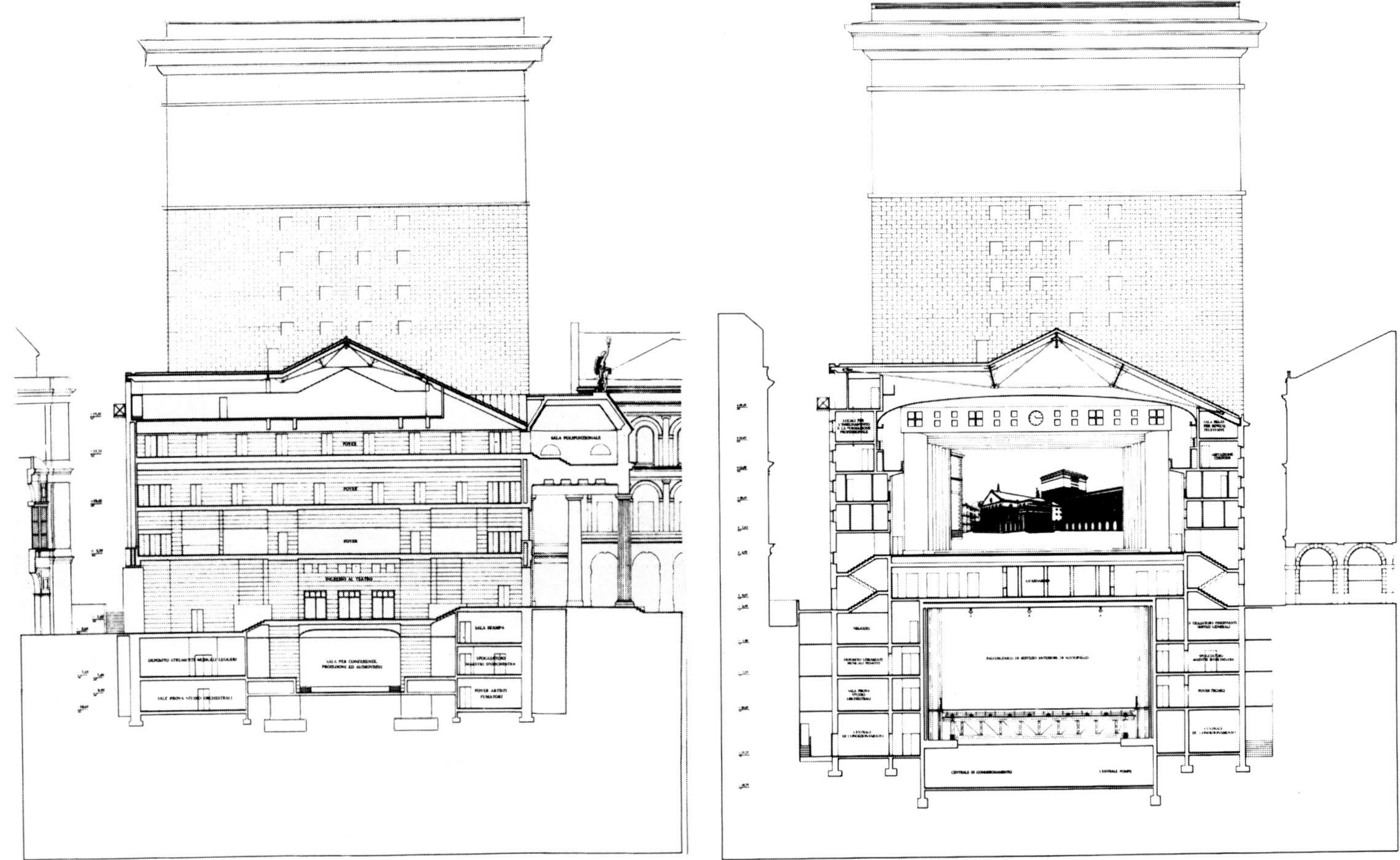

CROSS SECTIONS THROUGH THE GALLERIA

If we look at monuments old and new, we can give a single answer to the questions: What is to be done with the old towns? How do we create the new town? We must keep the old monuments and build the city through a series of fixed points, through large collective elements surrounded by ordinary housing. These monuments are symbolic forms which are stronger than their function: they are built above their time, or at least at a very different time. Roman baths became Christian basilicas, Diocletian's palace became a city, Roman amphitheatres became the sites for the Lombard's assemblies, and Adaloaldo was crowned in the Roman circus near the city walls in Milan, following a widespread tradition of holding political gatherings there.

In some places, the monumental form of the theatre became a palace, elsewhere, it became a citadel. Function and content can be altered without changing the form of the monument. Certainly we ought to be better acquainted with the importance of these major facts about urban transformation. The processes they set in motion and the meanings they take on should be subjects of scientific research into the city.

However, everyone can understand the force of the examples. Let us take the amphitheatre in Lucca. It is a singular square/market place/residential unit that retains its exact original form as a circus: the small staircases leading to the tiers of seats are still clearly visible.

We are beginning to pick out monuments even in modern architecture and the modern city which emerge as our experience of the city. Sometimes they are proposals for the idea of a city, but they are proposals which structure the growth of the city; the Alexanderplatz of Mies van der Rohe is an example. These monuments constitute a past which we are still experiencing, or a clearly glimpsed future, but this experience can occur only by means of a form, an architectural construction.

How is the construction of the city achieved through monuments? This is a problem of architectural composition which was perhaps first identified in modern architecture by Le Corbusier. He proposed the destruction of Paris and the construction of large buildings in green space. The city's monuments were to be placed amongst these buildings and used as part of the urban composition. In Venice, it would be like taking San Giorgio, Santa Maria della Salute, the Doges' Palace and St Mark's Square as fixed points of a triangulation around which to rebuild the city.

These fixed points are yet another way of understanding history and the rational reasons for what we are doing; they are the foundations of the city and of architecture. I am referring here to the logical building of architecture around the certainty of specific elements. The old cities constitute a great opportunity for architecture. Without them we would have to re-invent the whole problem of meaning in architecture. As it is, we can use their references as though we were putting them on a smooth and limitless surface and involve architecture gradually in new events.

Painters have understood this value of the city. De Chirico's Castle in Ferrara builds up, like the suburban reservoirs in Sironi, an urban landscape of precise planes and objects from which we glimpse the repeating and growing of the city part by part. The method I am referring to here is completely different from collage in painting; in collage an object dissolves in the composition of the painting.

A comparable method can be found in architecture in a consistent form of stylistic imitation; the construction of certain forms which can direct and predetermine certain feelings. This insistence on a certain form because of the feelings it can arouse seems to me largely the meaning of Romantic architecture and the sense of any 'revival'. The architecture of Romanticism was just as dominated by psychology as certain architecture is today. I am referring to a stronger form of the various feelings which bind us to this architecture and which, being autonomous, may also be available for successive transformations. These feelings are purely architectural and derive from the logic of architecture.

What then should be done with the old cities? The historic and pic-

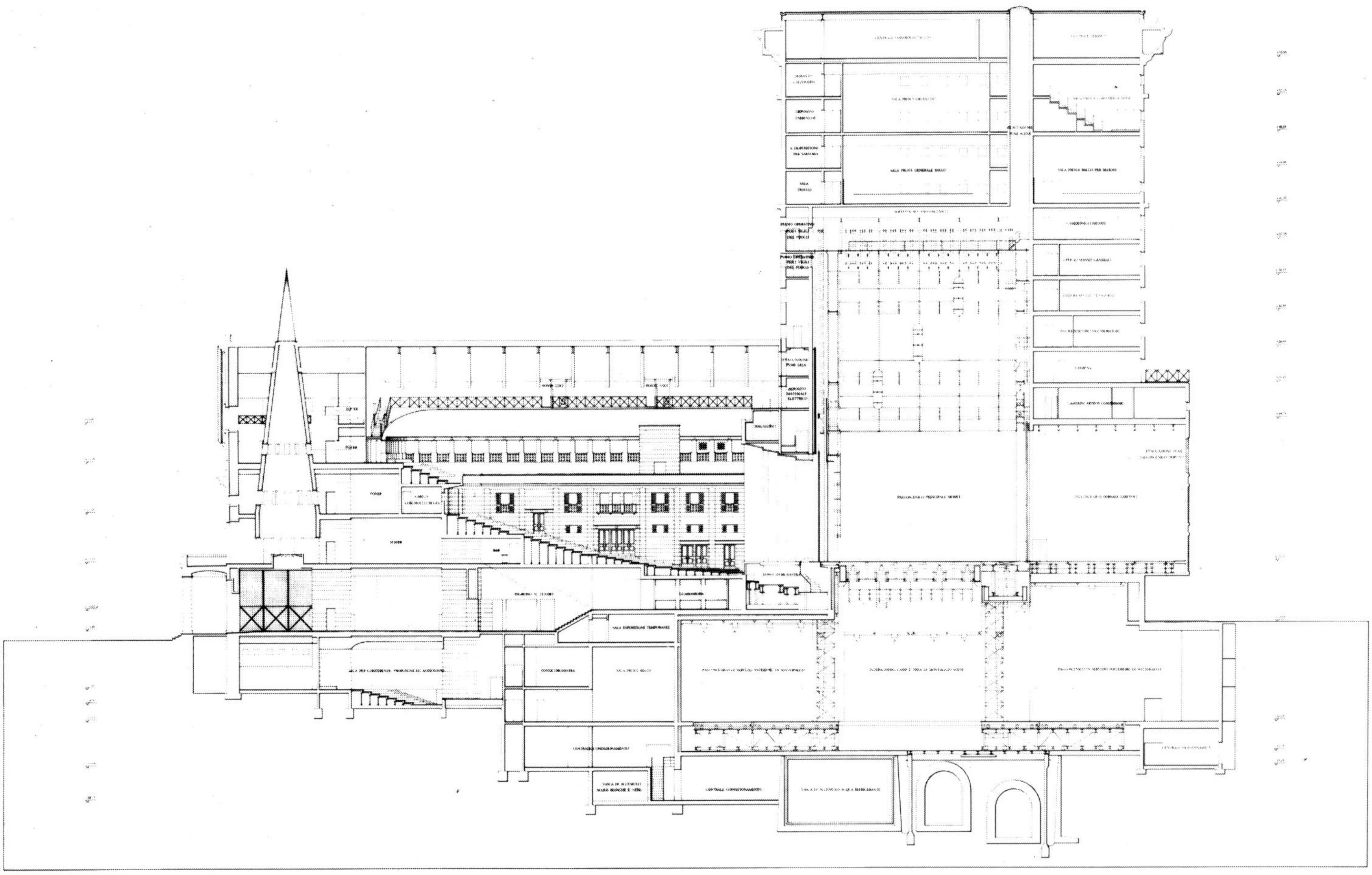

LONGITUDINAL SECTION

turesque parts should either be quickly destroyed to enable the monuments to play a direct part in the building up of the modern city or they should be retained in their entirety, whenever possible, as museums. It is obvious that this operation will have greater scope if we are able to reduce monuments and monument-cities to their most authentic values, with an economic and cultural function of their own as museum objects.

I do not believe that the problem is how to make Venice habitable. Rather, I believe that the problem is how to abandon it immediately or transform its every function and reduce it completely into a monument-city, like the Alhambra or the Kremlin. On the one hand we shall have the museum-city as an increasingly precise reference, a singular capital locked, like treasure in a cathedral, within a territory that is in a state of continuous change. On the other hand, we shall have old monuments as fixed points in the new cities, mingling and completely merging with new monuments and new collective facts in the urban composition of the great modern cities.

FRONT ELEVATION OF MODEL

MODEL INTERIOR, VIEW OF AUDITORIUM (TOWARDS STAGE)

# LUCIANO SEMERANI
## Hypothesis for Restructuring the Town of Mestre Altobello

NORTH-SOUTH VIEW OF MODEL

**A**NY ANALYTICAL EXPOSITION TENDS **to channel even the most tortuous process** into a succession of conventional choices. It also tends to use the mechanisms of rhetoric to gain possession of the reader's mind, giving him the illusion of remaining inside the rooms and enclosed gardens of the world he knows even after he has been dragged over fearful crags, through dark regions and into bottomless ravines.

We shall dispense with such artifices and, by artificially simplifying the course of our process, shall reduce our discourse to a series of oppositions which appear strange and paradoxical; a succession of choices each made within a series of elementary alternatives.

We shall outline just three choices, all of them concerning classic matters of town planning and architecture. The first choice is between the limitlessly developed metropolis and the city where growth is controlled. We support, experimentally, the first option. The second choice is between high-rise and low-rise housing. Here, we align ourselves with those in favour of detached one-family houses. The third choice is between architecture and context, or, remembering Ernesto N Rogers, between the project and the pre-existing features of the environment. We take the orthodox line respecting the character of the place.

Professor Panos Koulermos of the University of Southern California, who is a frequent visitor to the IUAV, has projected the city of Los Angeles onto the same scale as the Veneto region to prove that, in physical terms at least, they can be superimposed: *a region = a city*. We designed the Mestre project as if we were designing a section of Los Angeles and this is how we regulated its positioning in a *topos*, the Veneto, for whose history and geography we have great respect. The Veneto, much more than Venice itself, forms the context of the town of Mestre.

## Rules and Principles

The IUAV has been studying Mestre Altobello for about ten years now. These studies have produced the following recurrent hypotheses:

1 There is a need to link the potential plans with the existing social facilities, however inadequate. Mestre has a church, parish offices and a small square.

2 There is a need to retain the railway land running diagonally from the south-west to the north-east for transport circulation.

3 There is a need to provide services and green spaces for the new zones, partly to meet building standards but mainly to fulfill a collective image of the city: hence the provision of squares, commercial centres and multi-use centres of a social-cultural nature.

These three hypotheses have been re-examined in the present project, but one recurrent theme has not, namely, the idea of using a sort of inhabited bastion (a layer of building of medium height that would echo the complex circulatory structure of Aymonino's project for the Gallaratese) to provide a 'visual limit' to the town, a *shape from the outside*, for anyone coming from Venice. This idea was put forward by authoritative architects (such as Ludovico Quaroni in the Barene di San Giuliano competition), and it is also at the heart of the project already built by Gianni Fabbri on the edges of the area. But although it may seem inevitable or inspiring at first sight, the hypothesis that Mestre should be 'seen from Venice' in the same way that Venice is seen from the causeway, an unmistakable form and skyline, is somewhat ingenuous because the walls and boundaries of cities have always constituted mere stages in their development.

**Collaborators:** Luciano Semerani, Giovanni Fraziano, Giuseppe Rocco, Giovanni Testi, Guido Zuliani.

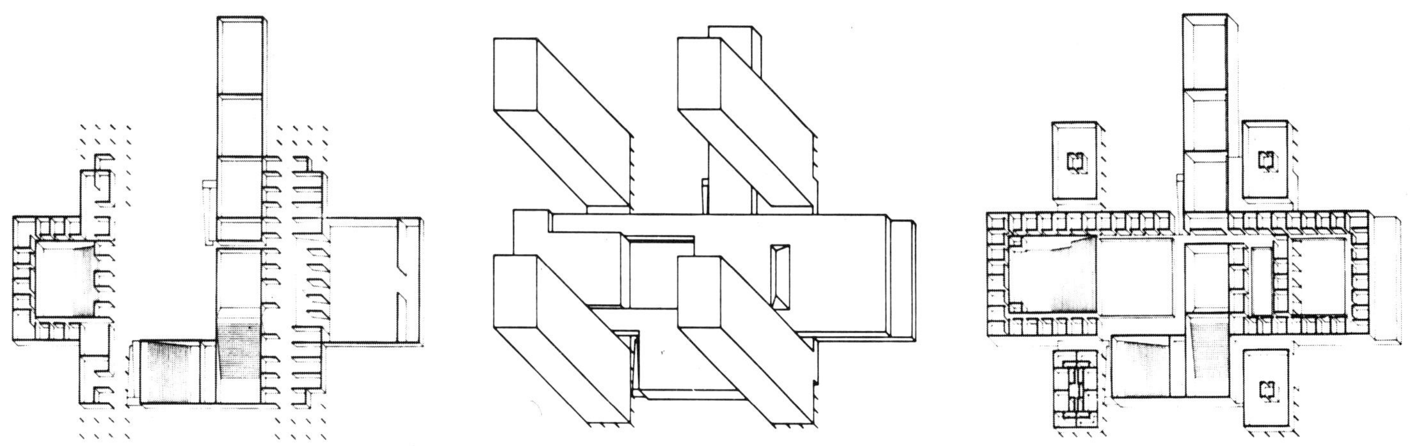

SCHEMES RELATIVE TO ELEMENTS WITH TOWERS. LEFT: GROUND FLOOR ISOMETRIC. CENTRE: COMPLEX SCHEME. RIGHT: FIRST FLOOR ISOMETRIC

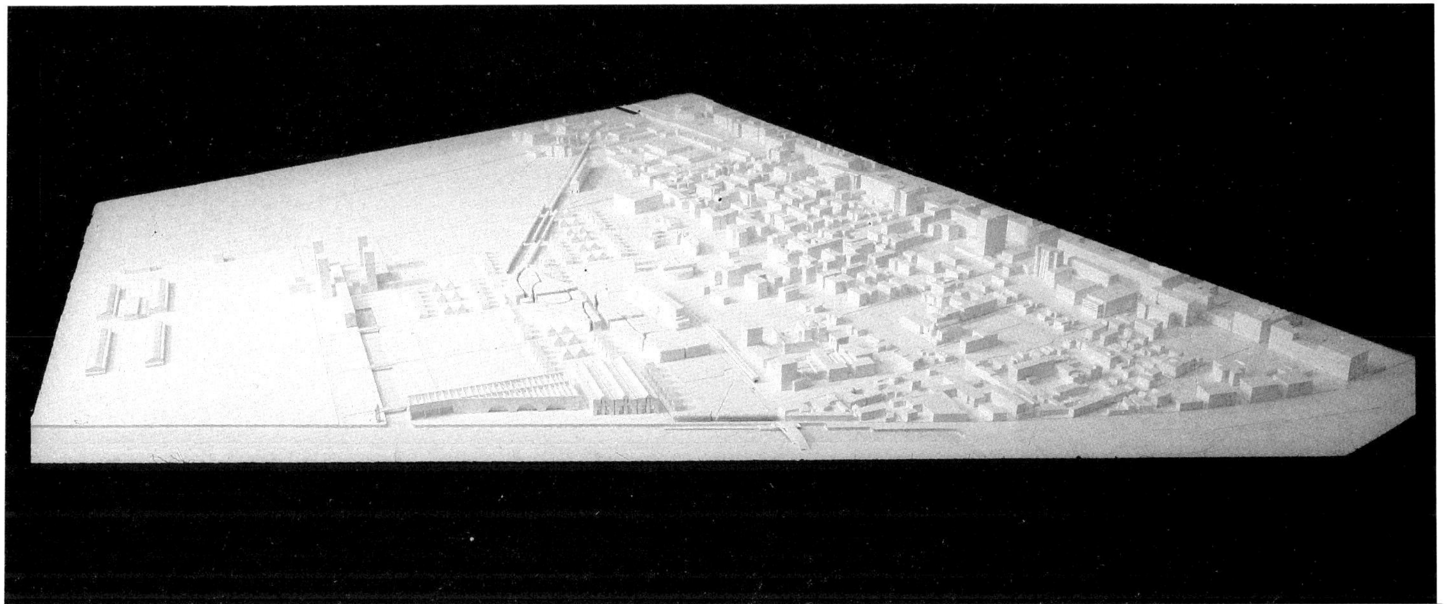

THE LIMITLESSLY DEVELOPED CITY. FORT WORTH, TEXAS. 19TH-CENTURY BIRD'S EYE VIEW

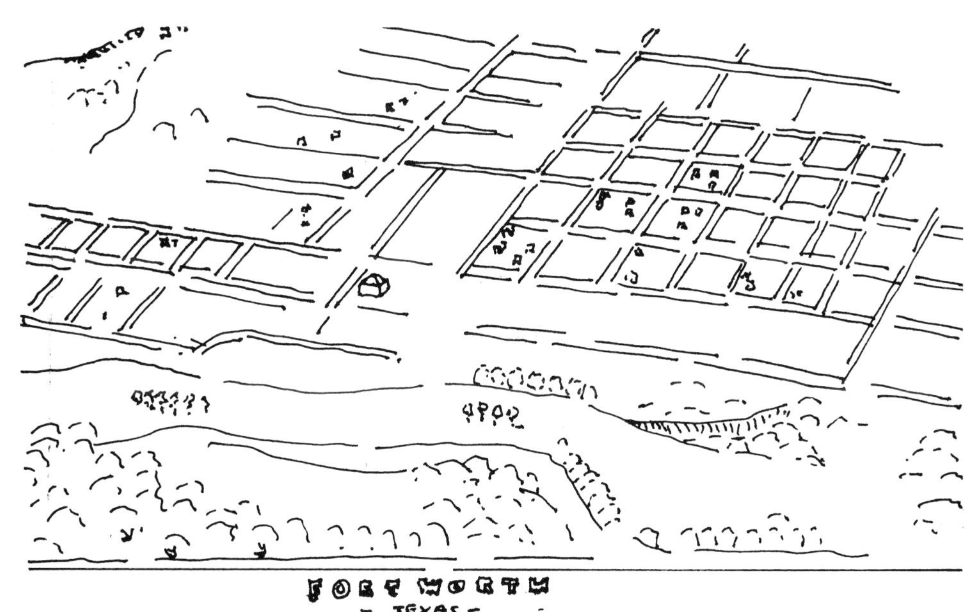


AERIAL PERSPECTIVE SHOWING THE LAYOUT OF FORT WORTH, TEXAS

AERIAL VIEW OF MODEL

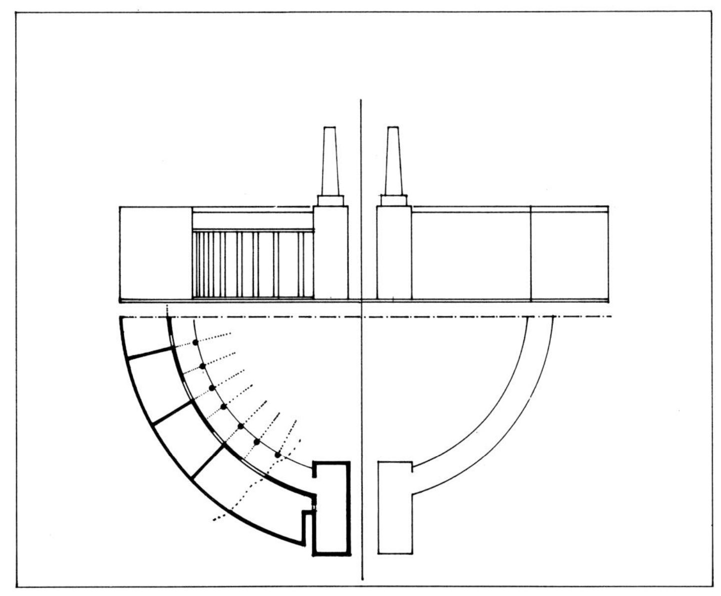

STUDY SKETCH FOR AN ARCHITECTURAL TYPE: THE EXEDRA WITH COLONNADES

EAST-WEST VIEW OF MODEL, WITH THE SALSO CANAL AND WAREHOUSES IN THE FOREGROUND

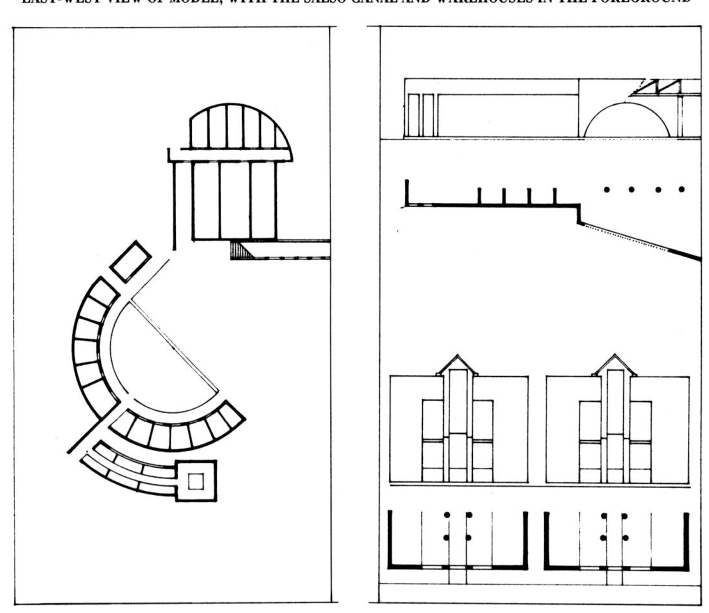

STUDY SKETCHES FOR ARCHITECTURAL TYPES. LEFT: AN EXEDRA, RIGHT: SERIAL ELEMENTS (WAREHOUSES)

GREGOTTI ASSOCIATI, MODULAR DIAGRAM OF THE SETTLEMENT SYSTEM

# THE TERRITORY

# VITTORIO GREGOTTI
## Territory and Architecture

**W**HILE PRESENTING MY PROJECT FOR THE **University of Calabria, I thought again of some of the theoretical reflections I had made in** *The Territory of Architecture* ten years earlier, in 1966, for they seemed relevant to many aspects of the overall layout of the Calabria project.

The theory of the materials of architecture and the pre-eminence of the figure as their organisational structure was central to *The Territory of Architecture*, but it did not resolve the specific organisational problems at Calabria. It concerned itself primarily with questions of theory and history, whether as hypotheses of the organisation of personal and group memory, or as a specific history of the discipline—the vacillations of its margins and the shifts in its centre of interests, its territory and its privileged relations with other disciplines. However, the physical spirit of history is the built environment which surrounds us, the manner of its transformation into visible things, its gathering of depths and meanings which differ not only because of what the environment appears to be, but also because of what it *is* structurally. The environment is composed of the traces of its own history. If geography is therefore the way in which the signs of history solidify and are superimposed in a form, the architectural project has the task of drawing attention to the essence of the environmental context through the transformation of form.

From 1963-64 onwards I began to put these problems at the centre of my reflections on architecture: my first opportunity to experiment with their consequences in planning was at the XIIIth Triennale in Milan in 1964. Since then, I have always tried to keep the relationship between my theory and my work open, if not consistent. I have attemped, for instance, to understand what one could conclude from reflecting on the idea of landscape and nature as the sum total of all things and of their past configurations. Nature, in this sense, is not seen as an indifferent, inscrutable force or a divine cycle of creation, but rather as a collection of material things whose reasons and relations architecture has the task of revealing. We must therefore modify, redouble, measure, situate and utilise the landscape in order to know and meet the environment as a geographical totality of concrete things which are inseparable from their historical organisation.

This can only be done if we abandon the sociological or ecological or administrative notion of the environment as an imprisoned element and think of it instead as material for architecture. It should be made clear that this idea of the environment is not a system in which architecture is dissolved, but is on the contrary a load-bearing material for the architectural project, enabling new planning principles and methods to accommodate the spirit of the specific terrain.

The spirit behind these new methods is *modification*. Modification reveals an awareness of being part of a pre-existing whole, of changing one part of a system to transform the whole. Through its etymological root, *modus*, modification is linked to the concept of measure and the geometrical world of regulated things. It is modification which transforms *place* into *architecture* and establishes the original symbolic act of making contact with the earth, with the physical environment, with the idea of nature as a totality. Such a concept of the project sees architecture as a system of relations and distances, as the measurement of intervals rather than as isolated objects. Thus the specificity of the solution is closely related to differences in situation, context or environment. We do not, therefore, conceive of space as a uniform and infinite extension where no place is privileged: space is not of identical value in all directions, but rather is composed of differences, discontinuities considered as value and as experience. The organisation of space, therefore, starts from the idea of *place*: the project transforms *place* into *settlement*.

The origin of architecture does not lie in the hut, in the cave or in the mythical 'Adam's house in paradise'. Before a support was transformed into a column, a roof into a pediment, and stone heaped upon stone, man put stone on the ground in order to recognise place in the midst of the unknown universe and thereby measure and modify it. Like every aspect of measuring, this required a radical simplicity. From this point of view, there are essentially two ways to place oneself in relation to the context. The instruments of the first way are mimetic imitation, organic assimilation and visible complexity. The second way uses measurement: distance, definition, rotation within complexity.

In the first case the problem is mirroring reality, in the second it is establishing the double. The latter mode is based on restless division:

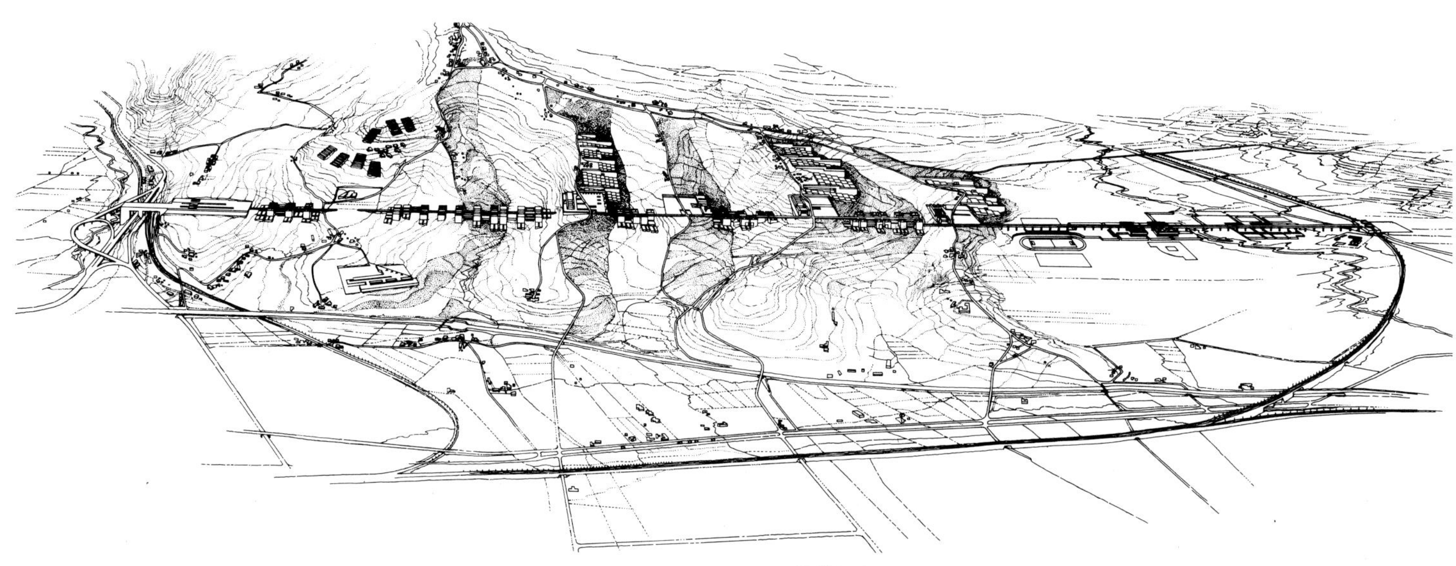

GENERAL VIEW OF THE CRATI VALLEY

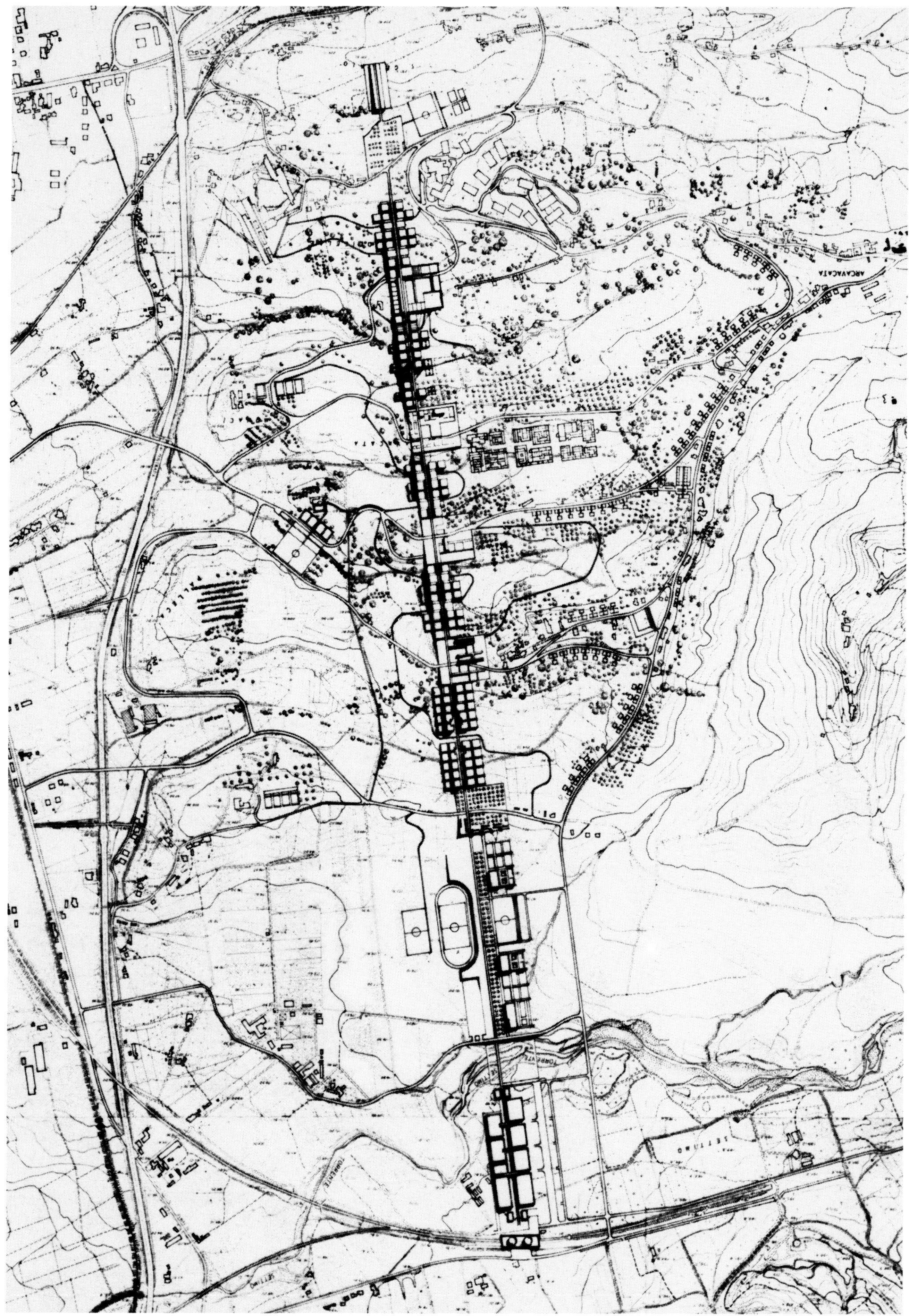

SITE PLAN OF THE PROJECT

putting up a wall, building an enclosure, defining regions, producing a densely articulated interior which will correspond to the fragmentation and differences of behaviour. A simple exterior will thus appear as a measure of the larger environment's complexity. For this reason a material is not actually a thing of nature: it is more earthly and more abstract, alluding to the form of the place, to things as they are combined, but also to what is beneath, to the stable geological support, to a nature which is historically transformed, to a nature which is the product of thought, and which as a result of being frequented or settled has become a shared memory.

The project, then, must be established upon the regulating tradition of style and métier. But what gives architectural truth and concreteness to this tradition is its meeting with the site, for only by perceiving the site as a specific environment can those exceptions which generate architecture emerge.

My current work explores the implications of developing an architecture of context. This has led me to confront the problem of implementing large-scale works and to examine which principles and methods would stand up to the realities of production. I have been especially concerned with work environments in industry and universities, and was involved with the important competition for the University of Calabria. The project's main proposal was to base the design of the new university on a principle of settlement. This principle is evinced by an irregular alignment and by the connection between it and the sinuous terrain of the countryside. It functions as a way of gauging the landscape and regulating and characterising a large-scale design. Alignment and discontinuity are, moreover, ancient and characteristic methods of regulating settlements in Calabria.

The project also attempts to bring about an interaction between morphological and functional systems. The first system consists of a linear succession of university departments running across the hill system to the plain of the River Crati. The blocks housing the departmental activities accommodate the varying levels of the land and are laid out on a square plan on the axis of a bridge. The second system considers the morphology of the hills, the succession of their slopes and peaks (which carry the local road system) and their relationship to the fabric of the low-tiered houses along the northern slope intended as university residences. Since the southern slopes are cultivated with olive trees, an alternating succession of residential units and natural spaces results. The university services, which are open towards the exterior, are situated at the junctures between the bridge system and the hilltop roads.

The 7m-wide upper lane of the bridge caters for public transport and goods traffic; the lower lane is for pedestrians and internal student traffic. Between the two lanes, the various installations run along a conduit with a triangular section. The tall blocks of the university departments are linked to the bridge by a narrow body of services placed perpendicular or parallel to the bridge depending on the type of cube.

The whole layout of the university is regulated by a grid of 25.20 × 25.20m extended over two modules to the two sides of the axis, forming a settlement strip 110m wide. The tall blocks vary between two and five storeys to maintain a constant height of 232.40m above sea-level and project onto the line of transverse section of the valley below. They are enclosed by load-bearing reinforced concrete walls measuring 21.60 × 25.20m at distances of 3.60m on centre. The horizontal structures are supported by metal beams with a span of 19.60m for internal linkage. These control the positioning of the structures of the floors, spaces between floors and intermediate floors. In the second type, the internal structures are also reinforced concrete, and pillars divide the interior into two different articulated spaces: on the one hand, small spaces for studies and offices; on the other, large collective spaces for laboratories, lecture halls, libraries, etc.

The natural lighting for the interiors is obtained through large open-

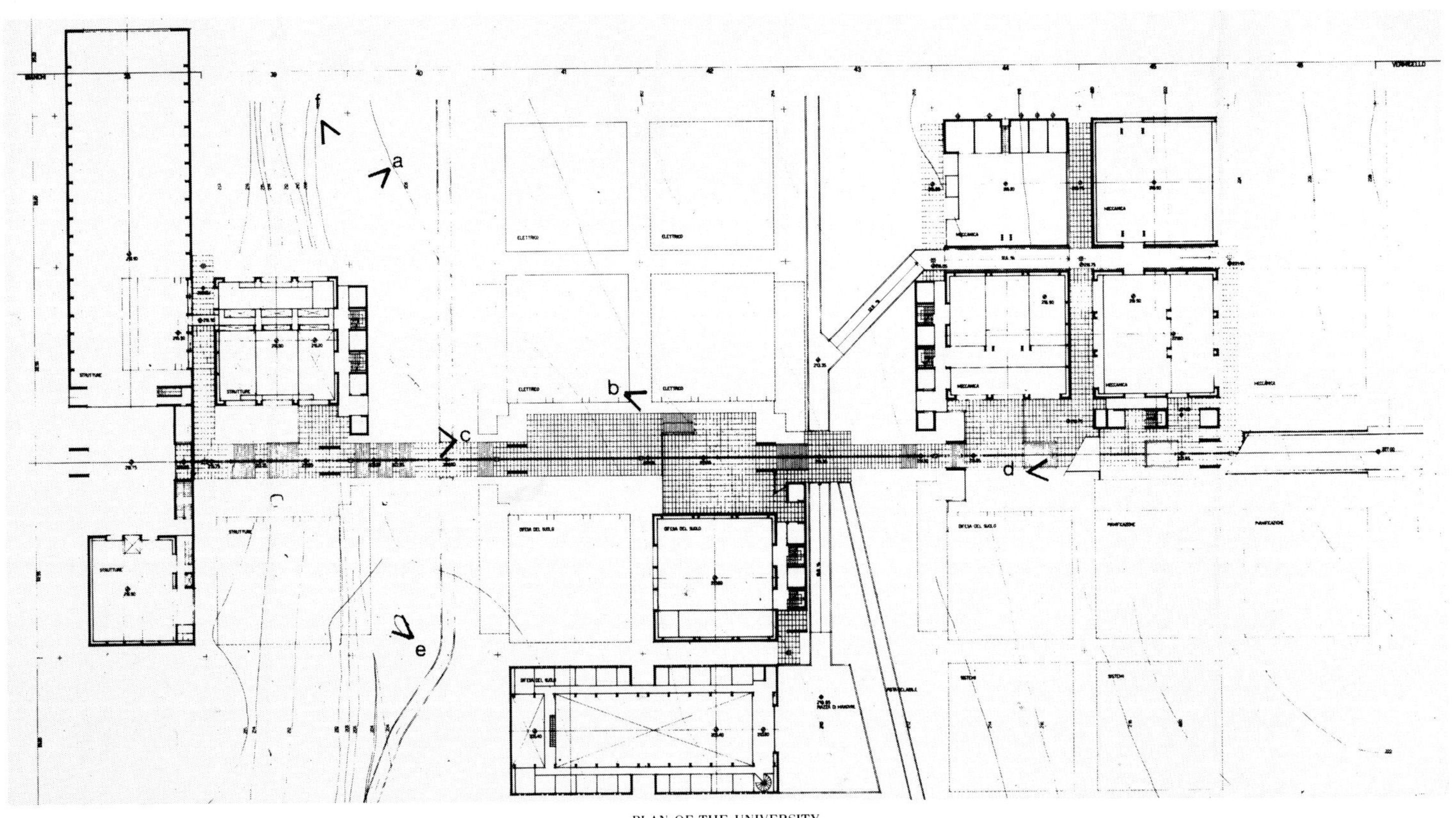

PLAN OF THE UNIVERSITY

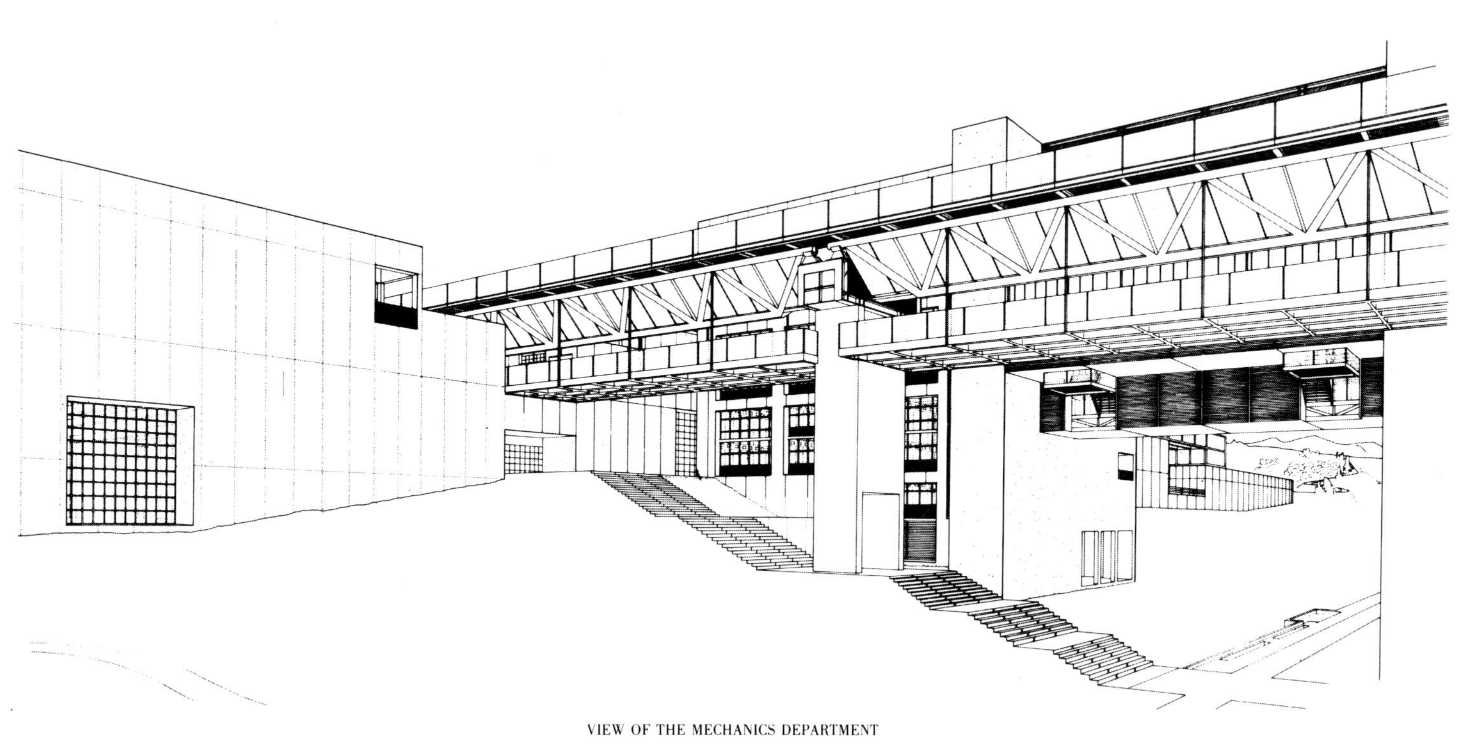

VIEW OF THE MECHANICS DEPARTMENT

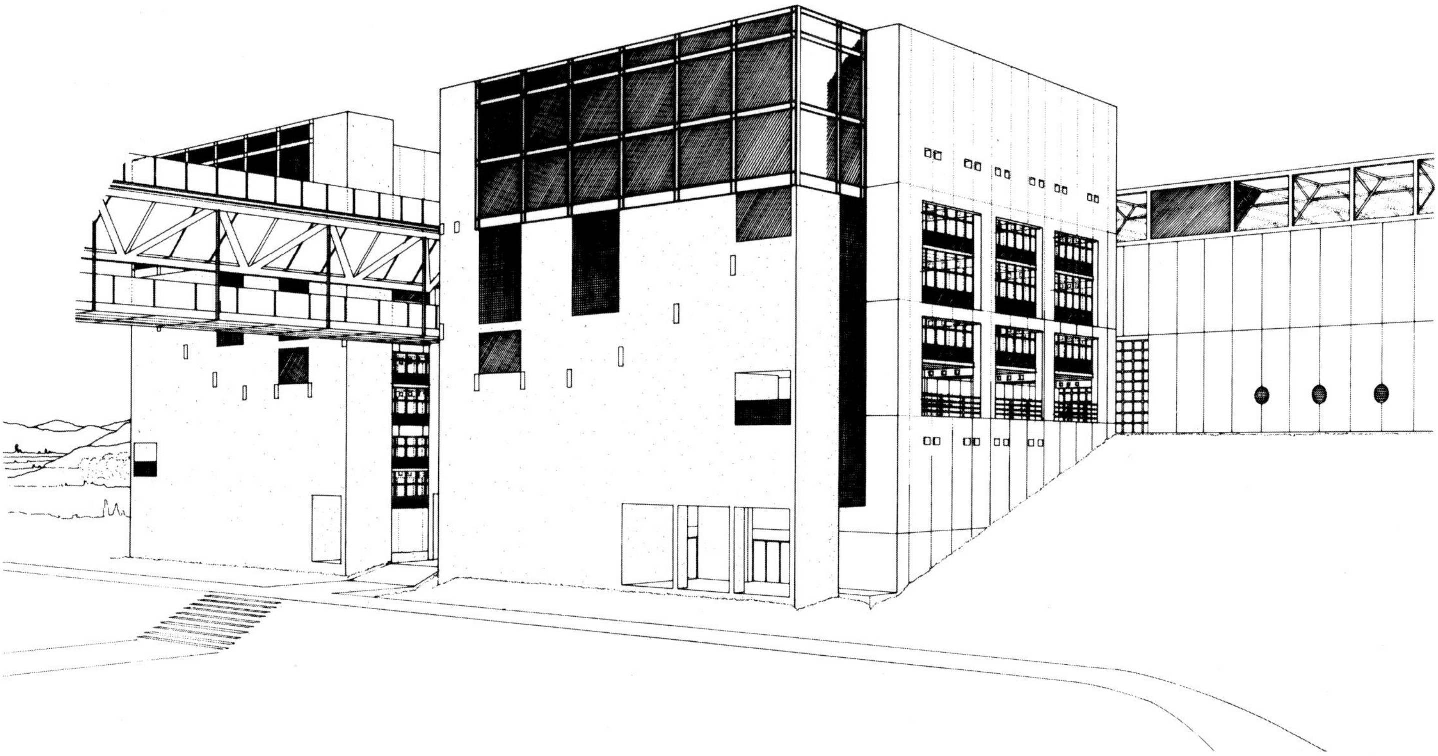

SIDE OF THE MECHANICS DEPARTMENT, DESIGNED FOR JUNCTURE WITH THE REINFORCED HALL

VIEW OF BRIDGE

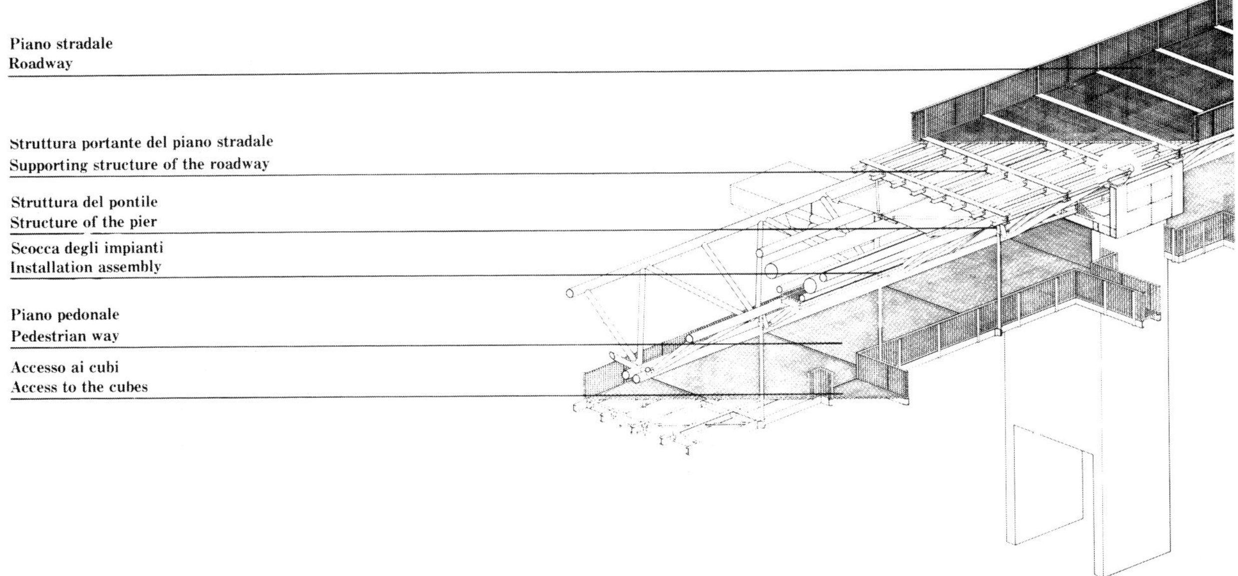



SECTION THROUGH BRIDGE

HUMANITIES DEPARTMENT, BRIDGE AND CUBES WITH MAIN HALL IN CENTRE

ings in the perimeter wall and the transparent, partially sun-screened roofing. This strategically regulates the view of the natural landscape and external architecture.

The outer modules of the grid are occupied by the extension of the tall blocks on the ground floor to form a support base and house the more cumbersome technical equipment. The 250-seat lecture halls are suspended between the volumes of two lateral blocks in order to leave the continuity of the slope unbroken and form a passageway below the tiered arches. The blocks which house the various departments and a whole range of teaching and research activities form the basic element in the grouping and set up a morphological referent for the university's future growth and change of layout. The final phase of project, providing accommodation for 12,000 students, suggested the doubling of the departmental spaces. In this projection, a rapid link-up service would replace the bridge and would continue both to the new station with parking facilities at the mouth of the Paola tunnel and to additional parking at the Cozenza tunnel. The level part of the northern area would house the buildings and supply areas of the main regional sports centre and the laboratories of the national research centre.

At this stage in its development, the university organism would be making full use of two access systems deriving from the settlement system: the two ends of alignment would be linked by a fast, efficient urban transport system while the hill roads would continue to function as they had in the first phase. The squares would be the meeting point of the two systems.

The plan for the University of Calabria was the result of a competition won in 1974 by a group consisting of E Battisti, V Gregotti, H Matsui, P Nicolin, F Purini, C Rusconi Clerici. Urban planning was by Laris.

**Collaborators on the project**: P Cerri, V Gregotti, H Matsui (Gregotti Associati); G Grandori, G Ballio, A Castiglioni, G Colombo (Structural Engineers); Tenke VRC (Engineers).

GENERAL VIEW OF THE HUMANITIES AND CHEMISTRY DEPARTMENTS

JUNCTURE OF THE BRIDGE WITH THE LIBRARY SQUARE

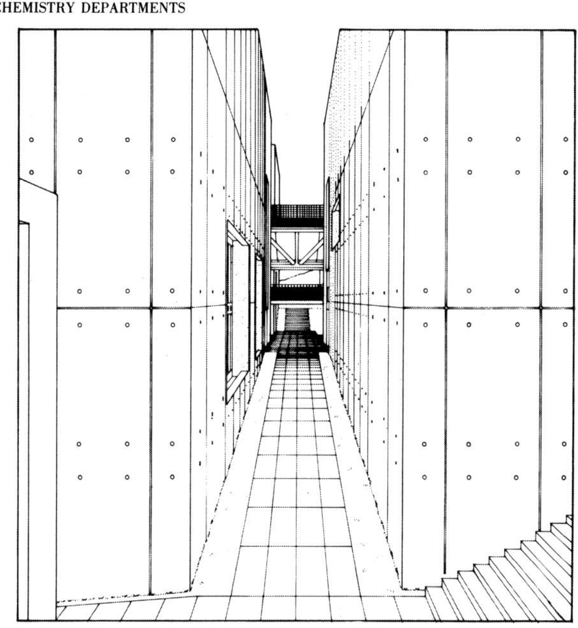

MAIN HALL OF THE MECHANICS DEPARTMENT

RELIEF MODEL

LOW CUBES, LOAD-BEARING STRUCTURE

# VITTORIO GREGOTTI
## Project for the Venice Lagoon
## A Student Thesis

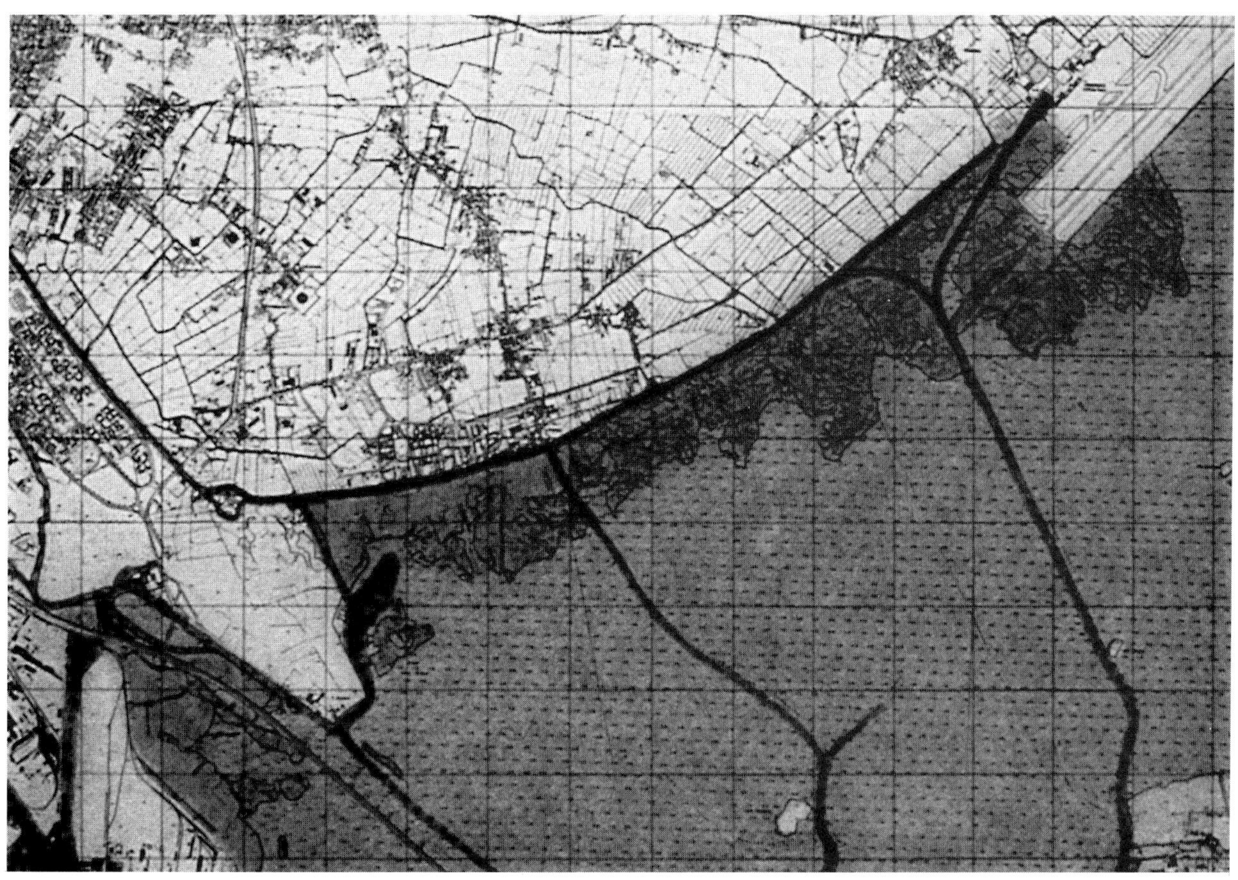

PLAN OF THE AREA COVERED BY THE PROJECT. IN BLUE, THE LAGOON AND PENETRATING CANALS

**T**HE PROBLEM OF THE LAGOON'S ACCESSIBILITY **affects two specific areas: the complex of large and small islands beginning with Venice itself and the whole strip of** border area which defines the breadth of the lagoon basin, the so-called *gronda*. The area requires a communications system between the various islands, as well as close communication between the settlements on land and those on the islands.

In the past few years attention has been concentrated on Venice and its malfunctions. At best, researchers have taken into account the totality of the islands, but they have rarely, in tackling the problem of the lagoon's accessibility, put themselves on the side of the mainland and tried to provide an answer to the serious dearth of relationships and linkages between the territory of Mestre and the Venice Lagoon. It is not simply a matter of solving the problems caused by the demands of tourism, but of overcoming the present-day division of the territory into parts, ensuring the permeability of the *gronda*. The articulation of the problem of accessibility must be based on the creation of a range of possibilities which take into account the complexities and specific nature of the context and geographical structure.

We believe that the system of intersection points (terminals) on a territorial scale should be integrated with another system to provide more frequent penetration on an urban scale. If this is to be achieved, there

must first be a review of the mainland road system to ensure the maximum permeability of the main routes that link up with the lagoon. All the areas of the *gronda* are of particular significance in this hypothesis because of their characteristic position on the borders between the mainland and the lagoon. It is in these border zones that the relation between the streets and the canal system must be resolved, and the selection and planning of the intersections must be made.

The area between San Giuliano and Tessera is the most significant for examination of the aims described above because of its position on the edges of the built-up centre of Mestre and the sizeable settlements of Campalto and Tessera, and because of its physical structure (the Canale Orsellino runs its entire length and is crossed in turn by a series of canals draining into the lagoon).

This proposal envisages a terminal at Tessera. This would link up with future airport offices and facilities and serve as an intersection for road, air and water traffic used almost exclusively by tourists. At San Giuliano a more urban terminal would be built specifically for all those commuters who come into Venice by shuttle train and are currently crowded out of Piazzale Roma or Tronchetto. At Campalto and at San Giuliano along the canal of Seno della Seppa, there would be two intersection points on an urban scale for the residents to use as mooring zones.

The main role of the *gronda* in the overall system of built-up areas would once more coincide with its role in the morphological system of the territory: that of mediator between land and water. Its primary function would be to create, in various ways and for various needs, a series of communications with the whole of the lagoon.

Any action on a section of *gronda* immediately brings up the old question of boundaries, because this is an area which by its very nature emerges as an element of division and mediation between two distinct geographical realities. The theme of the boundary recurs constantly in all the projects; from San Giuliano to Tessera it is the principle on which the whole proposal is structured. On one hand the limit, experienced as an element of division, tends to emphasise the specific nature of each single area; on the other, it clearly picks out the points of rupture where relations occur. These points would acquire a definite identity because they are sole elements of connection and linkage.

The relation between the mainland urban settlement and the lagoon settlement will be neither direct nor identical over the whole area of the lagoon. On the contrary, it will be highly differentiated, leading to a precise hierarchy of possibilities and situations.

It is the canal which determines the opportunities of access and the areas most suitable for intervention. With a penetrating canal, the system opens up, something happens. Without a penetrating canal, there is neither a direct relationship nor an immediate visual relationship between mainland and lagoon. The lagoon is sensed negatively through the presence of a series of frontier elements; one has to get up on a barrier or go through barriers to get a view of it. These limits, which are made up of earth (embankments) or buildings (raised roads), indicate the lagoon's outermost borders, that is, they define exactly the field of action.

This thesis offers an opportunity to consider closely a series of choices resulting from experiments carried out in recent years. An attempt is made to test certain principles of method as well as more general theoretical principles which are considered fundamental for planning in architecture.

The relationship between architecture and planning is undoubtedly one of the larger problems facing anyone starting from the supposition that architecture is essentially work on environmental wholes which concentrates on formalising and making sense of physical space. It is difficult to establish theoretically which tasks concern town planning and which concern architectural planning. The various planning scales cannot be established unequivocally by arbitrary measurements but must be defined on the basis of the problems to be solved. In any case the architectural scale should be the instrument of every process aimed at the transformation of the physical environment.

We believe that it is important to introduce figurative aims right at the start of the planning process and that this is indeed the architect's province. When we embark upon an operation of this type it is often necessary to go beyond considerations of a functional nature and attempt to tackle the environment as a formal reality to be known and organised, and to pinpoint a principle by which to structure the whole planning operation. In our proposal the principle of settlement (as a synthetic act of positioning oneself with regard to context and as a parameter of judgement) becomes the 'thread' holding the various actions together, the element giving unity to the overall operation and the key to interpreting the whole project.

The principle of settlement can be applied over a range of situations; its strength is its ability to absorb the diversity each case presents, while preserving the specific quality of each single project.

**Student thesis by**: Michele Reginaldi, Daniela Saviola, Mario Tassoni

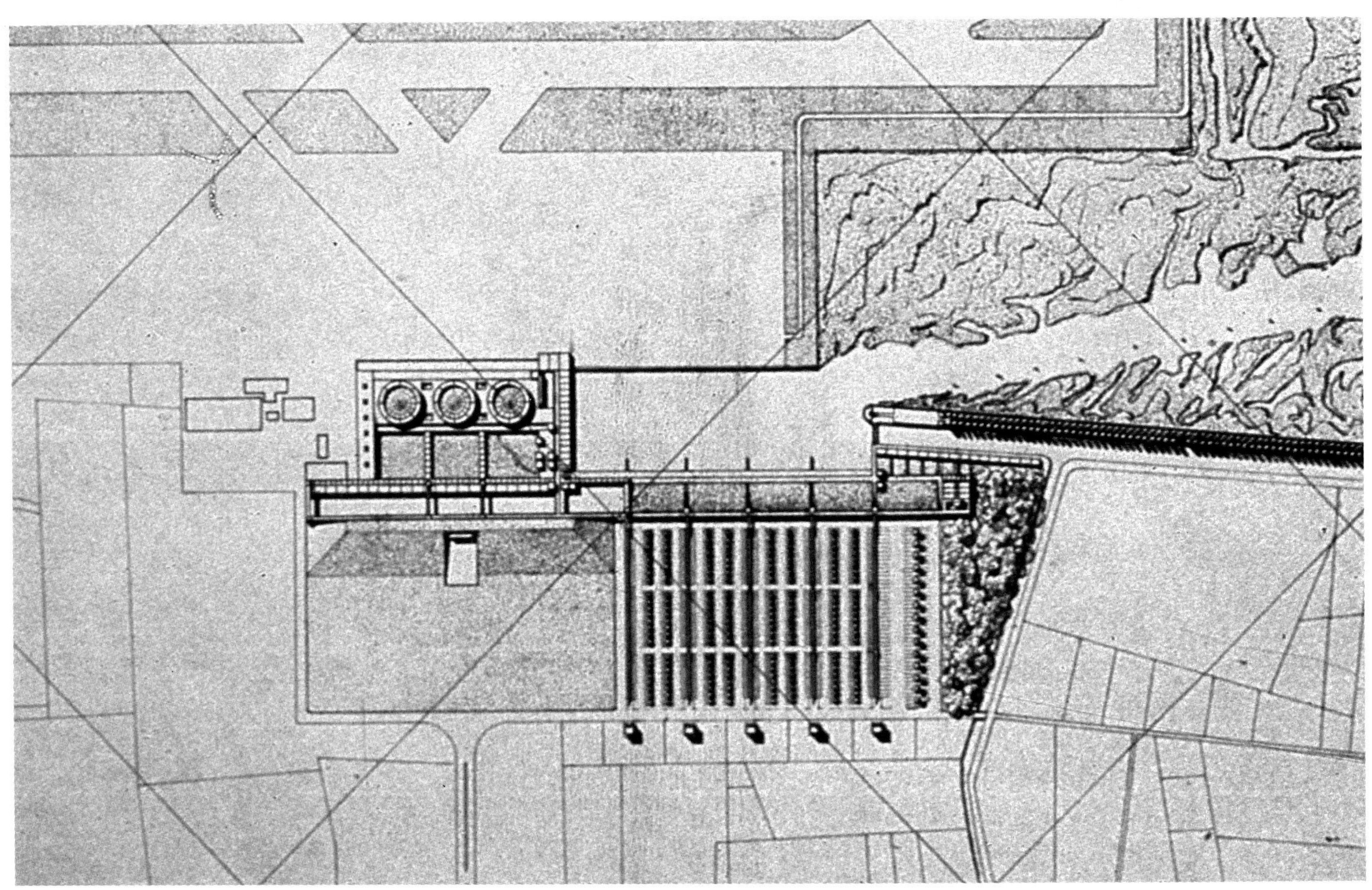

TESSERA, GENERAL PLAN OF THE INITIATIVE

HEAD OF THE VAULT SHOWING INTERNAL FACADE

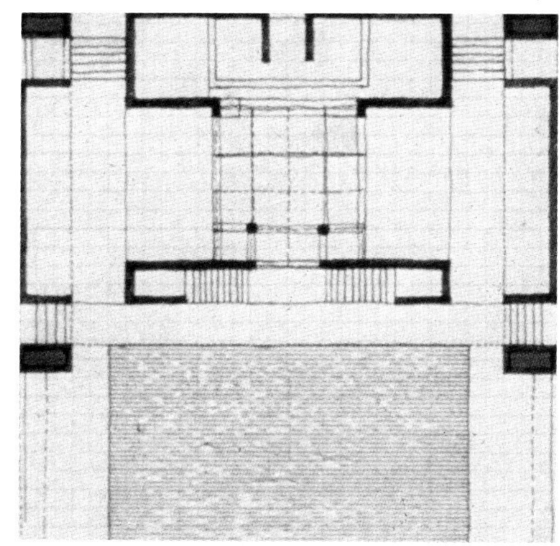

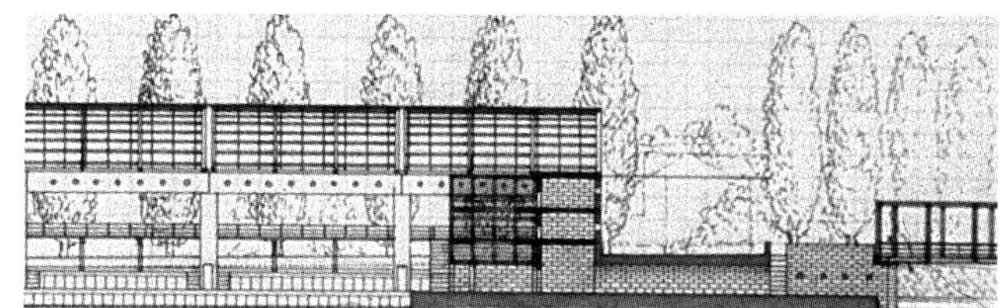

SECTION

PLAN AND LONGITUDINAL SECTION OF THE VAULT AND SERVICES

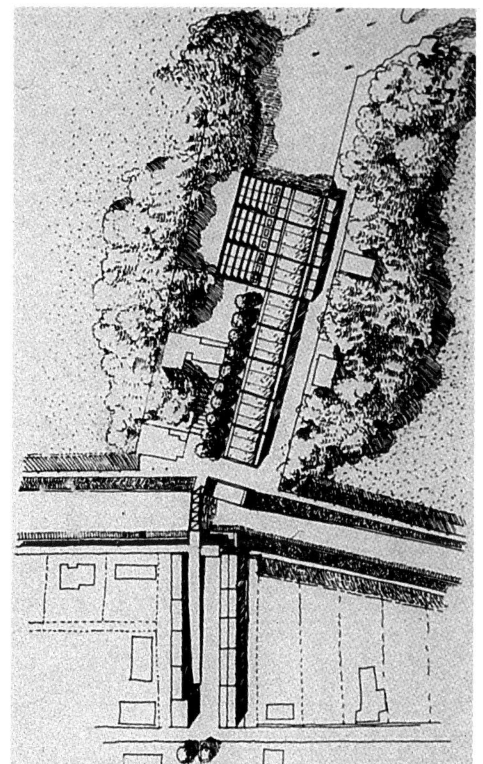

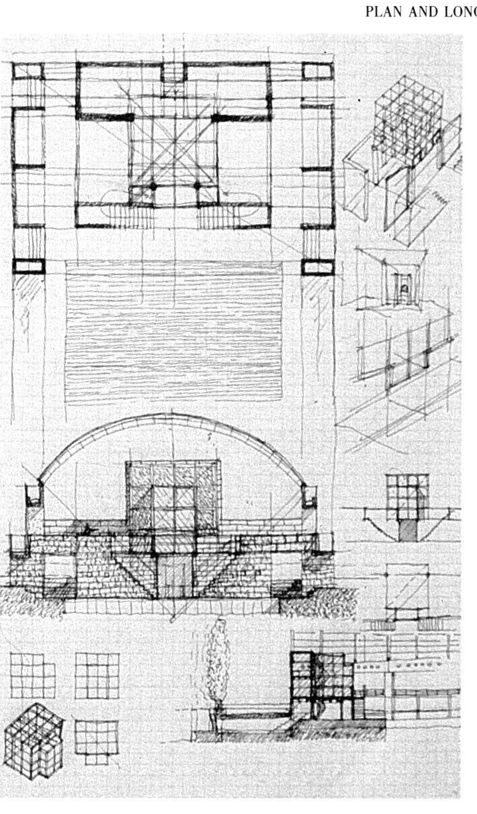

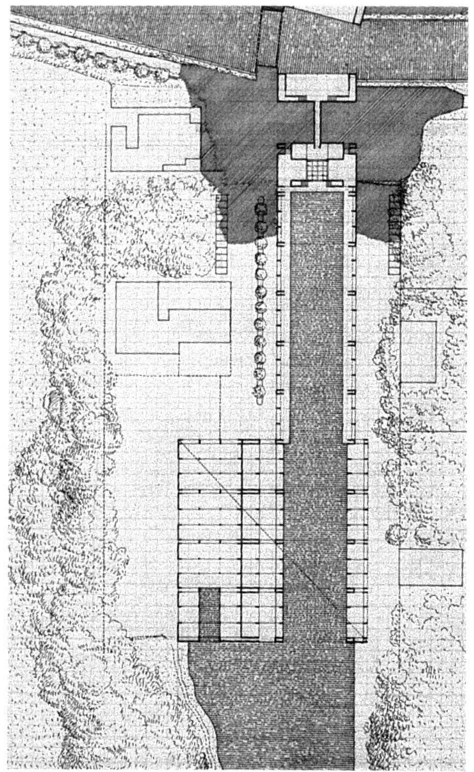

AERIAL VIEW OF PROJECT

STUDY SKETCHES

PLAN OF PROJECT

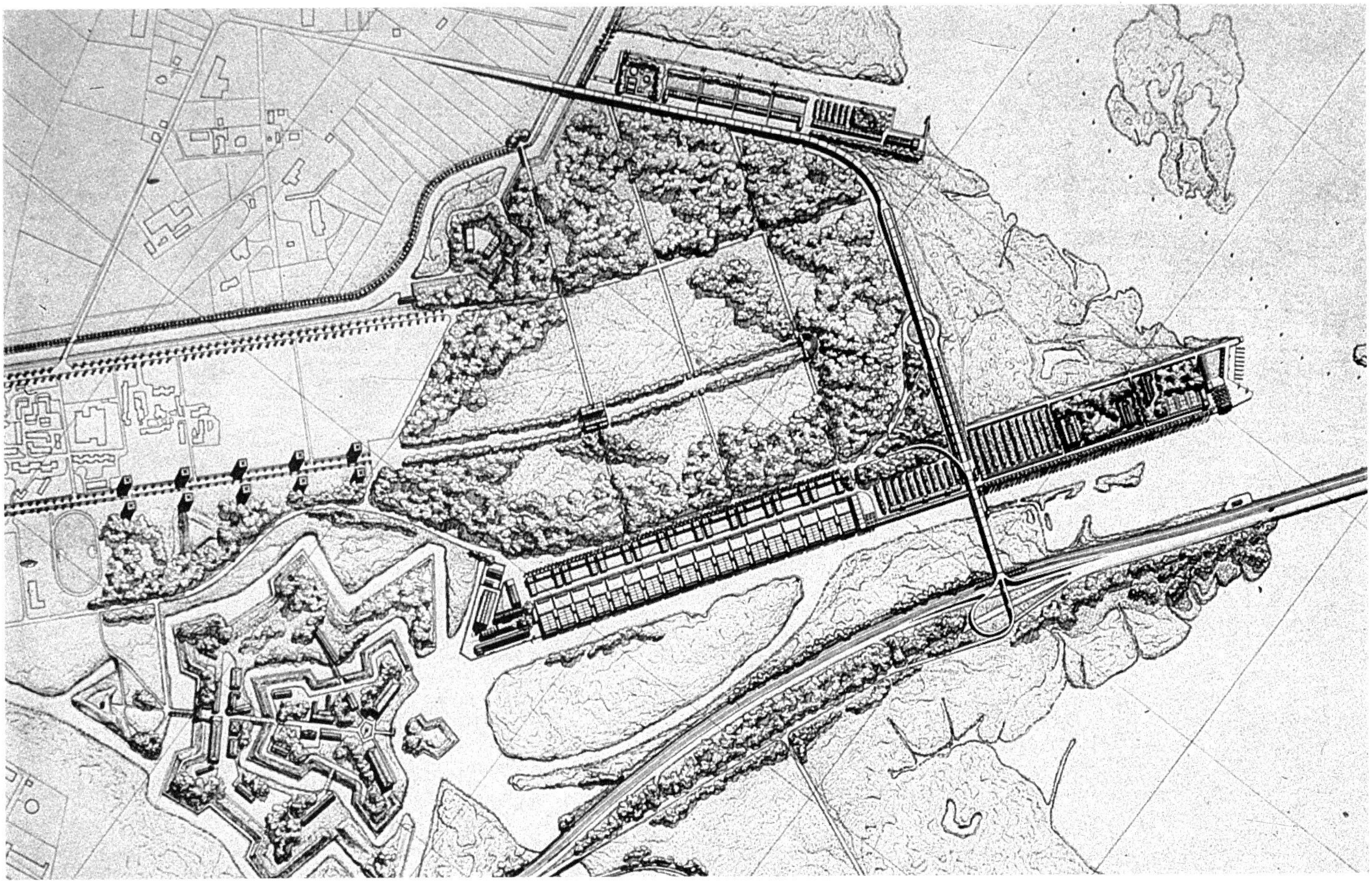

SAN GIULIANO, GENERAL PLAN OF THE PROJECT

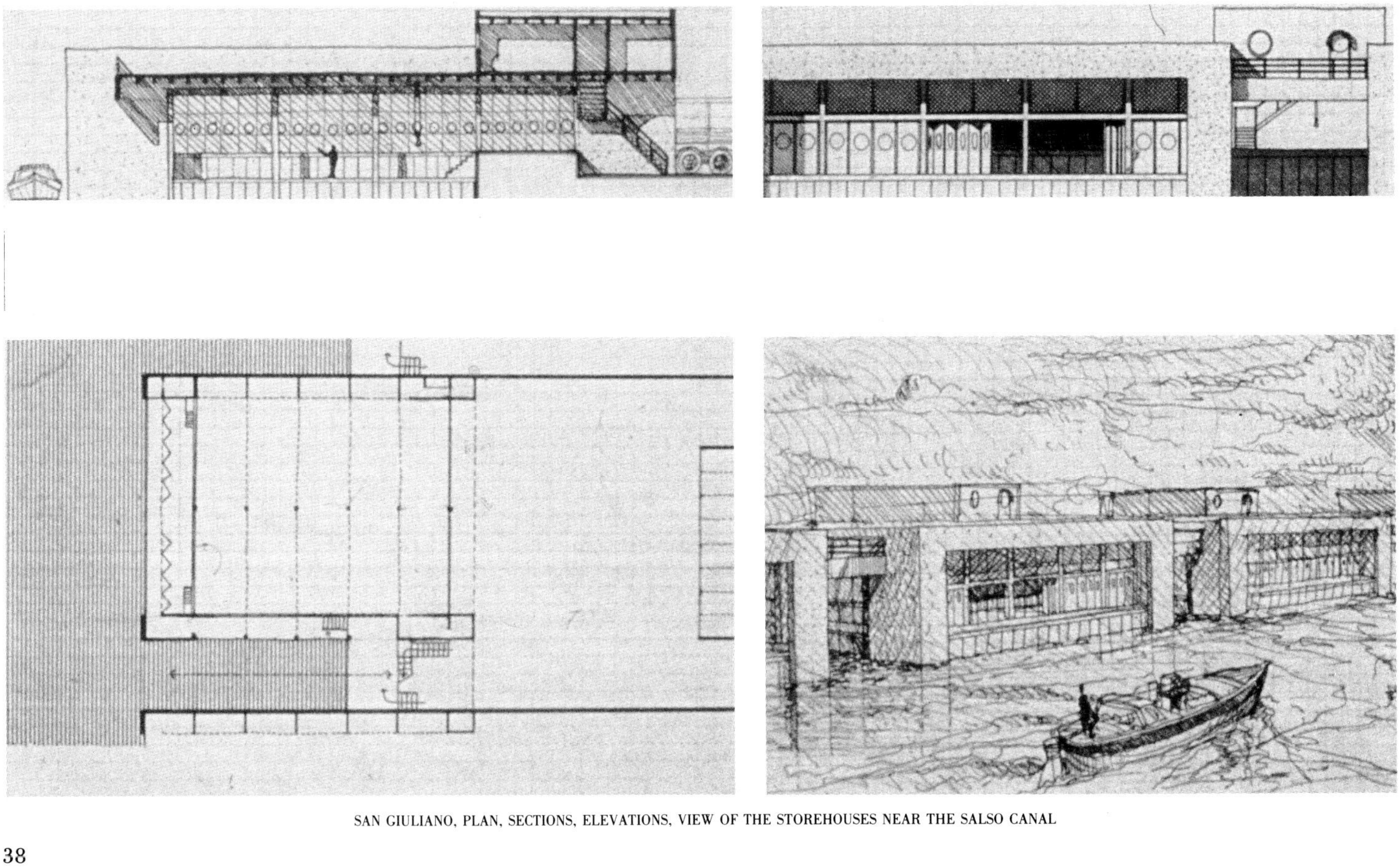

SAN GIULIANO, PLAN, SECTIONS, ELEVATIONS, VIEW OF THE STOREHOUSES NEAR THE SALSO CANAL

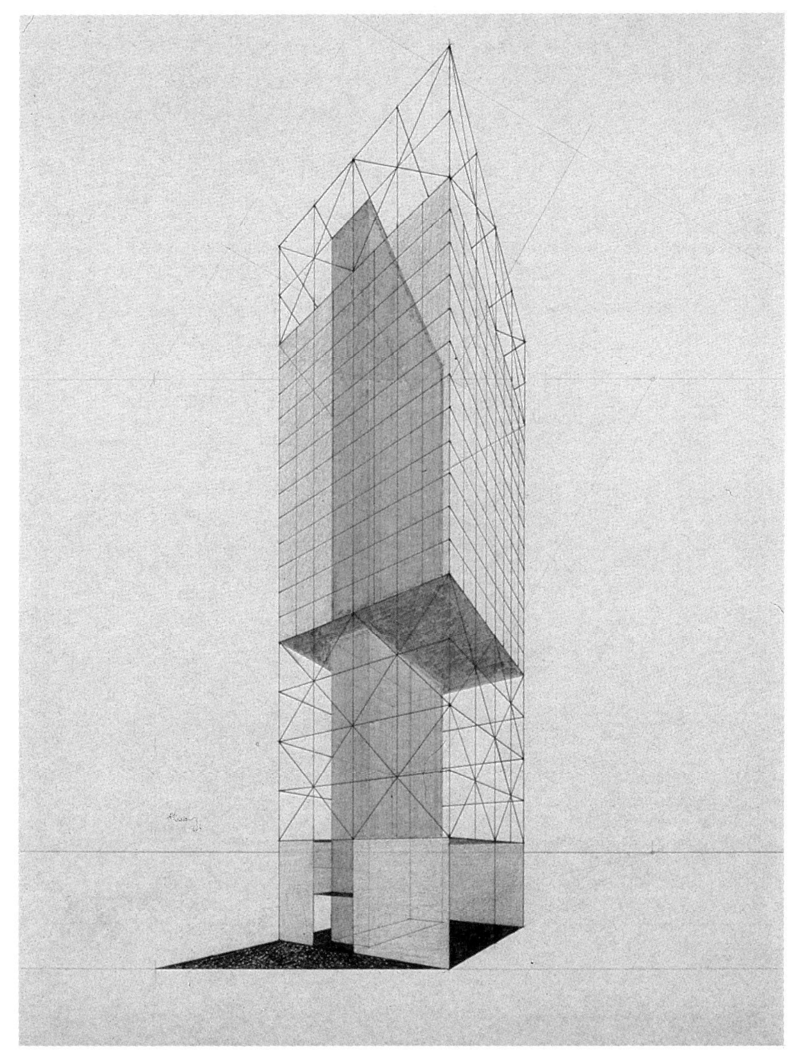

GIANUGO POLESELLO, STUDY FOR A TOWER TYPE

# THE TYPE

# GIANUGO POLESELLO
## Typology and Composition in Architecture

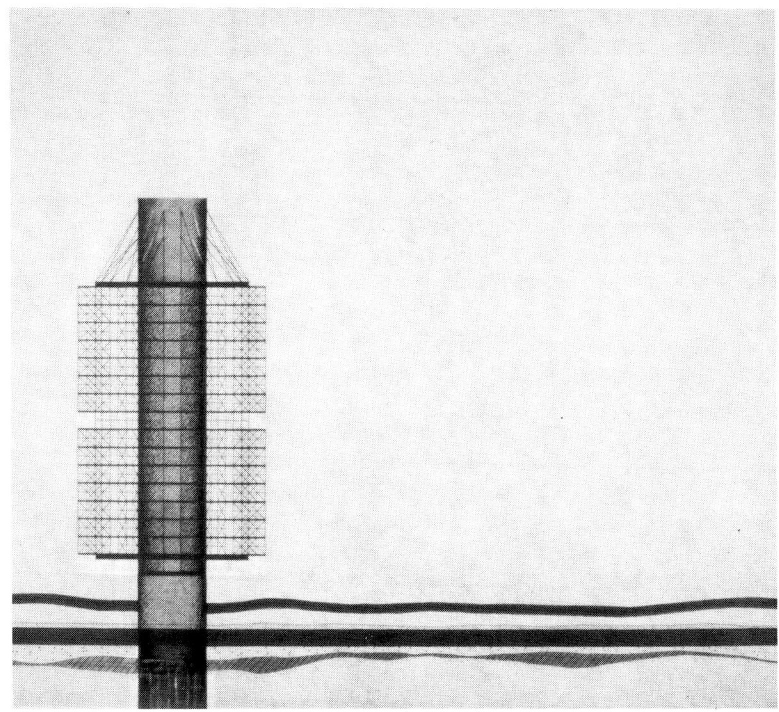

GIANUGO POLESELLO, STUDY FOR A TOWER TYPE

**T**HESE PROJECTS REPRESENT EXPERIMENTS IN **Architectural Composition rather than experiments in Architectural Planning. The distinction between Composition** and Planning is subtle; furthermore, I believe Architectural Planning and Composition share the same 'basic' structure which constitutes a precise frame of reference for all the intercoordinated technical operations that make up a project. It is also true that building techniques and architectural projects condition each other. Those who have talked of architecture as the *art de bâtir* (art of building) have been obliged to add *chez les Romains* (of the Romans) etc to designate the specific material and constructive aspects of Architecture and Architectural Planning in a particular society.

I have tried to distance myself from any connection between ARCHITECTURE and CONSTRUCTION based upon building technique. However, these projects are examples of an experiment that sustains the connection. Here, TECHNOLOGY assumes the role of a variable in the composition. In other words, TECHNOLOGY is taken to be subordinate to the final figure in the compositional planning process. In these experiments, I have been able to use different technologies currently available on the building market.

What serves, then, to stabilise the connection between ARCHITECTURE and CONSTRUCTION is the general geometric configuration, GEOMETRY. However, this premise alone does not explain these architectural projects, which I persist in considering as 'examples' of Architectural Composition and as partial experiments of an investigation into Architecture. I must add that they refer to ideas which can be summed up as follows:

1 Typology refers directly to Architecture itself, not to its use. It should be clear that I am not claiming that the study and experience of functions in the procedures of architecture should be excluded. I simply mean that I am concerned with typology as 'architectural typology' in particular.

2 The 'architectural typology' to which I am referring is a typology which has been built up in the form of an archive of 'given types'—architectural figures which have been reduced to their elementary geometrical nature. As a rule the 'given types' have their origins in history, but they may also be the product of invention. They are however always 'givens', that is, elements which may be part of a system (the compositional project) but are also independent of it.

In Architecture, the building up of an archive of 'givens' is equivalent to the building up of a poetic. It is therefore important to define the nature of this poetic: it is equivalent to saying, 'This is how I made some of my architectural projects' or 'This is how I formed an archive that may be helpful to me in planning.'

It may be interesting, at this juncture, to reconsider some procedures for formalisation that are similar to those already mentioned. The first of these procedures is contained in the writings of the Abbé Laugier (*Observations sur l'Architecture* and *Essai d'Architecture*, both written around 1750). Laugier examined the logic of the 'architectural orders'; his work was characterised by a description of the 'constants' (that is, the orders) in the construction and function of a building in the city. In the first case (the construction of a building) the planning consisted of a combination of elements. This combination could be expressed in a model using a single plane of projection (the horizontal) provided that

40

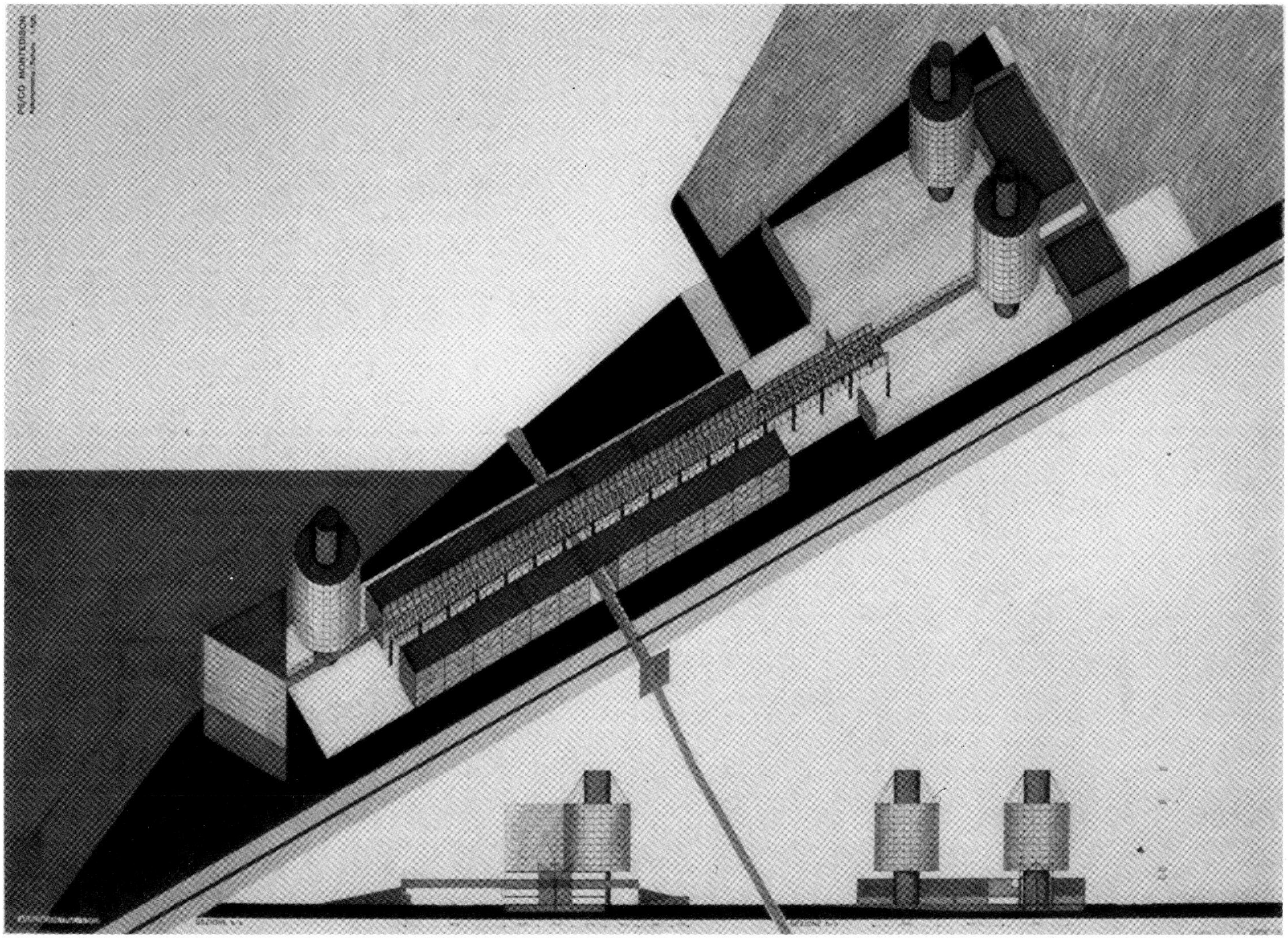

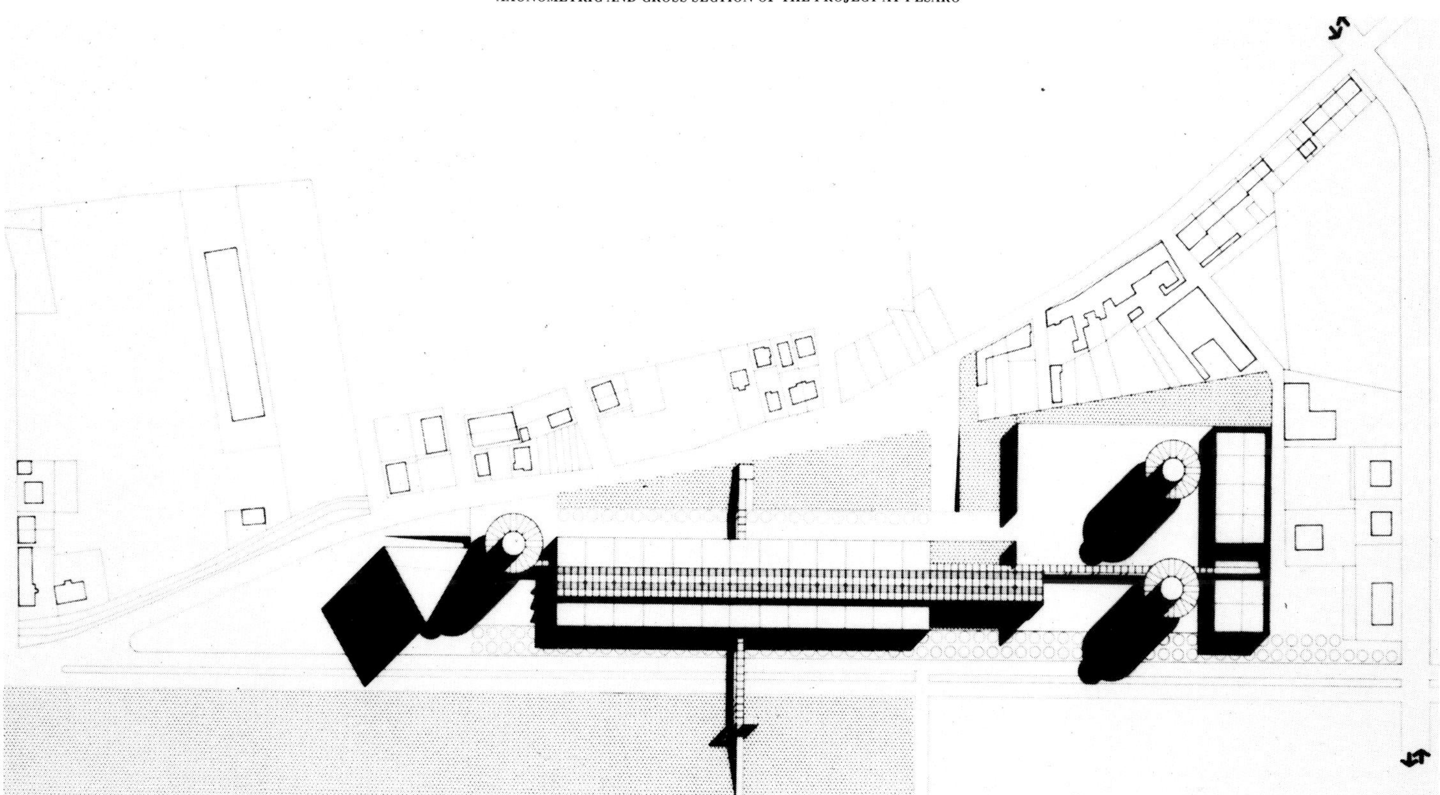

**AXONOMETRIC AND CROSS SECTION OF THE PROJECT AT PESARO**

**SITE PLAN**

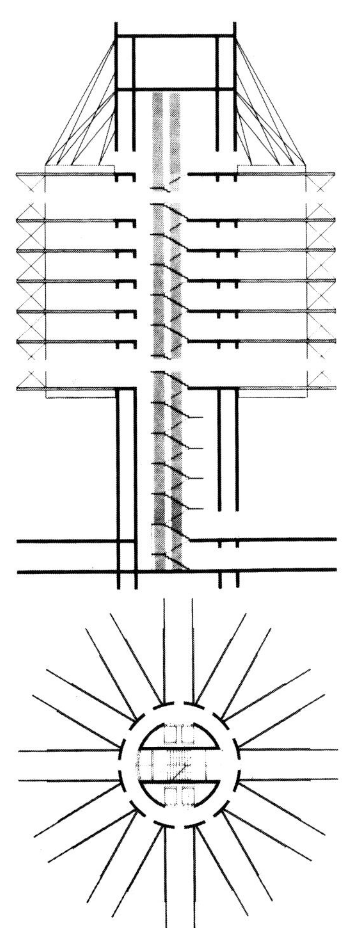

LEFT: THE TOWER TYPE, PLAN AND SECTION. RIGHT: SKETCHES FOR NEW CHAMBER OF DEPUTIES, ROME

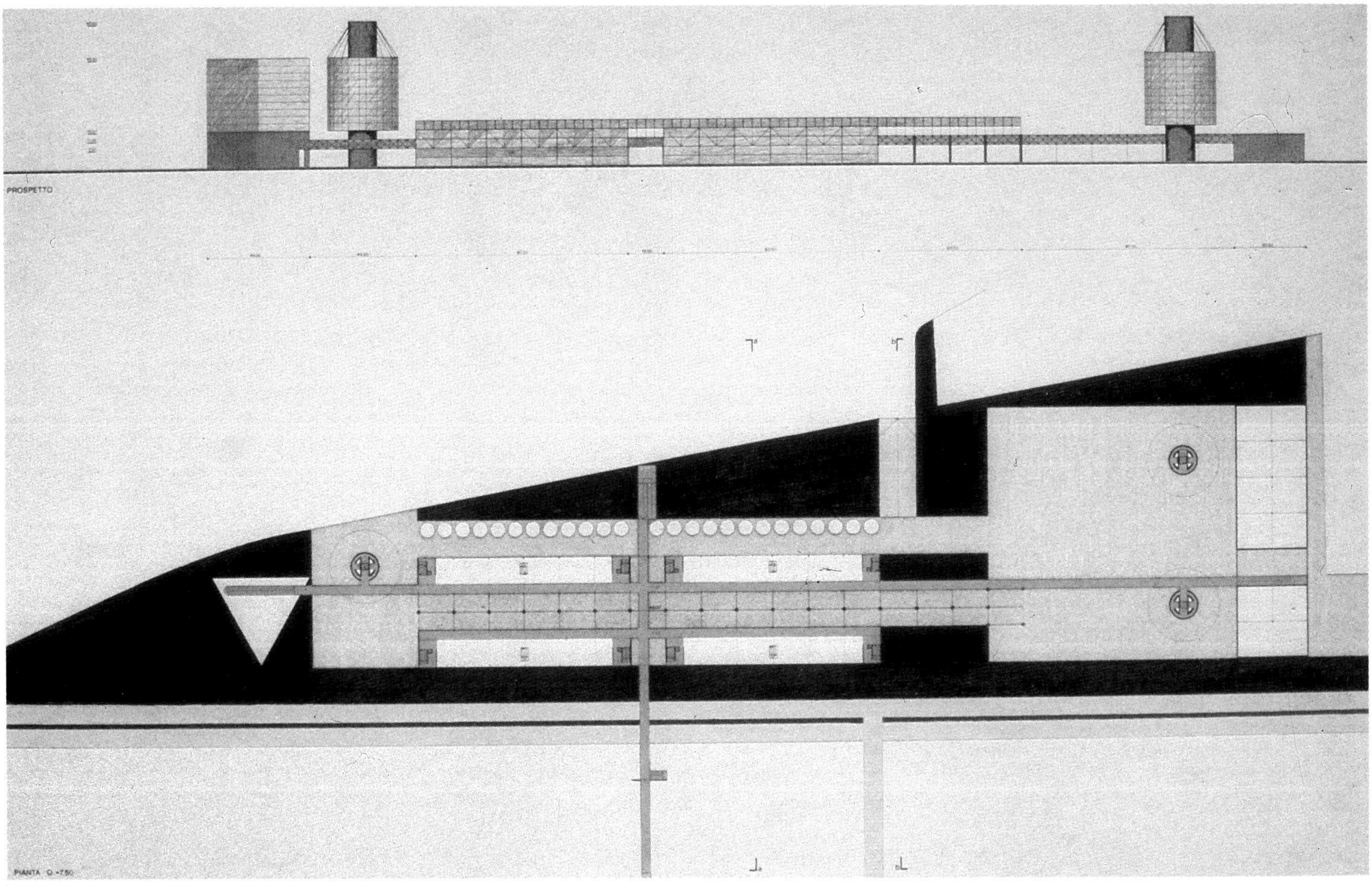

TOP: LONGITUDINAL SECTION. BOTTOM: PLAN OF GROUND FLOOR, PESARO

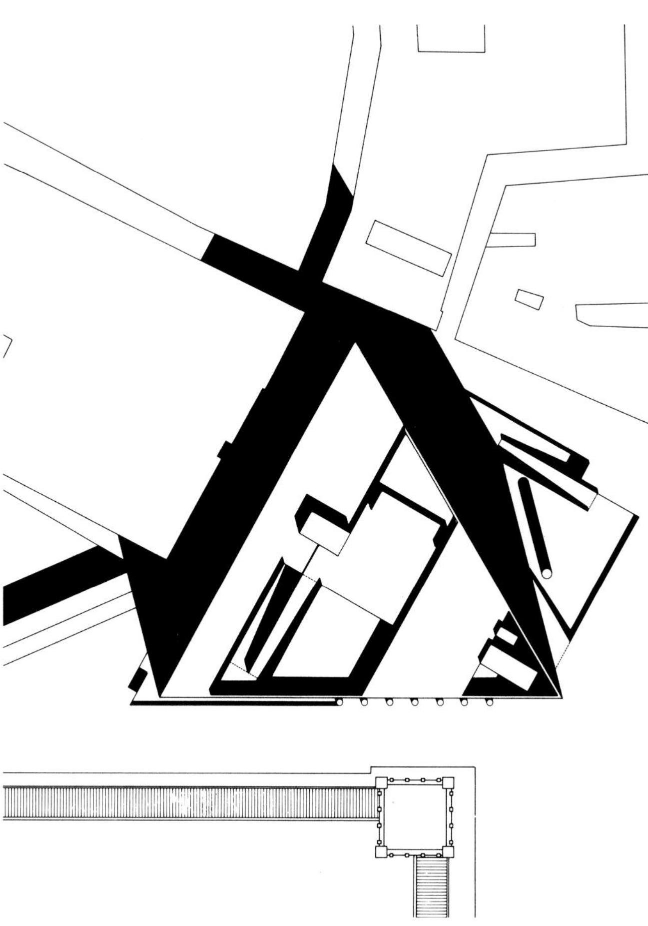

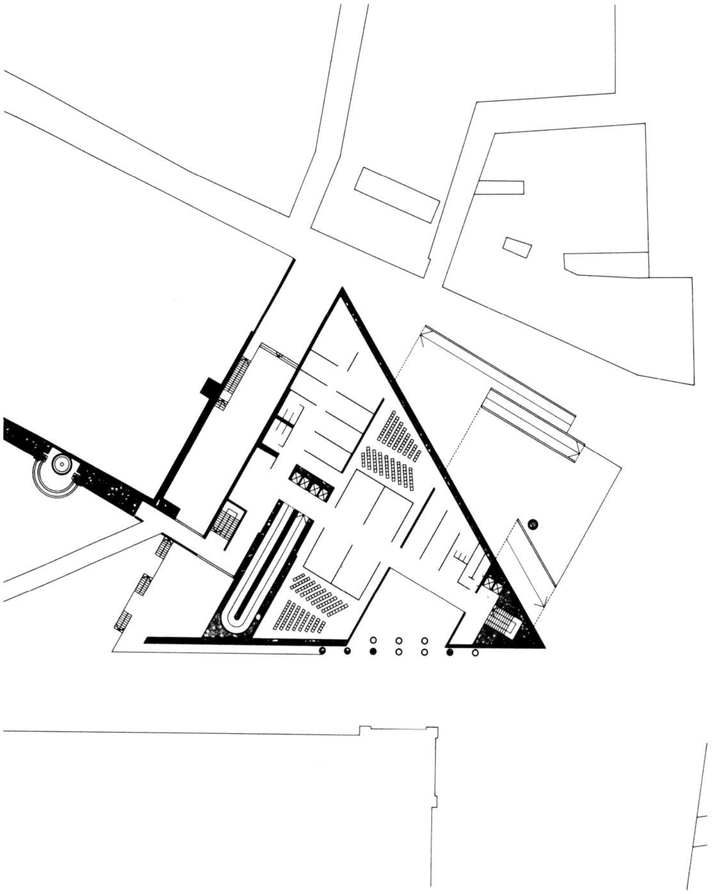

LEFT: PLAN OF INTERMEDIARY FLOOR. RIGHT: FIRST FLOOR PLAN, ROME

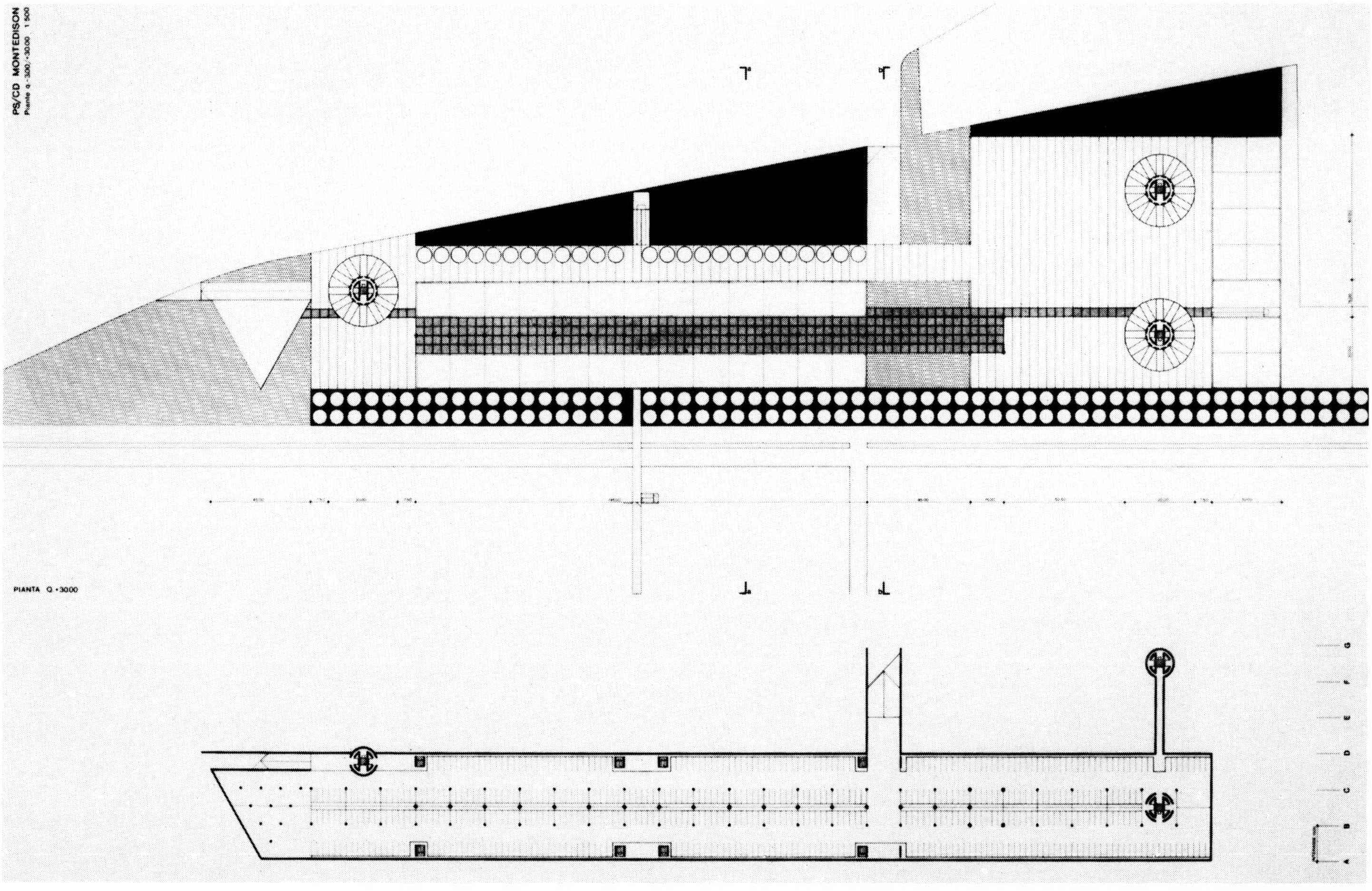

TOP: PLAN OF COVERS. BOTTOM: PLAN AT LEVEL + 30.00, PESARO

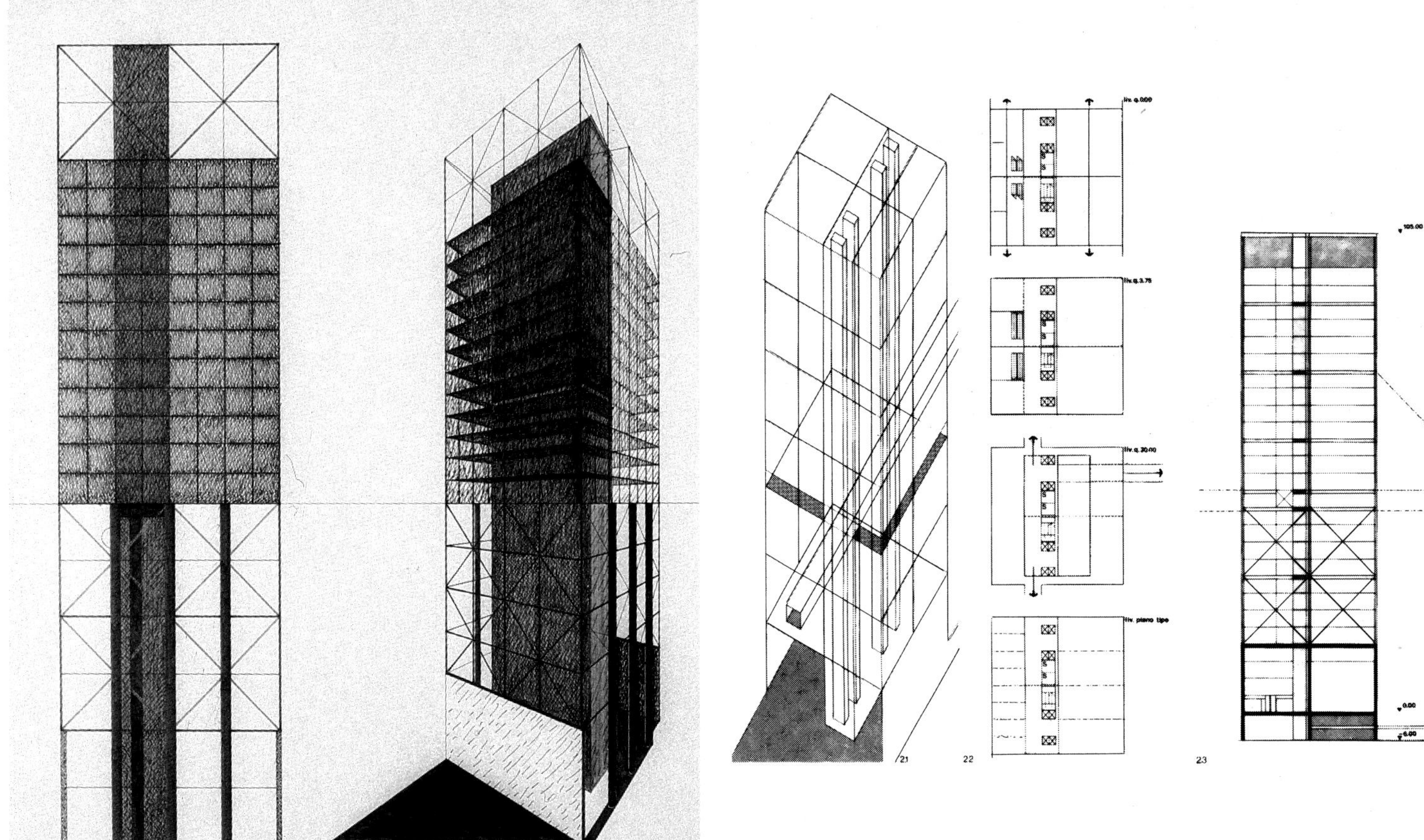



PROJECT FOR THE NEW HEADQUARTERS AT FLORENCE (1977 COMPETITION). LEFT: STUDY FOR TOWER TYPES. RIGHT: SECTION AND AXONOMETRIC OF ONE OF THE NINE TOWERS

the elevations and sections were determined by the rules of proportion. In the second case (construction in the city or of the city) the planning would follow the well-known maxim of unity in the whole and tumult in the detail.

About seventy years after Laugier, J N Durand made an important contribution to the formalising of compositional procedures. This formalisation, which was proposed and taught at the Ecole Polytechnique in Paris, can be summarised as follows:

1  initial adoption of the elements which make up the trilithic system;
2  subsequent adoption of non-trilithic elements;
3  analysis of the trilithic system (that is, analysis of the architectural orders);
4  examination of the superimposition of the orders in relation to the theory of the proportions of the column, and adoption of the rules for intercolumniation and interaxes;
5  derivation, from theory, of the proportions defining the shape of internal spaces;
6  proof that Architectural Composition may coincide with a combination of trace-elements in the plan, making it possible to define Architectural Composition as *Ars Combinatoria;*
7  examples of complex compositions built as 'compositions of buildings by means of buildings'.

If one ignores Durand's tendency toward the axiomatic and bears in mind the contemporaneous (or nearly contemporaneous) experiments of Schinkel, Semper, Von Klenze, Persius and Gilly as well as the great epoch of the architecture of the French Revolution (Boullée, Ledoux, Lequeu), it is possible to see a very important question in the last proposition: the composition of buildings by means of buildings is, in addition to being a new theory of types, also a critique of the theory of types as expressed by Quatremère de Quincy.

In Durand's proposition the building itself becomes a 'type', and conversely, the combination of 'types' becomes a combination of 'ARCHITECTURES'. The study of 'building types' is then indispen-sable for the formation of an ARCHIVE. At the same time, the formation of an ARCHIVE is the formation of an ARCHITECTURAL TYPOLOGY. The undifferentiated nature of the 'architectural type' refers back to 'composition-by-types'; that is, composition/planning as *'Ars Combinatoria'*. The place where the combination of types is ripest for this type of experiment is, in my opinion, the city. The previous statement can therefore be summed up in this second way: the question of the typology of architectural actions in the city can be viewed (and investigated) through a combination of types and their locations. This procedure sets out from Le Corbusier's experiments and patient research into the placing of given and available elements (*outils*) in a pre-existing or newly formed context. Le Corbusier's experience stands at the threshold of modern typology, examining both the single building (elementary or complex) and the city.

This obliged me to consider at length Le Corbusier's appeals to architects to look first of all (or only) at the elementary figures of geometry. I first set myself the task of considering the elementary figures of spatial geometry using their outlines on the fundamental plane (the ground) as my starting point. This helped me understand that the relationship between building and ground could be reconsidered by contradicting Le Corbusier and examining every spatial relationship starting from its location on the ground. Consequently, buildings in their different locations assume the functions of operators in the transition from 'ground' to 'site', that is, they take on the role of 'signs' whose meaning is defined by their reciprocal (or internal) relationship. This is the only sense in which it is right to say that Architecture is a finite system, a closed system, or that you can limit architectural/building action in the city to certain of its parts. This is the heart of the logic of 'measurement' and the principle of groups.

In these projects, the 'site' is only a configuration marked by precise limits. These limits depersonalise geometric space, making it merely space that is perceptible and intellectually graspable.

# AUGUSTO ROMANO BURELLI
## Unearthing the Type

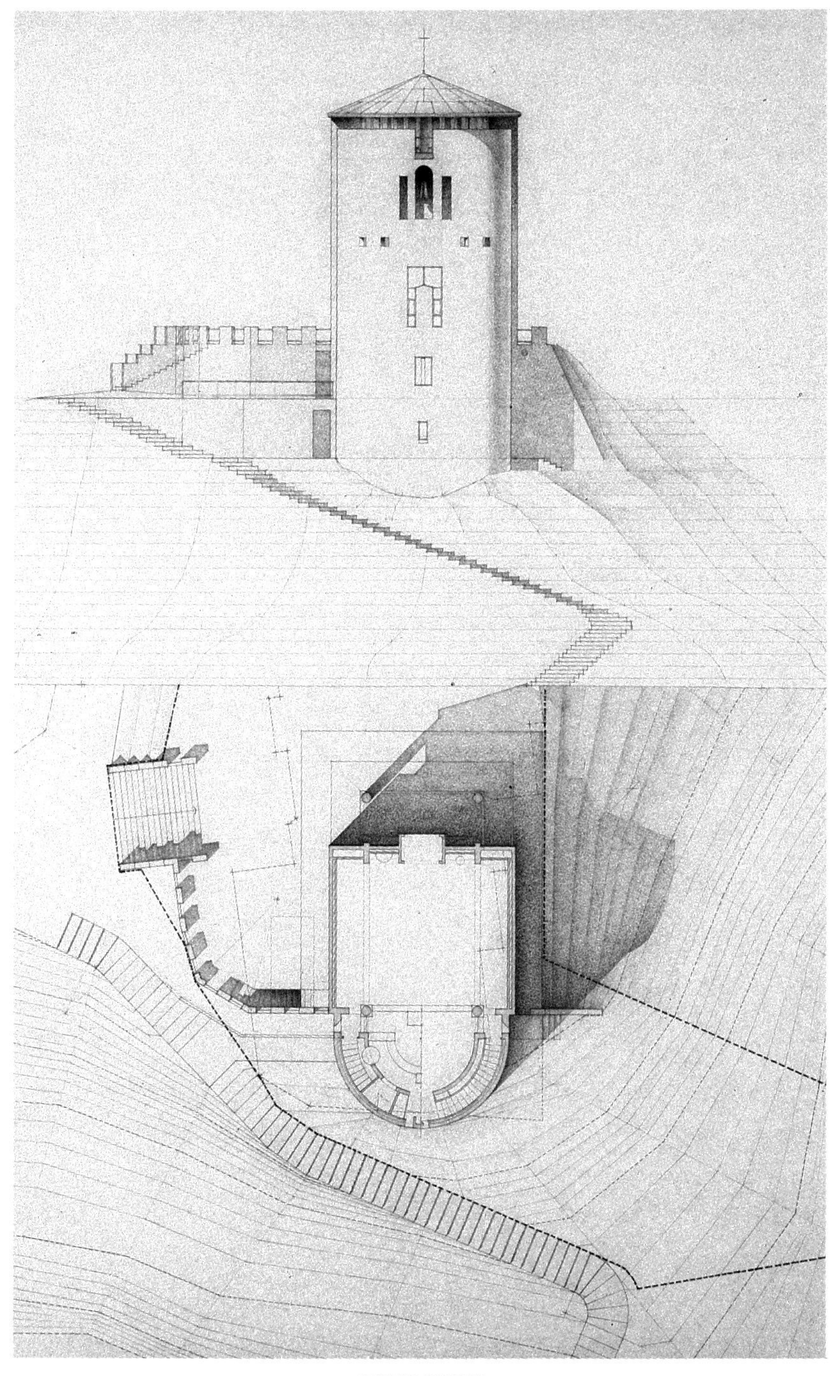

S ELENA CHURCH

**T**HE CONCEPT OF TYPE IS A FORTUNATE **combination of two imperatives: the principle of individualisation and the principle of classification. It is** well known that the first principle is dear to Romantic thought and the second to positivist thought. However, the double nature of the type has been responsible not only for its success, but also for its degradation and vulgarisation.

In the study of types architecture has tried to instil order into its own materials and eliminate evolutionist doctrines and stylistic classifications in order to concentrate exclusively on the essence of a work. For the

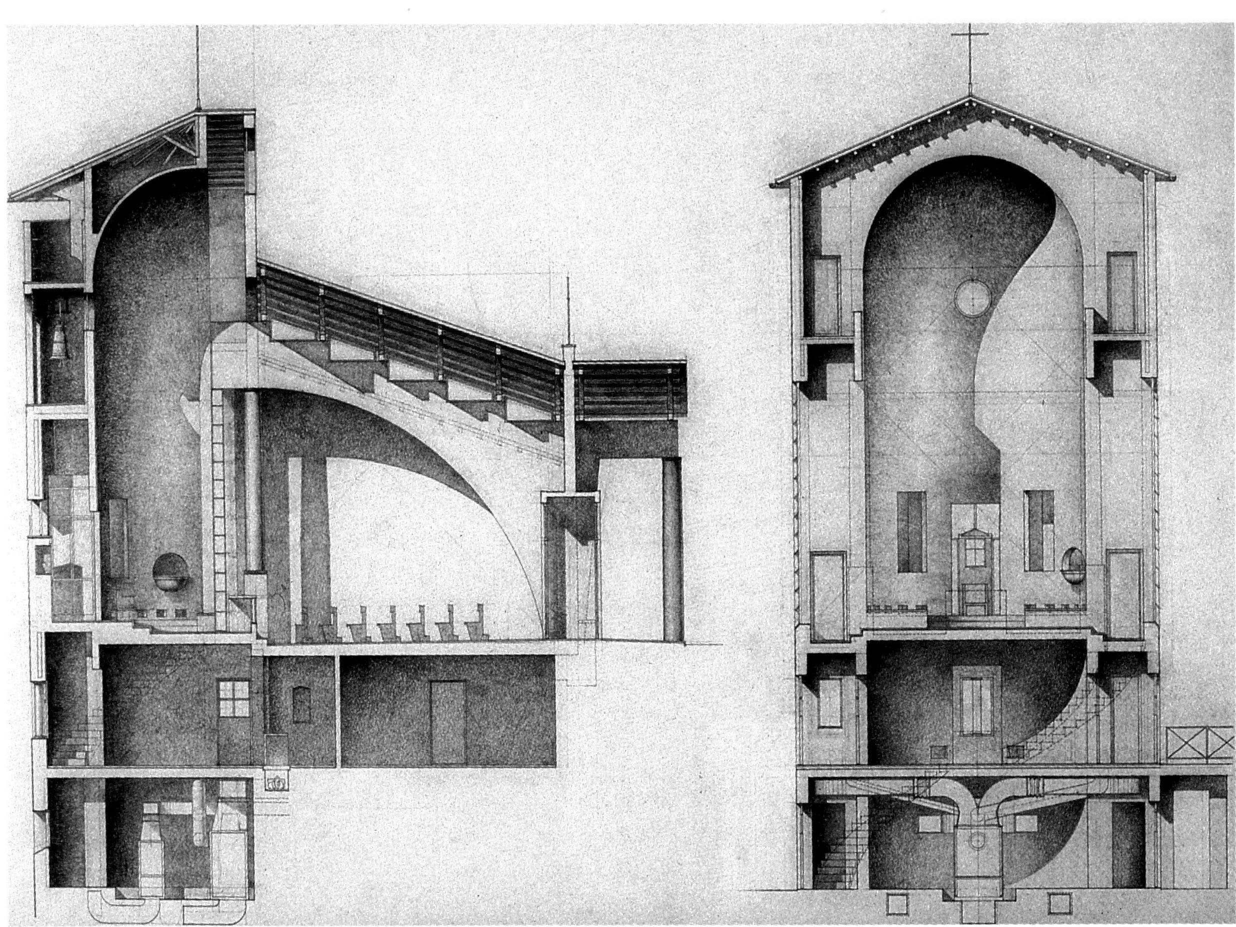

CROSS-SECTIONS

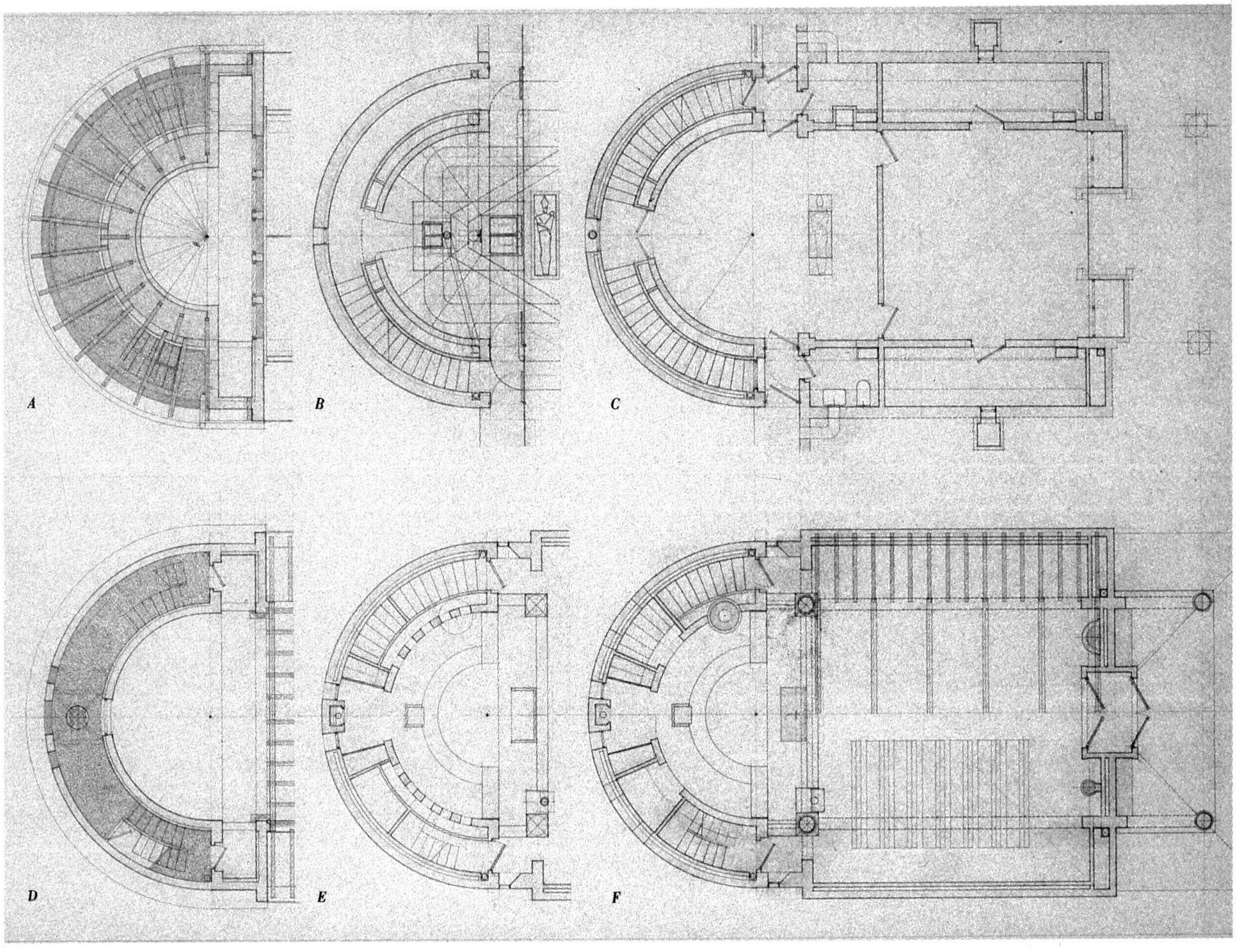

*A* THE APSE – TOWER AT THE LEVEL OF THE OPEN GALLERY. *B* THE APSE – TOWER AT THE LEVEL OF THE BELL-ROOM. *C* THE BASE OF THE APSE – TOWER *D* THE APSE – TOWER AT THE LEVEL OF THE CHOIR *E* THE CRYPT *F* THE AULA

ELEVATION FROM THE CHURCHYARD

SECTION THROUGH THE TRANSEPT TOWARDS THE ENTRANCE

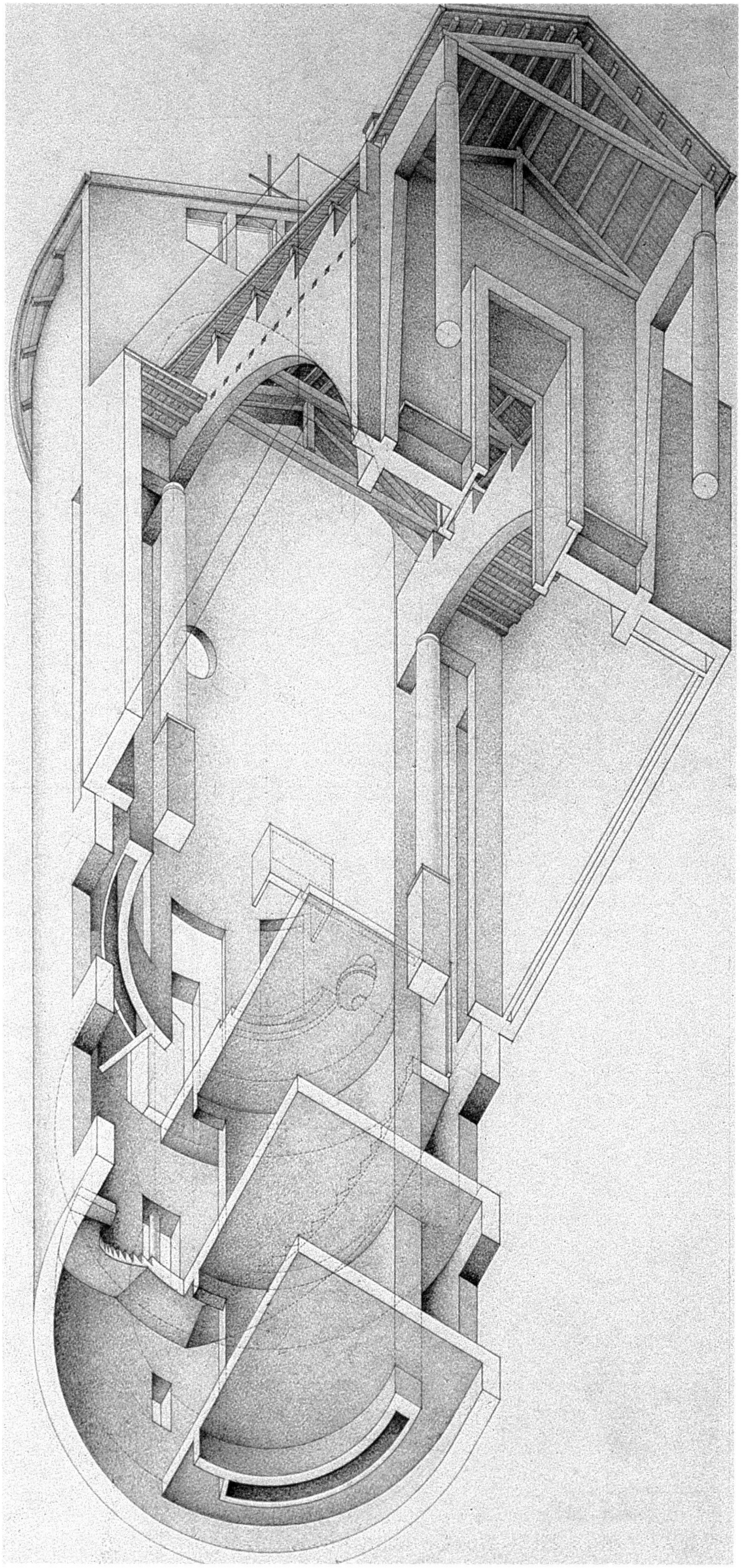

ISOMETRIC

first time architects can move among the materials of the history of architecture without getting confused. They are in a position to direct their own interests towards the conceptual nature of phenomena, discovering invariances, compositional problems and spatial principles by looking at transient or historically determined elements. Now that they are freed from the tired conventions of styles they scrutinise the material of history in search of that *alius semper et idem* which does not change conceptually, which always re-emerges as itself.

However, the other side to the type is classification. In the overall process of creeping nominalism, architecture has allowed itself to join in the game of imitating scientific method (at least since Durand's teaching deteriorated to the level of the manuals of the Polytechniques). The impulse towards classification is so strong now that it makes one forget that no worthwhile work of architecture has ever entirely corresponded to a type. Indeed all the typological regurgitation contained in the present-day manuals is the result of cataloguing and rationalising, with scant attention being paid to figurative problems.

The problem with classification is that it evades the aesthetic question and reduces the study of types to mere technical protocol. Outside the aesthetic sphere of play and appearance, everything has to be essential and technically provable. Aping scientists, jargon-ridden minds are busy classifying the technical elements necessary to the architectural plan and compiling long bureaucratic lists of their social aims. This amateurish and pretentious activity puts typology in a frontrank position in the bureaucracy of building regulations.

The root of the concept of type, the *principium individuationis*, is moreover a directive, not a ready-found *de facto* state. In other words, the concept of type contains within itself the essence of its various manifestations.

This kind of abstraction calls for both training and inspiration: the intellect reflecting upon the type is combining an exercise in logic with an exercise in evocation. In this way typological thought becomes bound to the project, and this is the source of its fruitfulness. Logic restricts irrational invention but does not stifle it. The architect's reputation as creator has always wronged him because it makes his deliberate decisions seem to be arbitrary discoveries, which they are not.

The advent of the type coincides with the re-evaluation of the plans of buildings, or rather their site plans. The first abstraction to be determined is always that of the plan, which is virtually the hallmark of the idea of the type. At the end of the nineteenth century Auguste Choisy represented the Greek temple with points and lines alone, and in so doing supplied an ethic for architectural planning; namely, the parsimonious use of figures and a conceptual means of representation. One principle of this ethic is that everything can be described in, or inferred from, the plan. It is perhaps only natural that this principle should have established itself as the norm, becoming somewhat tainted with didactic intent. However, this method of reducing architecture to a unit of signs in order to make measurements and seek out proportions appears less than ingenious to those who know that measurements and proportions are not the essential elements in a project. The didactic aspect of the study of types has nothing codified or incontrovertible about it; it is a mental exercise, just as the measurement of the units of signs is more rhetorical writing than a system of rules.

The distinction between type and individual is a very recent theoretical dissociation that was invented to raise the type to the position of an absolute schema. Schematism can be kept at bay only by recognising that the type allows itself to be articulated part by part. In architecture articulation guarantees the multiplicity of the whole, whereas the unarticulated whole is a schema. In general a project becomes more clear and explicit when it is more articulated, when there is nothing left in it that is dead or shapeless, when there is no portion that has not passed through the work of configuration. The impulse towards classification which is closely allied to the type must therefore be oriented towards its articulation.

If, for example, we examine the theatre as a typological building we notice that in all its manifestations in the history of architecture, it is articulated in various combined parts. Of these parts, two are basic to the configuration: the auditorium and the stage. The distinction between the individual types can begin from the physical conflict between these parts (which always raises complex compositional problems) and from their resolution. Naturally the type is always engendered by the historical needs of the materials. In the case of theatres, new types are born when the frequent conflict between the amphitheatre/auditorium and the deep stage become irresoluble. In addition, the conflict between stage and auditorium may be aggravated by new historical needs (the foyer, triumphal entrance, etc). It is however the articulation and different configuration that give rise to the new types; one need only think of the typological lesson given by Gottfried Semper, to whom the modern theatre owes much.

Returning to the distinction between the type and individuality of a project, we can see that it is in the way the parts are articulated and shaped that the whole is diversified. The unmistakable and irreplaceable element in each single architectural project is in fact the deviation from the type. If the deviation is not to overthrow the project and eclipse the idea of the type, it must be based on the alteration of the project's parts.

The terms of deviation and alteration can be clarified with an analysis of the articulation of the parts in the typological family of a church with a nave using the processional succession of narthex-nave-presbytery-choir. We can indeed distinguish the types from the different articulation of the parts, but the single project becomes explicit only when the parts are altered and given different spatial values. If the alteration is sufficiently penetrating the project may reach the very point where one type tips over into another. This is illustrated by the reconstruction of a recently destroyed church with a nave. In this project, the experiment pushed the nave type to the point of changing it into the type with a central plan. The choir, which traditionally completes a large nave, grew enormously in size and height. The nave leant upon it and the transept was reduced to a brief interval between the two parts. The length of the nave was shortened, tipping into the height of the tower-apse, the processional route was compressed onto the choir, with its point of equilibrium in the central altar. The conflict between the nave and choir is the deviation from the type; the result could be defined, in a literary fashion perhaps, as the project for a tower-church.

The current crisis in the concepts of type and typology bears witness to the reduction of aesthetic classifications to techniques. The only way to restore their speculative strength is to fight off the vulgarisation for which they seem destined.

The one solution is to put the rich evocative aspect alongside the logical aspect at the centre of theoretical reflection on the type. The type has a mythical dimension and should be seen in its historically undetermined atemporality. Its meaning is not that of scholastic perfection or exemplary rule. Rather, it is a form of the spiritual life of architecture, an original atavistic model in which future works may recognise themselves. Therefore it is a myth, since the essence of myth is return, independence from time and perennial presence.

**Collaborators on church: A R Burelli, P Gennaro.**

# CARLO AYMONINO
## Type and Typology

ENTRANCE TO THE JUSTICE COURTS AT FERRARA (PHOTO POZZAR)

**I** HAVE TRIED TO DEFINE BUILDING TYPOLOGY AS **'the study of the possible associations of elements in order to attain a classification of architectural organisms by** types.' I would now like to clarify how applicable this definition is to the field of urban studies, bearing in mind the numerous contributions on the subject which have recently appeared.

In this case the word *element* clearly indicates a part of a whole which can be isolated by analysis. Although the element possesses some characteristics of individuality, it is in general only valid in relation to the whole, and not in itself. In typological definitions elements may be, roughly speaking, identified by two different procedures, one stylistic and formal, the other organisational and structural.

The first procedure is valid in research on architecture as an autonomous phenomenon, while the second method, as we shall explain shortly, is applicable to research on architecture as an urban phenomenon. There are of course exceptions to this rule: there have been times when the specification of a stylistic and formal type has influenced or indeed determined the development of a particular city. According to Chastel, the Sultan Bajazet and Michelangelo met each other, so the development of Istanbul and Rome might well be con-

nected in terms of resolving the two greatest monuments of the respective cities with a centrally planned building; the basilica of St Peter's and Bajazet's Mosque.

*Classification* indicates an act of abstraction that puts order between different entities—each one identifiable in itself—and arranges them in classes in order to identify their common data and make a comparison possible. In specific cases, classification does not concern development of a single *theme* in time (the house, temple, theatre etc, as for example in the manuals of distributive features of buildings). Rather, it deals with concrete examples of a single theme in a period bounded by the permanence of constant characteristics (the Gothic house, nineteenth-century road, Romantic garden etc). It is therefore a regulating instrument of phenomena which compares different entities in terms of their relationship with urban form.

In this sense the original definition of building typology can be transformed into 'the study of the artificial organisational and structural elements (meaning not only buildings but also walls, avenues, gardens etc—the whole built fabric of the city) with the aim of classifying them in relation to the urban form of a specific historical period (or a particular urban form, which is the same thing).'

GALLERY INTERIOR

A single definition is therefore not valid. Building typology should be redefined in terms of the research to be undertaken as the occasion arises. It is an instrument and not a category: in our case it is one of the instruments needed to be able to carry out studies on urban phenomena.

The numerous contributions to a typological definition may therefore be regrouped, as we have already indicated, according to two classifications with different aims: classification by formal types—or *independent* typology—which provides a critical method for the analysis and comparison of phenomena of art; and classification by functional type—or *applied* typology—which provides an analysis of the phenomena which make up a whole, independently of aesthetic value judgement.

In the first case the classifications are arranged according to certain formal constants. One example is Wittkower's constant for centrally planned Renaissance buildings, where the reduction of the formal variants to a basic form or common schema was the result of a comparison between concrete cases. In the second case the classifications are grouped according to structural constants, like the one proposed by Babelon and Gallet for Parisian residences to describe the constituent elements and locate the types in the Parisian context. In this case, the constancy of the phenomena is also the result of a comparison of concrete cases, but it is used as an instrument to confirm the duration of the phenomenon more in relation to the city than to itself. This classification is therefore an instrument which can establish a relationship between different entities.

Regarding independent typology, Argan's observation is valid: 'The aim behind typological grouping is neither artisitic evaluation nor historical definition in that works of a very high level and common buildings of any period and place may enter the same class of typology.' However, in applied typology, historical definition does come into play, for although the time and place are fixed they are determined in the precise terms of the applied typology to be used. Furthermore, Argan contradicted himself when he made the following observation: 'Only in the second half of the nineteenth century was there an attempt to find a classificatory typology with regard to previously fixed practical functions (the typical schemes of hospitals, hotels, schools, banks, theatres etc). However this produced no important results, because the type was not deduced from a series of historical facts, but was deter-

50

VIEW OF THE INTERIOR

EXTERNAL ENTRANCE TO THE COURTROOMS

mined in relation to a positive calculation of its expediency.' Argan's claim may be negated by the observation that much of modern and contemporary architecture has been grafted precisely onto this classification and, unlike nineteenth-century productions, it has achieved exemplary artistic results.

*Applied* typology makes it possible to establish a relationship with urban form as a dialectical term. The relationship between building type and urban form is not constant in principle or in fact. It should however be noted that formal typology is not to be excluded *a priori* from specific examinations. In fact, *formal* typology is more useful than *applied* typology in some cases, particularly in the examination of phenomena belonging to the Renaissance and Mannerist periods.

It is certain that architectural products tend to affirm themselves in relation to a period rather than a precise and differentiated place: they are opportunities rather than solutions. In this sense the Florence of Brunelleschi, the Vicenza of Palladio or the Rome of Michelangelo do indeed bear a relation to the form and history before them, but they are above all the architecture of their authors.

'One of the chief lessons of Brunelleschi's humanism was its considera-

tion of the pre-existing city as an unstable and available structure, ready to change its overall meaning once the balance of the Romanesque-Gothic *continual narration* had been altered with the introduction of compact architectural objects.

Urban history and new interventions are therefore still complementary, but in a dialectical sense. And one can go further: given that the dome of Santa Maria del Fiore, the two basilicas of San Lorenzo and San Spirito, and the rotunda of the Angeli were conceived as architecture on a city scale, one may understand how it was that neither Brunelleschi nor Alberti should have felt the need to codify urban utopias. In fact the rigorous organic nature of perspectival space is reinforced in early humanism as a new and polemical truth, complete in itself. The architectures which are co-ordinated around rational postulates confront and compete with the pre-existing urban fabric. There is no need to extend the unitary co-ordination of space to the whole city, since those architectures demonstrate visibly their ability to beam their rational qualities over the polystratified medieval fabric.'

# ALDO ROSSI
## The Architecture of the Squares in the Veneto
## A Student Thesis

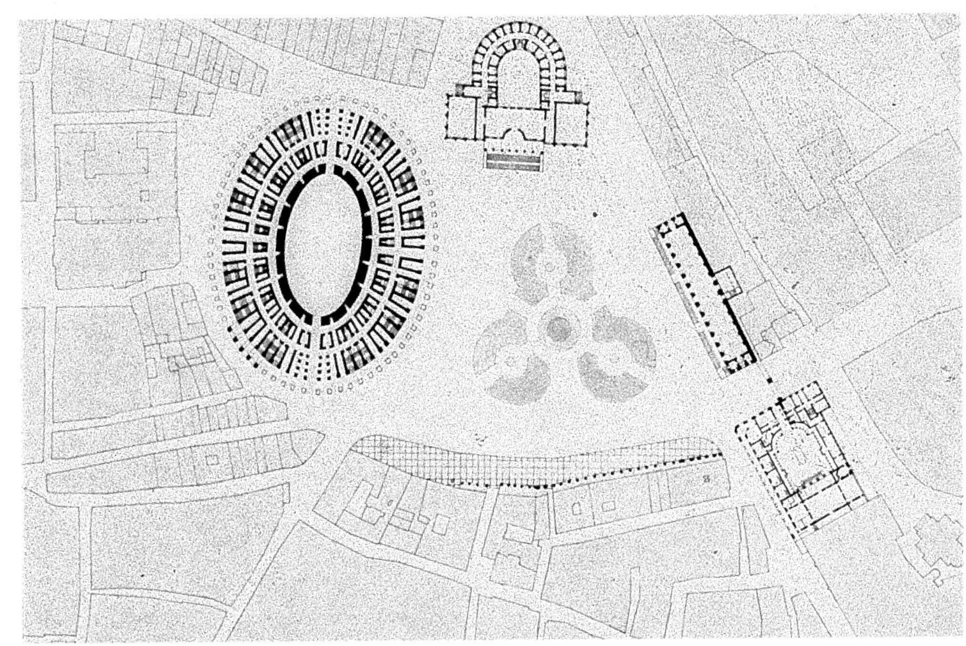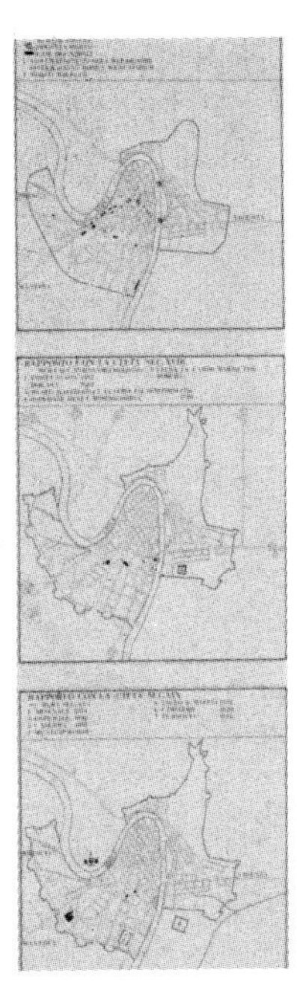

SITE PLAN OF THE PROJECT IN PIAZZA BRA IN VERONA

**T**HE AIM OF THIS THESIS WAS TO pinpoint the architectural and compositional elements of the squares in the Veneto.

Planning rather than pure analysis was the final objective, but the students still made use of urban analysis because it gave them a knowledge of the squares, a definition of their morphology and an understanding of the roles they have played in the city in various historical periods. Once they had singled out those squares in the cities of the Veneto which 'spoke more of themselves than others spoke of others'—namely, Piazza San Marco, Piazza Bra, Piazza della Frutta e delle Erbe and Piazza dei Signori in Verona, Piazza dei Signori, Piazza delle Erbe, Piazza della Biave and Campo Marzio in Vicenza and Prato della Valle in Padua — they drew up card indexes for each square, or system of squares, since the two were inseparable in the history of their constitution. Then the group concerned itself with determining the specific architecture making up the square and classifying it according to building type and position occupied in the square.

The typological elements they noted were, in the case of the perimeter of the square: a) curtain buildings b) basic buildings c) the loggia d) the means of access. The typological elements of the central space of the square were the central buildings. The typological elements of the square situated outside the perimeter were: a) buildings beyond the perimeter b) architectural relations between several buildings c) structural axes of the squares.

Piazza Bra, Caserma Pallone and Piazza Cittadella in Verona were chosen for the final stage of the project. However, the aim was not to plan new squares but to use the pre-existing ones to construct a building dense with architectural relationships.

The planned building has a curtain-building or facade with a two-metre base. It is aligned with the Gran Guardia and has two porticos which border a delivery gallery for shops on the first and second floors.

The project is linked with the open galleries in the Gran Guardia through walls which form a walkway as well as the set of a theatre where the fixed stage is the area of the complex of buildings in Piazza Bra.

**Student thesis by** R Libralon, C Pattuelli, F Dotti. Related by Aldo Rossi.

PERSPECTIVE TOWARDS PIAZZA BRA OF THE MULTIFUNCTIONAL BUILDING (MARKET AND RESIDENCES)

PERSPECTIVE OF THE MULTIFUNCTIONAL BUILDING

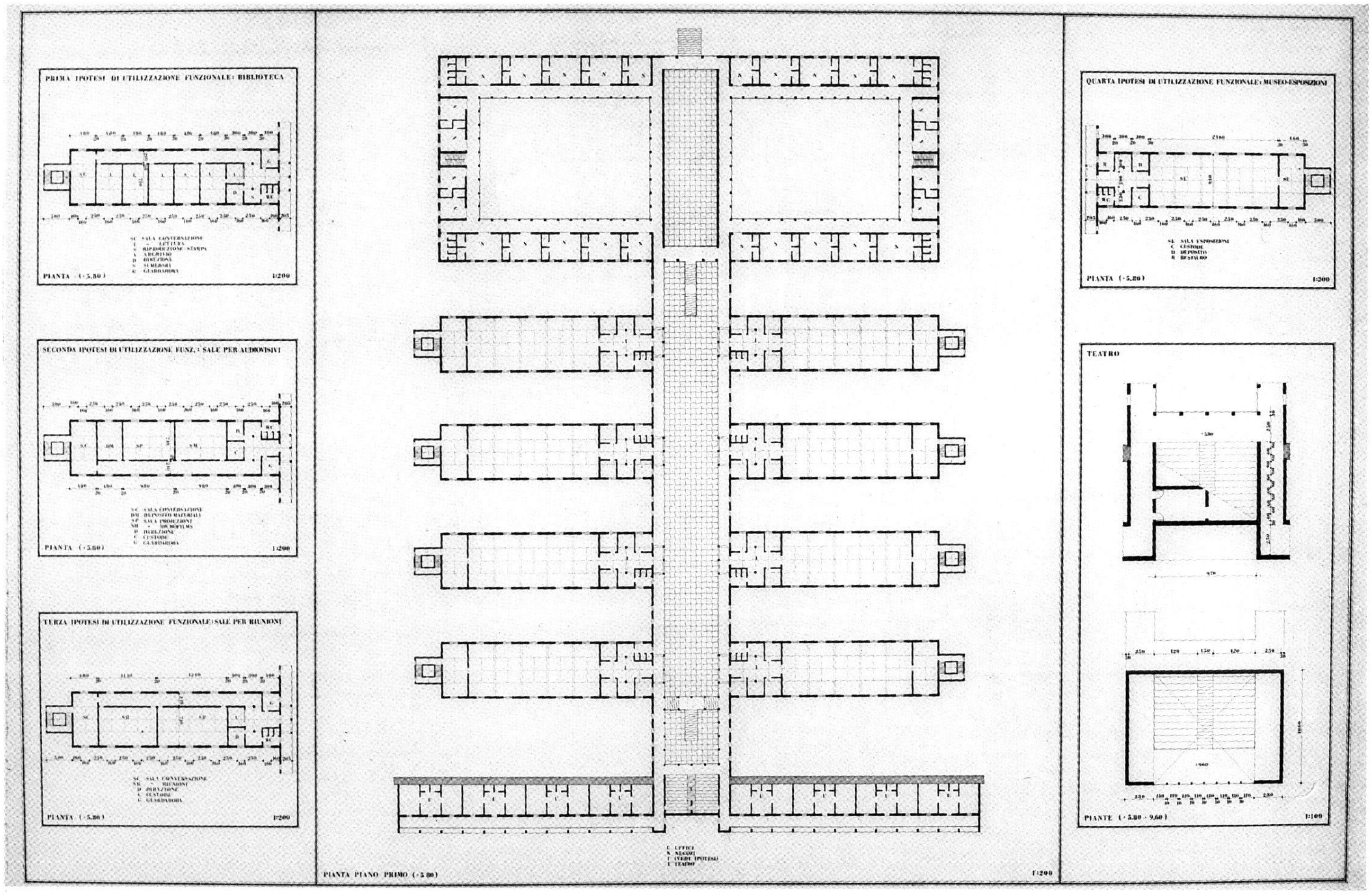

FIRST FLOOR PLAN SHOWING POSSIBLE USES

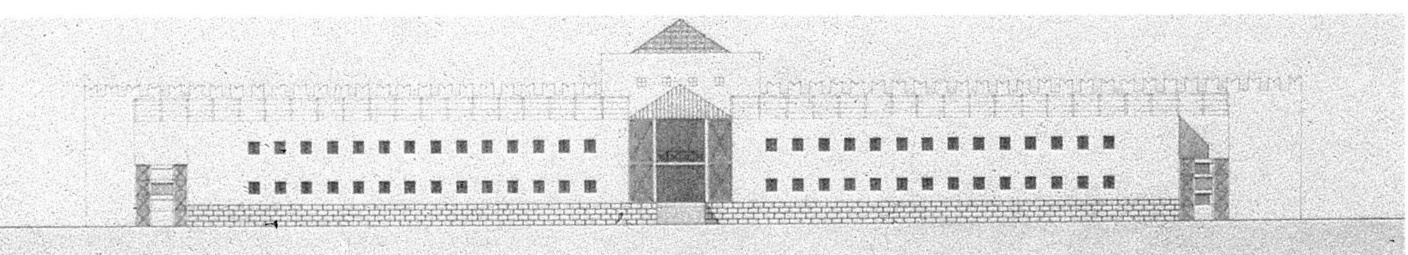

ELEVATION

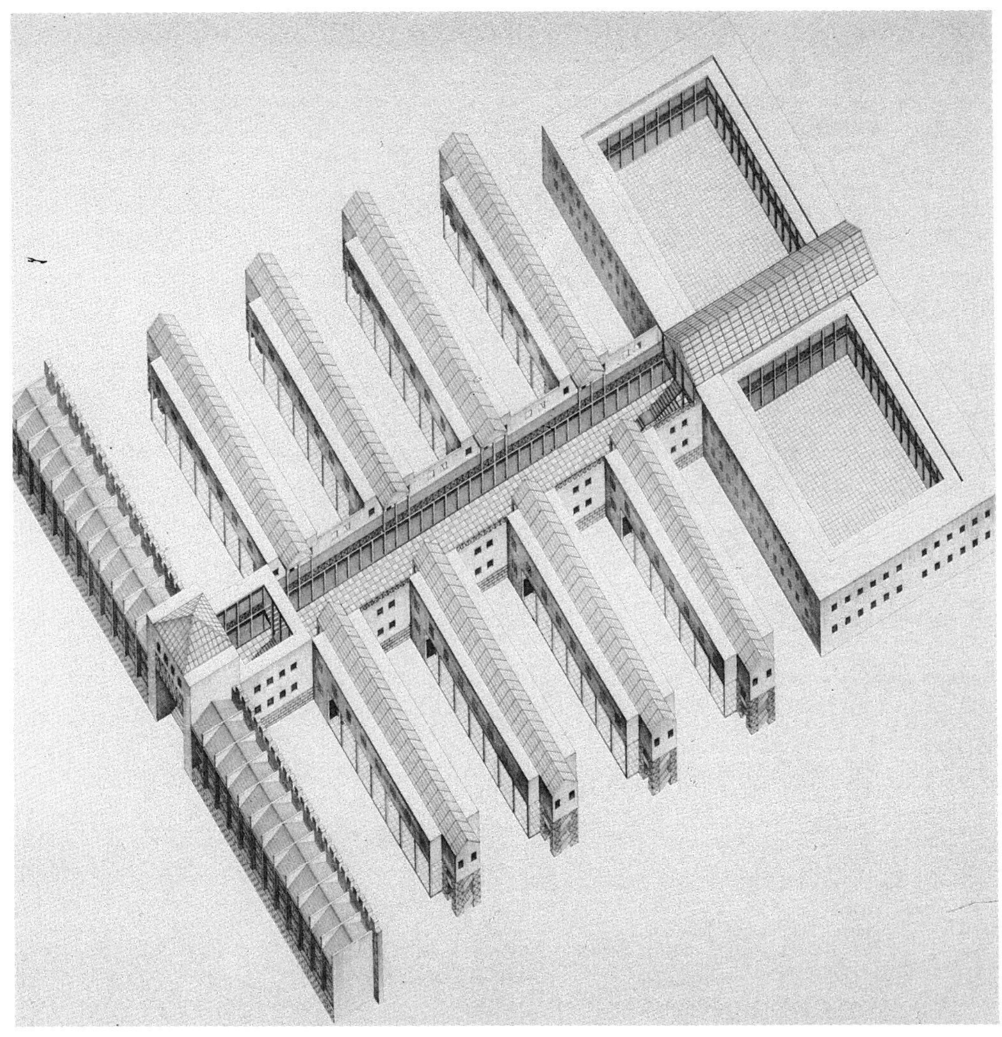

AXONOMETRIC

SIDE ELEVATION

LONGITUDINAL SECTION

GINO VALLE, OFFICES OF THE BANCA COMMERCIALE ITALIANA IN MANHATTAN

# FIGURATION

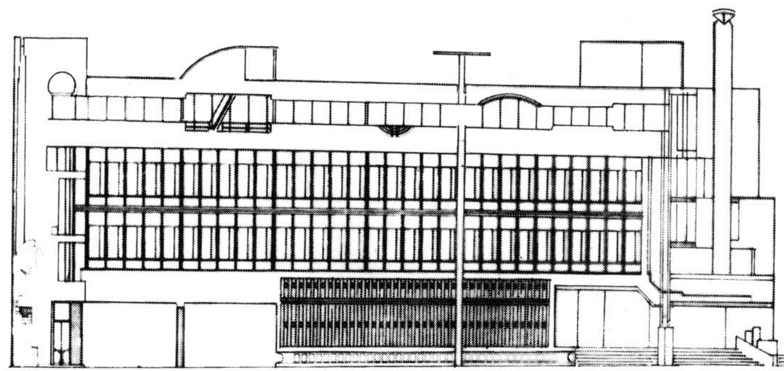

VIEW FROM THE RIVER

DETAILS OF THE FACADE

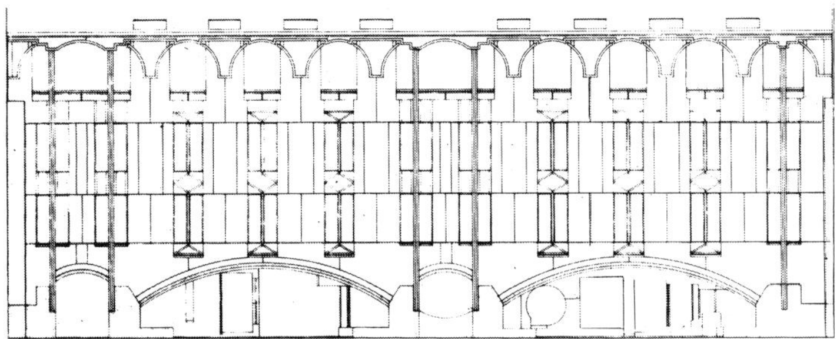

VIEW FROM VIA ROMA

# GIUSEPPE SAMONA
## Architectural Traditionalism and Internationalism

**I**N ORDER TO CLARIFY THE SPIRITUAL MEANING OF THE **modern architectural movement, one must consider modern industrialisation, which imposes a mainly utilitarian and econo**-mic character upon building and which makes speed of realisation consonant with the speed of current mechanisation. On account of these and other factors, the architectural profession has undergone deep and complex changes and has had to adapt to a scientism imposed by problems unknown in the past.

Architecture's scientific and technical tendency (today called rationalism, a broad word with many meanings) is not a phenomenon of one particular architectural movement: it is not the hallmark of a band of extremists, nor is it the academic concept of architecture described by Viollet-Le-Duc. Rather, it is one of the basic themes of all contemporary architecture, the unifying strength that binds architecture to life, the power that reconciles the artistic spirit with the practical and scientific tendencies of our century. The continuing vitality of all modern architectural movements is dependent, then, on them becoming 'rational' in this way.

In practical terms, rationalism culminates in the synthesis, bareness and simplicity of forms. It moves architecture towards a purely rhythmical principle of expression. Rational synthesis and simplicity are features of the two main contemporary architectural currents: traditionalism and internationalism. Both see rationalism as the means of translating their dreams into concrete form, but each interprets the concept very differently. Because of their spiritual balance, the traditionalists ought to be more capable of rationality than the internationalists. However, they are not always conscious of their own ability to adapt practical needs to the artistic needs of the spirit. This is possibly because they act rationally almost instinctively and are therefore sometimes led to criticise rationality as a defect of the internationalists. The internationalists, on the other hand, are possibly less rational in spirit because they are extremists and fanatics. They believe that they alone hold the secret of rationality and that is why they proclaim it as a measure of beauty to the bitter end. In doing so, they are exaggerating a very natural concept of modern life and arriving at conclusions which are absurd from an aesthetic and psychological point of view, such as transferring art from the realm of the human spirit into a colder field, a supremely anti-expressive field remote from the creative imagination.

It is, however, a mistake to try to look for the values of the modern architectural movement in these theories alone. A clear, sure judgement of the currents in modern architecture can be achieved only by a study of the psychological foundations which inspire architects and by a comparison of the works they create. Let us first examine two aspects of international architecture; the transference of the new architecture of the industrial building to civic architecture, and the appearance of a new set of aesthetic formulae dictated by the confrontation between modern architecture and new urban demands.

In recent years the construction of industrial buildings throughout the world has multiplied a hundredfold. The industrialist's need to use publicity to inflate his power has given rise to a new architecture which is beautiful in its own way and sometimes brilliantly inventive. This architecture is seen as an opportunity to affirm the industrialist's importance in a lasting manner. In all ages, one type of building has provided the salient features for the architecture of a civilisation. Today – because of the overvaluing of industrial architecture in artistic relations and the decline in the commissioning of great architecture – the industrial building is the broadest source of inspiration for all monumental architecture. However, the client's desire for economy means that the architect cannot match the monumentality that used to be required for certain buildings. The result has been a certain levelling-out of two genres of composition that are in fact very different: thus the powerful masses of the industrial building, where horizontal elements stretch for hundreds of metres along immense glass walls, are also to be found in public offices, museums and modern theatres, where the same horizontal glass walls contrast with extremely tall vertical elements. While this contrast of masses has given rise to a new monumentality, it lacks balance from a traditional point of view because it reverses ancient and static laws by putting, for example, huge windows at the corners of the building where it was usual in the past to give a greater appearance of strength.

The other aspect of international architecture is reflected in particular in small buildings, modest rented accommodation and mass-produced houses. For the internationalists, this lesser architecture must also be the expression of an ideal future, because modern civilisa-

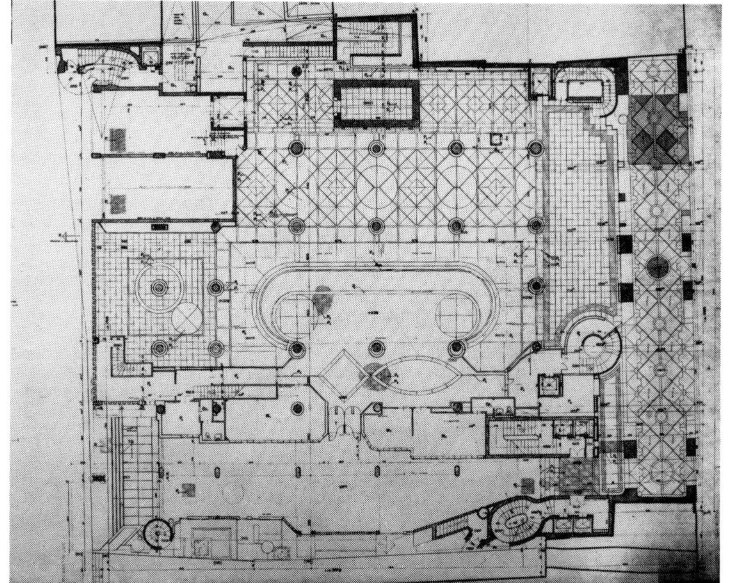
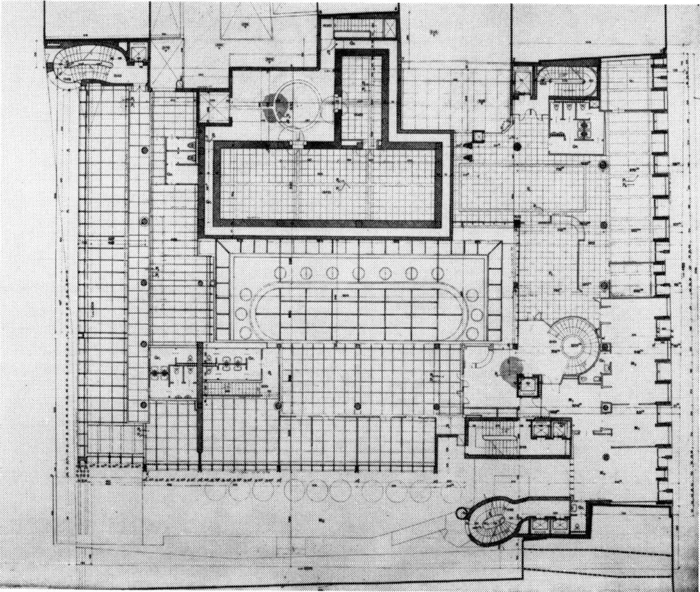

GIUSEPPE SAMONÀ, PLAN OF THE NEW BANCA D'ITALIA HEADQUARTERS IN PADUA. LEFT: GROUND FLOOR. RIGHT: FIRST FLOOR

PLAN AND VIEW OF THE TOWER AND STAIRS

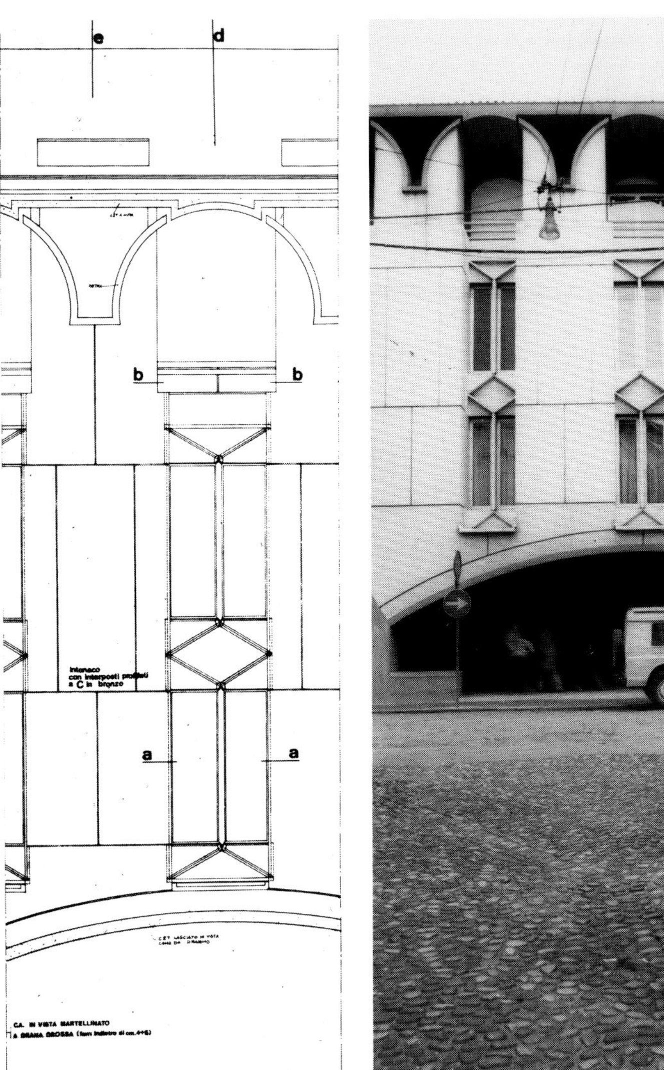

PLAN AND VIEW OF THE PORTICO FROM VIA ROMA

tion tends towards industrial goals. However, these goals change the physiognomy of the houses so radically that it seems absurd to think of them in forms inspired by the past. Instead, a whole new series of aesthetic formulae has developed, inspired by the forms of the new dynamic which is regarded as the most characteristic and basic exponent of future society. The internationalists reason that steamers, cars and aeroplanes have nothing in common with the past, and yet are beautiful purely because they have spontaneously adapted to the nature of the object in which every part has its value and nothing is superfluous or useless. For them, the aeroplane is a greater source of inspiration than the Parthenon. They see the future vindicating their belief that all style is absurd, and that the science of building the most daring forms with the minimum means will be triumphant throughout the world.

This is the standpoint from which Le Corbusier exalts a future society where everything will contribute to the logical and complete realisation of architectural rationalism and the house will be reduced to a tool like the car, beautiful in the same way that a tool is beautiful. This is the standpoint that makes Roux-Spitz write: 'The hour is approaching when a new internationalised architecture will triumph, with few variations from one country to another, an architecture whose unity will be the product of mathematics and intelligence'. To conclude, this trend in international architecture goes beyond daily life; it fixes its gaze upon the future and exalts it. Theoretically, it wants to transform the creative imagination into an artificial cerebral creativity in which feeling is opposed by the ingenuity of the scientifically organised brain. It has an impassioned rage for renewal based on an ideal scientific combination of architecture and engineering. At first glance, therefore, the stark contrast between the arid theory and the extravagant language

used to express it seems curious. If, however, we try to fathom the sense of the words, the strange dissonance no longer strikes us, because beneath the arid mathematical outer cover is the soul of this movement – a new romanticism.

This romanticism is evident in the transference of art and architecture to a sometimes paradoxical and fantastic future. Although the internationalists declare themselves rational to the end, despising traditional sentimentalism as romantic dross, and although they repudiate the old romanticism of Wackenroden or Schelling, Hayez or Ingres, a look at the innermost roots of the new movement reveals that it has the same bases as the old. The roots of the first romanticism lay in the need to re-assess art and free the creative process from merely imitating the classical traditions of the Enlightenment. Then, as now, the aim was to remove all the fetters of the past and transfer imagination to the future. Then, there was a return to the cult of beauty which idealised nature. Now, on the contrary, an attempt is being made to find a new form of art that will be a spontaneous creation of the object idealised in a distant future. The words 'creative imagination' have been replaced by the phrase 'mathematical brain', but the substance remains the same: the spirit is trying to break the fetters of an age-old discipline and direct all its impassioned exaltation at the unexplored regions of the future. In fact, the rationalists' idea of an art based on mathematics and science is founded not on contemporary life, but on a new life forged by the artist in his own way. This life is never in the present but always straining towards an imaginary future in which all modern possibilities are multiplied to the point of paroxysm. And yet, in the same way as the old romantics used to try to fashion themselves a nature which did not have its roots in reality but was entirely dictated by their imagination,

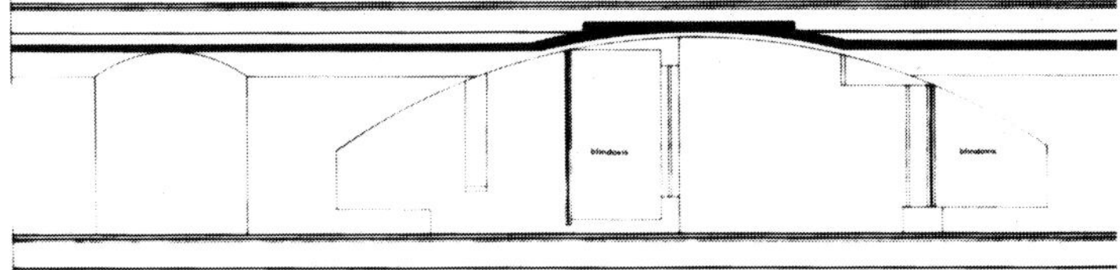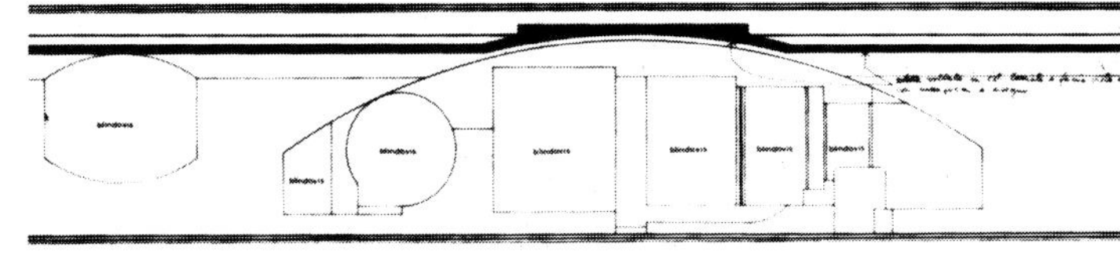

VIEWS OF THE PORTICO

the moderns base their construction not on present-day needs but on an ideal, an hypothesis poised towards the future, requiring a special state of mind that will take hundreds of years to develop. This feeling of being out of one's time was also very common in nineteenth-century romanticism. It was the sort of prophetic vision experienced by all those whose spirit was not truly in this life but out of it.

We may indeed talk of spirit now that we intend to consider the internationalists as the modern romantics of architecture. From this point of view, rationalism may still be art, but art would not exist if we were to take the theories which replace the heart by the brain and the spirit by reason literally. It is only possible to join together architecture and engineering by means of a spiritual current, in the form of art. Future generations will be able to judge how healthy this romanticism is and how far its rationality is capable of triumphing over the industrialist tendency of modern life. We can only state that internationalist architects, as romantics, idealise architecture by transferring it to a distant future of which they appoint themselves the prophets and from which they draw their inspiration. Thus this movement can only be called international in a broad sense, since in essence it is highly personal, reflecting the singular interpretation of an imaginary future in which each artist must feel and interpret his own way.

The internationalists are countered by the traditionalists, a group of calmer and more measured architects, who consider life as it is, accept its obstacles, and try to overcome them in art. These architects, who are convinced of the altered needs of architecture, try to find a balance between practical needs and spiritual needs because of the concrete nature of modern problems and because of their modest and utilitarian nature. Balance is the fundamental notion in this trend, which can be called classical inasmuch as it links up with tradition, not to imitate its forms in a sterile fashion, but to seek expression in it. What is characteristic of the traditionalists is their lack of preference for any particular era of the past. The modern traditionalist architect looks to the past for the concrete expression of a particular state of mind and takes it wherever he finds it, without worrying about whether it is baroque, Roman, Greek or romantic. This is a sort of new eclecticism quite distinct from academic eclecticism with its pre-established forms; it consists of the conviction that in art one can have the beautiful, the noble and the new, not by avant-garde practices, but by infusing one's own spirit into the material which the past offers. In short, it treats the past as a pure means, as a vehicle to attain personal expression.

From this point of view, the traditionalists are perhaps more daring vis-à-vis tradition than are the internationalists. The internationalists see the past as a threat to be avoided and try at all costs to forget it, while the traditionalists immerse themselves in the past with indifference, manipulating it as living material. More importantly, they do not reject modern expedients but often make use of them in their own work, just as they do with tradition. They have already designed many inspired buildings which combine aspects of the past with forms and rhythms taken from, for example, extremely modern industrial architecture.

Although conciliation may seem strange, it is in fact not so at all, if one grasps the most salient feature animating the traditionalists – their sense of measure. This gift allows them to plunder the past for what moves us today and plunder the present for what is most alive in it, rejecting aberrations out of hand.

*First published in* Rassegna di architettura *no 12, December 1929*

# LUCIANO SEMERANI & GIGETTA TAMARO

## The New Town Hall at Osoppo

VIEW OF EXTERNAL PIAZZA

**O**UR INITIAL DESIRE TO CREATE **something specific and original for the** new town hall at Osoppo grew with the development of the project. We were asked to use the character of this important public building to express not only a typical moment in the process of reconstruction but also the symbolic value which the town hall as an institution has held and will continue to hold in the democratic history of the community. The forms of the new town hall had not only to fulfil practical standards and requirements but also to fuse the modern times, future hopes and troubled history of the people of Osoppo. It had to be a political and cultural centre for the community and not merely a technical and administrative building.

Initially, the town hall was articulated in three blocks: the first block was on a square base, with four large corner piers supporting a pavilion roof; the second was on a rectangular base with a keel roof; and the third block, with a large deep arch running under it, was the essential bridge between the two. Later, this plan was refined when three characters of marked individuality emerged on the urban scene.

The figures were enlarged or reduced in relation to the models we referred to, namely, a small portico at Aviano for the pavilion, and the basilicas of the Veneto for the main hall. In our building, the pillars become a room, the facade turns into a face, the portico detaches itself like a husk from the volumes behind it and the bridge heightens the figure of the arch by making three great arcs itself.

The genesis of architecture from architecture is also genesis from the context. (In this case also genesis *of* context.) It was therefore obvious that the spaces external to the buildings could not be alienated from the planning. At the crossing of the two main streets of the historic centre is the new piazza Napoleone I, and behind it, a small square which joins up with the long house on via Andervolti. Together they form a continuation of the covered pedestrian spaces below the buildings, that is, the porticos under the council chambers and the vaults under the bridge linking the office and the hall. In face of this complex, suggestive urban space, the paving and lie of the land can offer themselves only as a comment, a measured underlining achieved through the combined use of porphyry and Cividale stone on natural valleys and ridges.

*Luciano Semerani*

**Collaborator**: Adalberto Burelli.

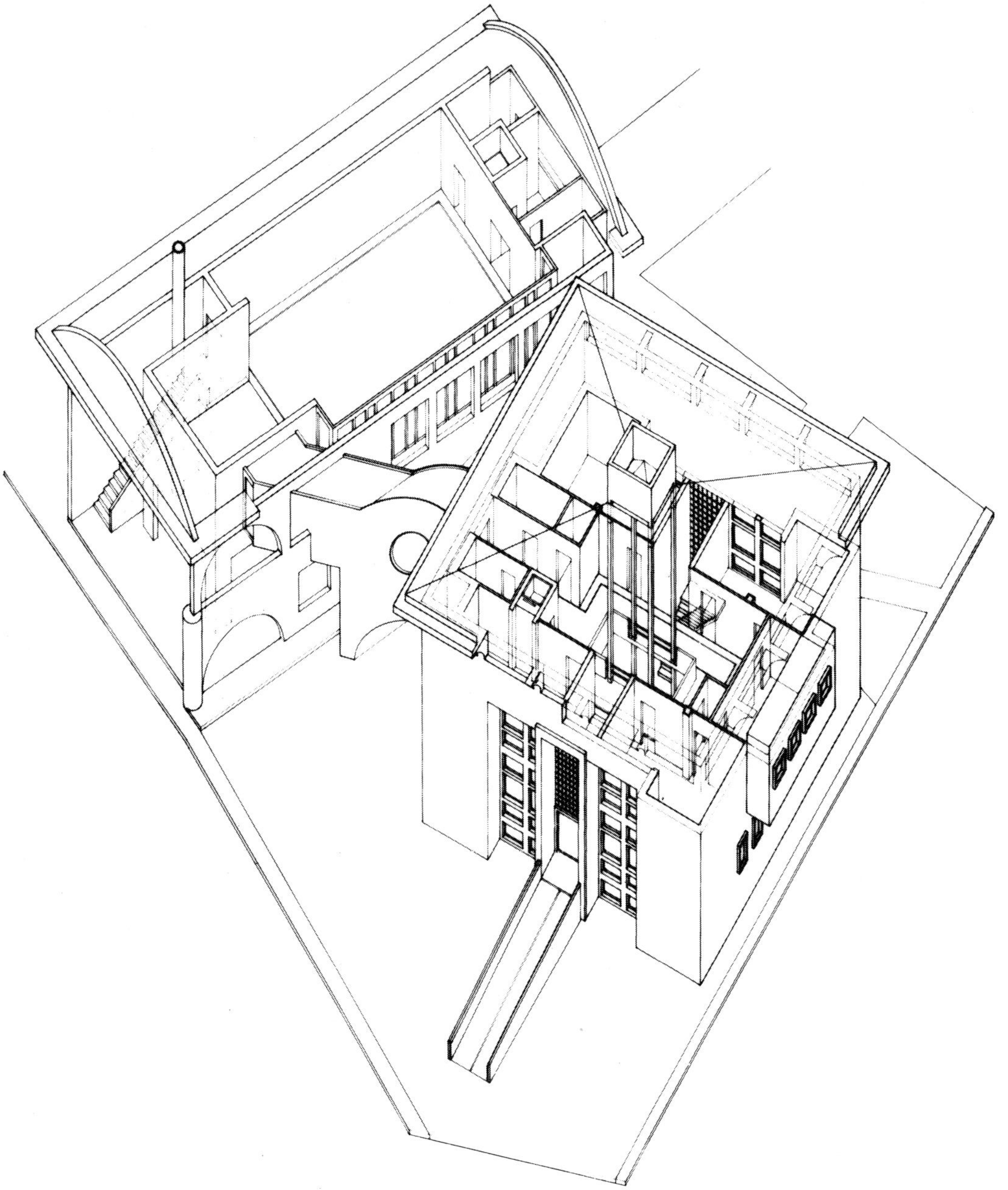

AXONOMETRIC SHOWING THE RELATIONSHIP OF BUILDINGS, CONNECTING BRIDGE AND COUNCIL CHAMBERS

DETAIL OF BRIDGE

DETAIL OF ACCESS RAMP TO OFFICE BUILDING

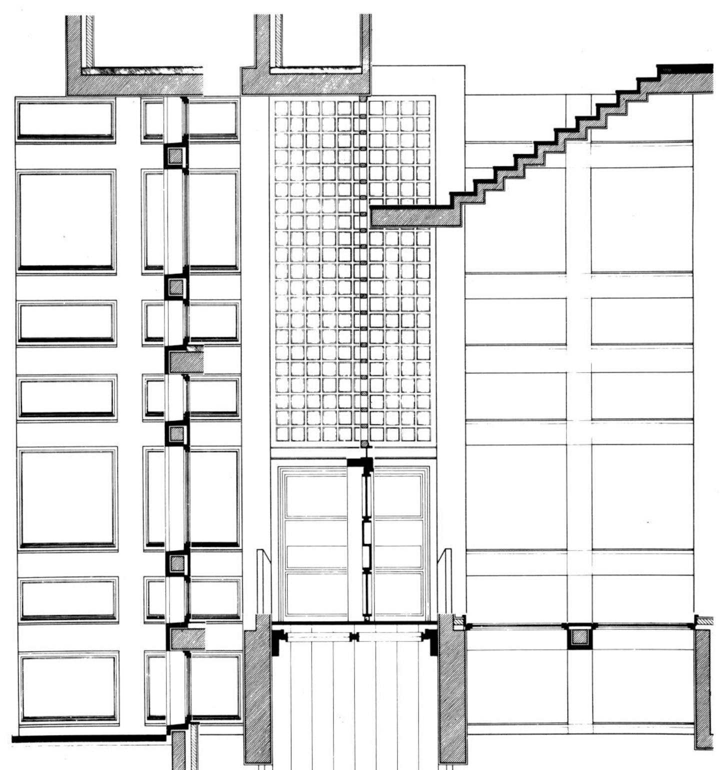

ENTRANCE TO THE OFFICE BUILDING

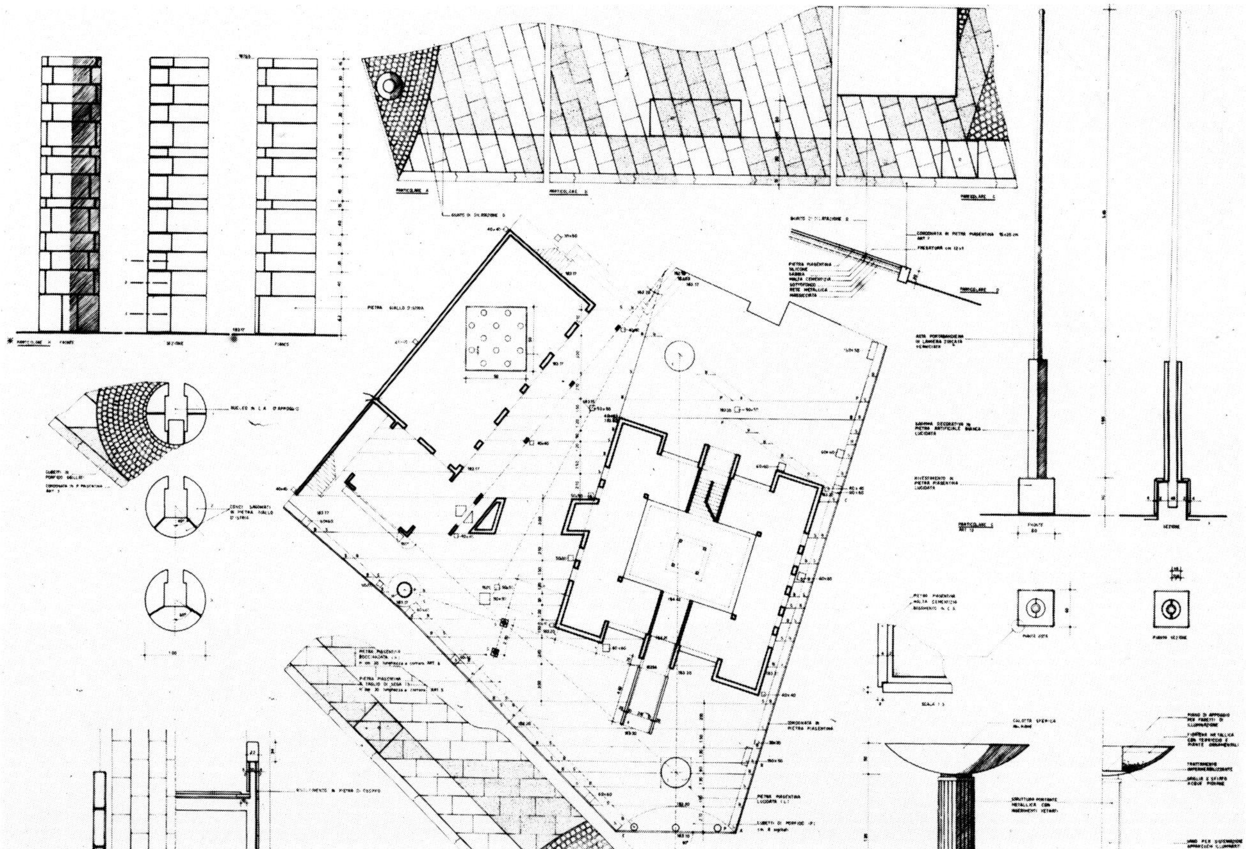

MATERIALS AFFECTING THE LAYOUT OF THE EXTERNAL PIAZZA: CYLINDRICAL COLUMN, FLAGPOSTS, DIVIDING PILLARS, PAVING

# OSWALD ZOEGGELER
## Competition for the Conversion of the Old Cotton Mill in Venice

VIEW OF THE PROJECT FROM GIUDECCA ISLAND

**T**HE SCHOOL OF VENICE HAS ACQUIRED the city's old cotton mill, which is an enormous industrial building in brick and Istrian stone dating from the last century. Inside, it has a regular pillared structure in the fascinating style of the earliest works in reinforced concrete and cast iron. Originally a three-storey building, each storey being five-metres high, it was partially destroyed during the First World War and has been two-storeyed in parts ever since.

This project was an entry in a competition to develop the cotton mill as a school of architecture. The mill has been treated as one of those great 'containers' which fit brusquely into the urban fabric of Venice and dominate its structure and skyline as exceptional elements, like the Doges' Palace or the Scuole. These great containers characterise the inner spaces of the Lagoon's islands; their unusual position in the region increases their importance. Postwar rebuilding has largely destroyed the image of the great container, making it more like a part of the urban fabric, and less like a monument. After wars, people are more afraid of the monument, the sign and the symbol, and because of this fear many people are still living in the immediate post-war period forty years on. The monument is, however, important and necessary, so we had no doubts about freeing this particular giant from its contorted, disabled image and restoring its original appearance with all its superior, serene dignity.

Internally, a new glass-enclosed gallery will increase spatial perception and link the three floors optically. The Zattere serve as a long terrace for Venice, opening up the whole city to the south and to Giudecca. At present, the cotton mill does not relate successfully with this important urban element. The small existing building with the chimney has been turned into a terrace which overlooks the sea and joins to the roof-terrace of the main building.

The figurative characteristics of the cotton mill have been retained because its industrial, factory-like appearance is very apt for a building producing architects. Only the palms that stand on the outer corners of the building, with their steel leaves and massive aluminium branches swaying gently in the wind and glittering in the sun, will give the industrial building the dignity of a public building and that premium of elegance and worldliness needed for a school of architecture.

The facade facing the Zattere is the only part of the building which needs a new form. This will be a symbolic sign, visible from a distance, which will recall a period when architecture was more absolute, more abstract, more timeless; namely, the French Enlightenment. The sign will bear a particular reference to Gilly's kiln.

### Architecture and History

The history of architecture is composed of two qualities of form. On the one hand, there are forms which belong strictly to a particular time, which are tied to a given age. On the other, there are forms which seem to avoid the passage of time, which speak of eternal values. These two qualities depend on the relationship between abstraction and decoration which exists within every piece of architecture. When abstraction dominates, architecture is freed from history. When decoration prevails, architecture is tied to an historical moment. The ideas that should be expressed in architecture have the same qualities: some are concerned with a given time and situation, others with an eternal and absolute truth. Quotation is the other technique which introduces elements of history into the architecture of today. It is useful when an architectural expression has already been said with such precision that it cannot be improved. However, quotations in architecture should be used as thoughtfully and deliberately as they are in prose.

A quotation is not clever just because it's in Latin.

Each form, volume and architecture has its own characteristics. Each contains an *idea*, a spirit. In architecture, figuration is the translation of a thought or idea into architectural language. Each idea or group of ideas can be expressed with architectural forms or spaces in the same way that it can be expressed with words, musical notes or pictures. Architecture should generate feelings and sensations. The idea contained in the architectural form should show itself and speak. It is a spiritual expression. It takes a position on its surroundings, on life. It is a response, an affirmation, a negation, an exultation.

When an architectural statement is constructed around one or more ideas, the building becomes the visible statement of these ideas. When the generating idea is absent, all that is formed is an empty statement, a casual result, a mask with nothing behind it. An architecture designed without regard for formal expression will have a poor, vague, sad and confused spirit.

The effects and tensions of forms and spaces can be measured by examples from the history of architecture. We can use history as a collection of formal expressions, but history helps us above all to examine and compare: it provides us with analogies for our problems. In the history of architecture, there is no form that has not already been devised, just as there is no architectural expression, situation or problem today that has not already been resolved in the past. For this reason, we cannot pretend that history does not exist, we cannot ignore the way in which it has developed, and we cannot begin again from an imaginary starting point.

*Oswald Zoeggeler*

**Collaborators:** Fritz Nagele, Alberto Mascotti.

SIDE ELEVATION

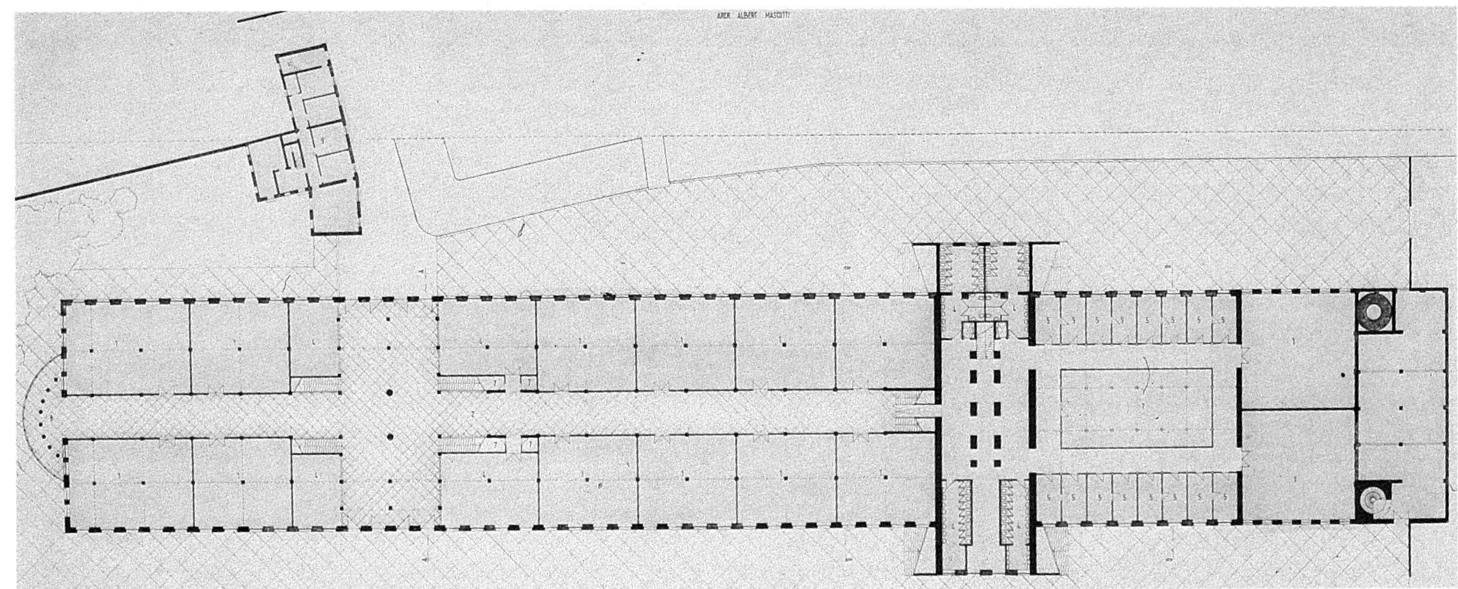

GROUND FLOOR PLAN

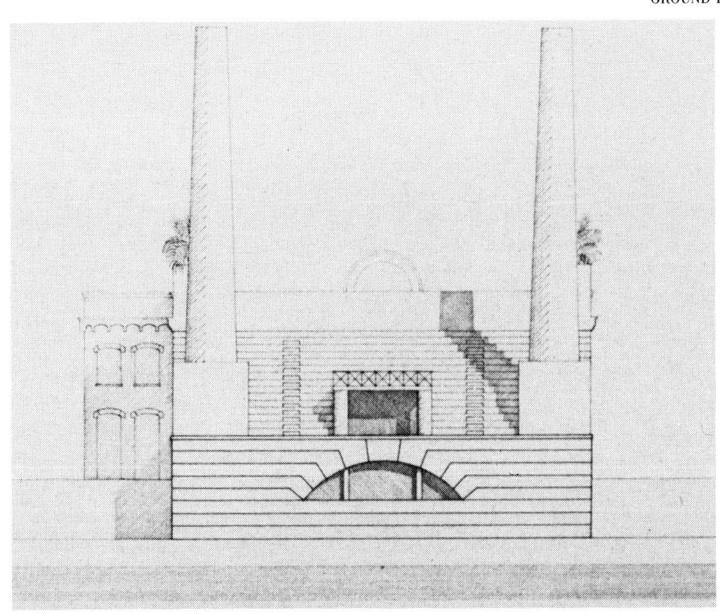

FRONT ELEVATION

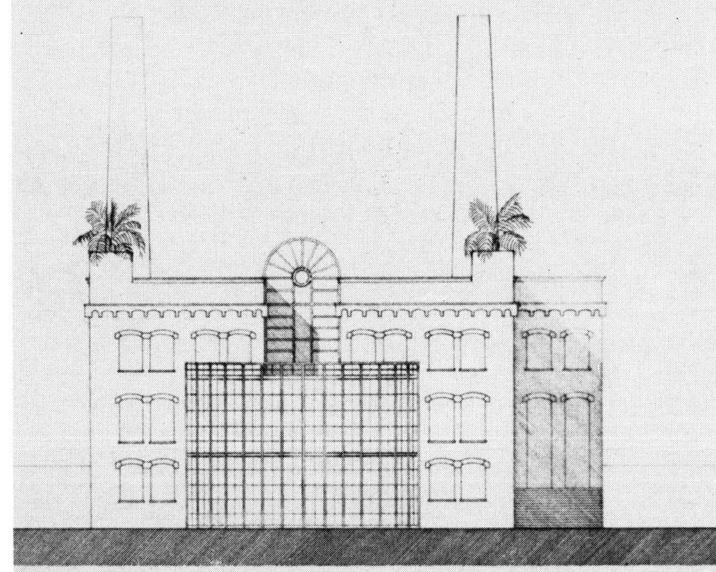

REAR ELEVATION

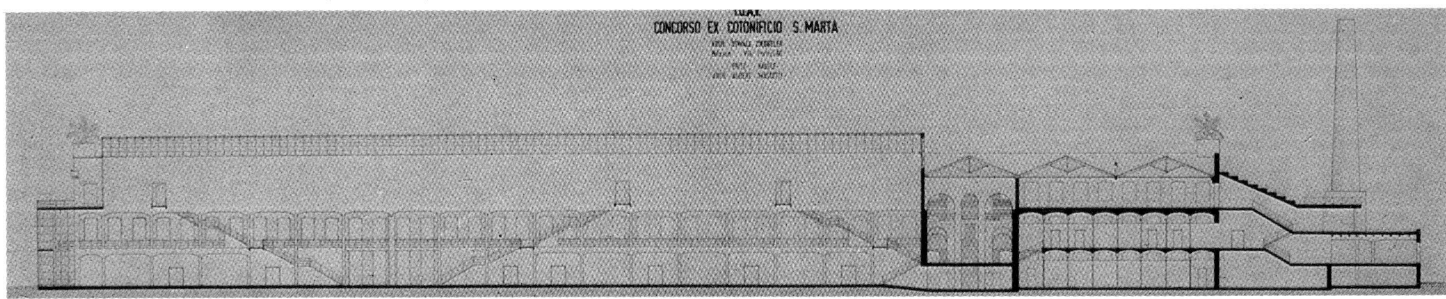



LONGITUDINAL SECTION

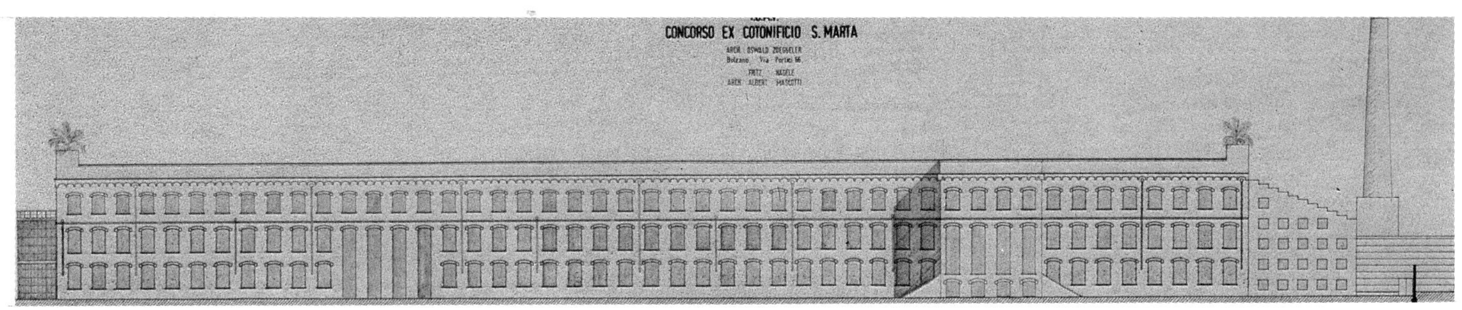


SIDE ELEVATION

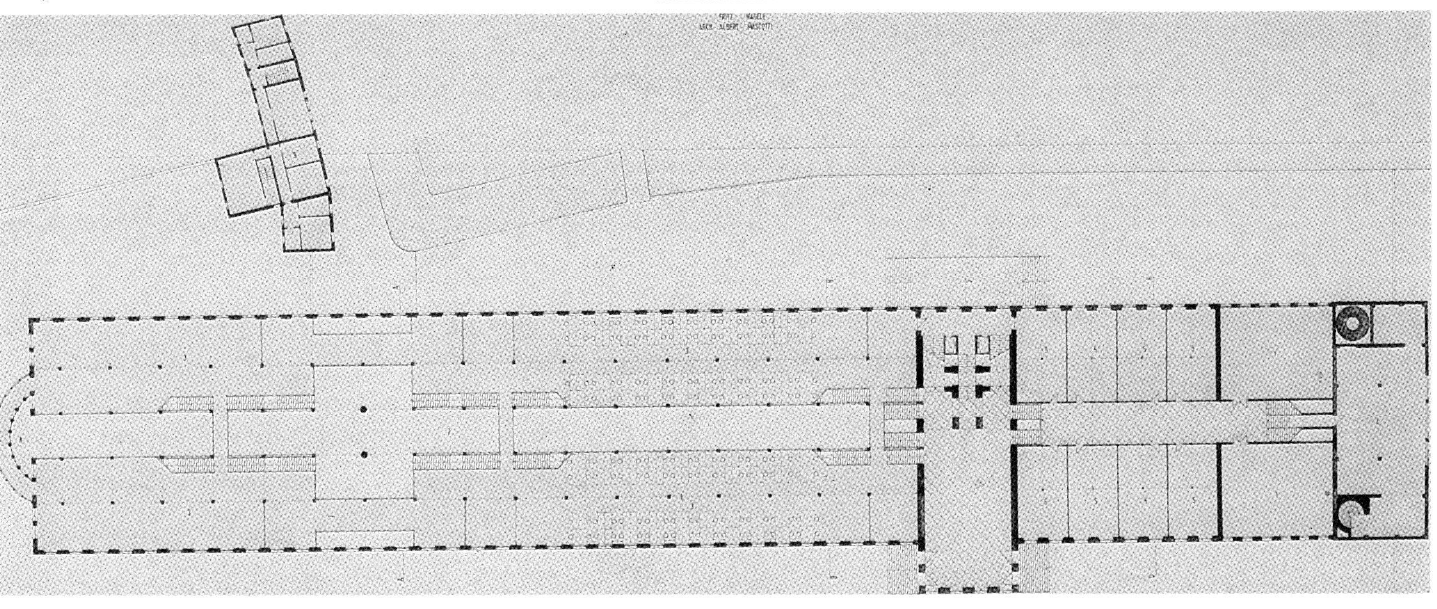


FIRST FLOOR PLAN

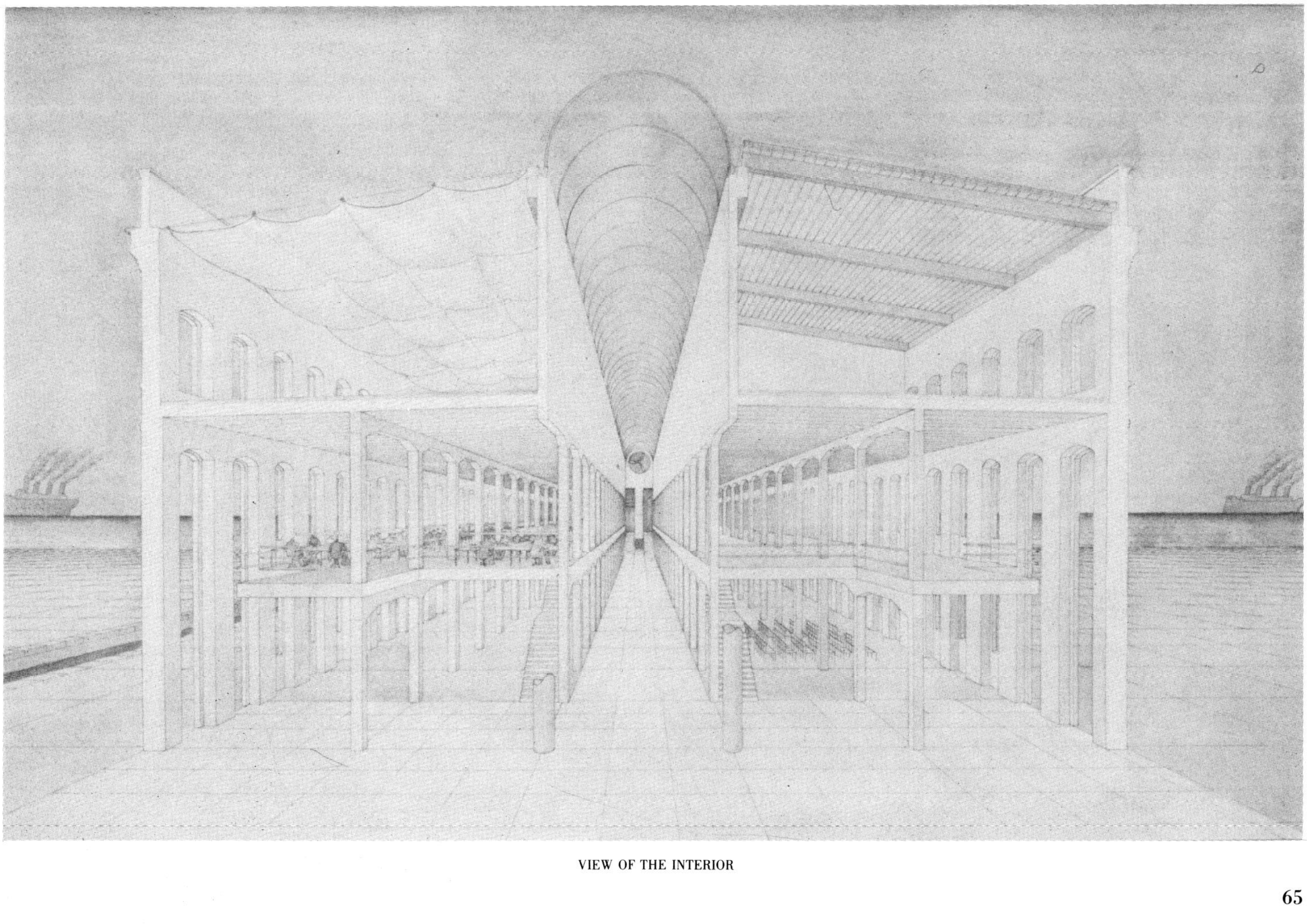

VIEW OF THE INTERIOR

AXONOMETRIC VIEW WITH THE NEW HOUSING IN THE LOWER PART OF THE ISLAND

# GINO VALLE
## New Housing on Giudecca Island

**P**EOPLE ARE WONT TO SAY THAT **Venice is a unique city, but this** uniqueness is really attributable to the Venetians and their life-style. Venice is like a piece of the Orient, partly because it is very difficult to get anything accomplished there, partly because nothing new has been built on the island or in the historic centre for the past fifty years.

Venetians see Giudecca island as a place outside their city, a place to gaze upon from the Zattere, a place to go with the first spring sun. The appearance of tables outside its pizzerias and ice-cream parlours is a sign that the best season of the year has begun.

The grand Giudecca canal is blue. At the time of the Republic, Giudecca was an island of villas, gardens, monasteries and orchards. However, industrialisation arrived in the nineteenth century, bringing with it the dockyards, the CNOM factory (where the Biennale was held), the Dreher brewery, and the Stucky mill which ground the grain that came in on the ships. Giudecca even had a railway running through it. The abandoned neo-gothic mill is an important part of the profile of Venice and the area around the Zattere. When I was a student in Venice in the 1940s I saw it as a strange castle on the water.

The buildings on Giudecca have maintained a very definite structure over time. Towards Venice, the buildings are as densely packed as the teeth on a comb. Towards the Lagoon and the south, there are green gardens or bleak *terrain vague* behind decaying industrial buildings.

The island is broken down into crosswise strips going from the Stucky mill in the north to the abandoned industrial buildings on the southern tip. Two narrow wall-lined paths connect the industrial fragments in the north with an established park. Hidden in the woods on one side of this park is a seventeenth-century house and garden surrounded by walls. On the other side of the park is a second, smaller house with a walled garden: this is the entrance to the Trevisan complex which covers the centre of the southern half of the island. The complex was originally a cement factory and is composed of well-designed late nineteenth-century brick industrial buildings.

There is another walled path which gauges the breadth of the island. After walking along it for quarter of an hour, the bridge that crosses over to the island disappears from sight and one enters the central part of the island. A short while later, the bridge leaving the island comes into view.

The project was conceived with great respect for this environment. The path across the island has been retained: access to the new houses will be from paths running along the boundaries of the two old houses in the park. A new canal will separate the new houses from the abandoned industrial buildings at the tip of the island. These buildings will however be restored to provide more room for the continuation of productive activity.

The site is a rectangle measuring 120m by 60m. The long sides are on the north (which overlooks green space and is the direction of access) and the south (which overlooks the Lagoon). Overlooking the canal on each of the short sides is a simple four-storey facade.

The project calls for a compact grouping of buildings on a module of 1.65m. The principle relations between the urban complex and the natural surroundings will be stabilised by the centre section, a rectangle measuring 100m by 35m. This section is called the 'carpet', and is composed of three facades running from east to west and decreasing—as the rows of buildings move from north to south—from four storeys to two.

The houses will be organised around an open space oriented towards the south. The living rooms and kitchen/dining areas will be located on the top floor and the kitchens will have terraces facing south above the roofs of the next row of houses. The areas open to the north will have insulated windows with views of the historic centre of Venice. The middle facade will be interrupted in the centre to make room for an open green space. Access to this section will be from the open space and two porticos linked to pathways. The third facade is oriented towards private green spaces which slope towards the south. Part of the section adjoining the canal is given over to an open space, the remainder is composed of buildings arranged in L-shapes to form small courtyards facing the canal.

**Collaborators:** Giorgio Macola, Maria Caterina Redini, Giuseppe Camporini, Alfredo Carnelutti, Carlo Mauro.

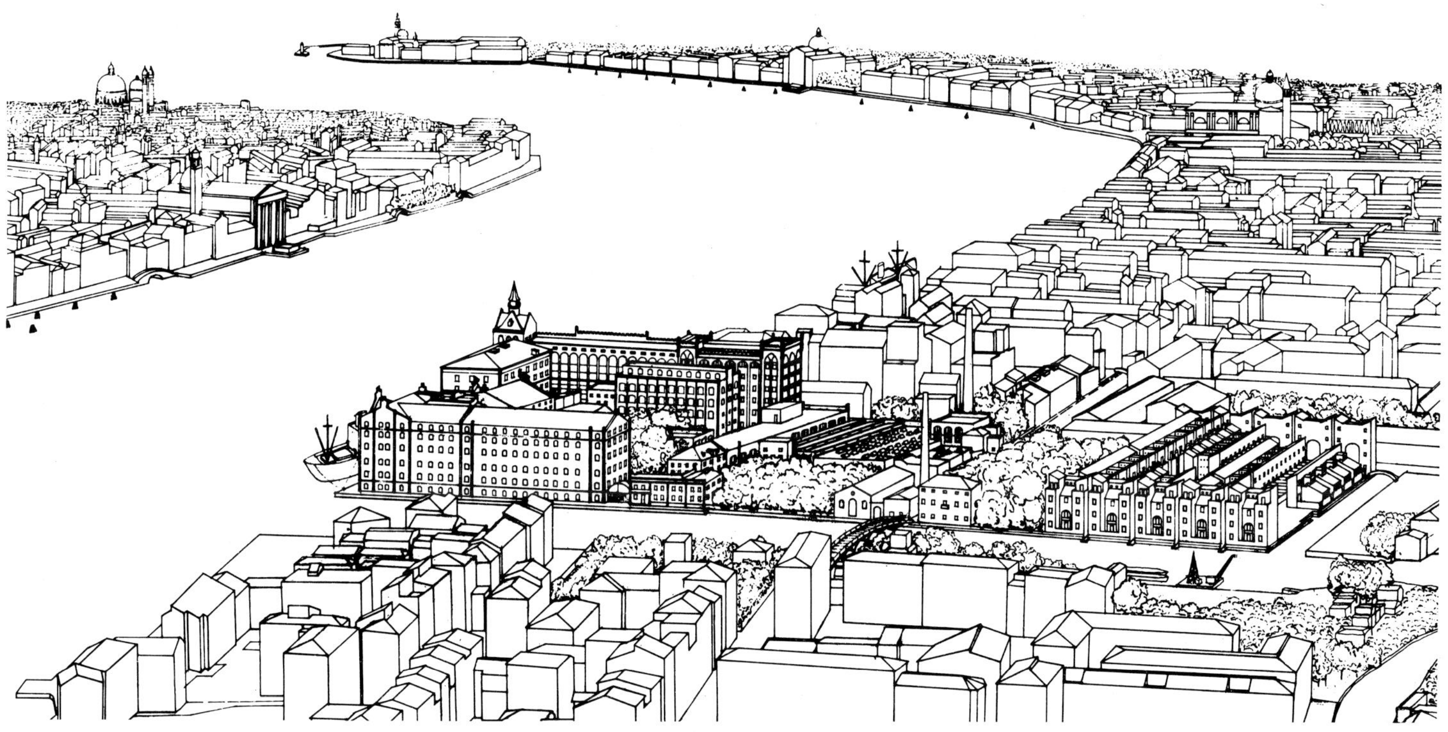

PERSPECTIVE OF GIUDECCA ISLAND AND THE CANAL THAT SEPARATES IT FROM VENICE

EAST PROFILE FROM SAN BIAGIO CANAL

GROUND FLOOR PLAN

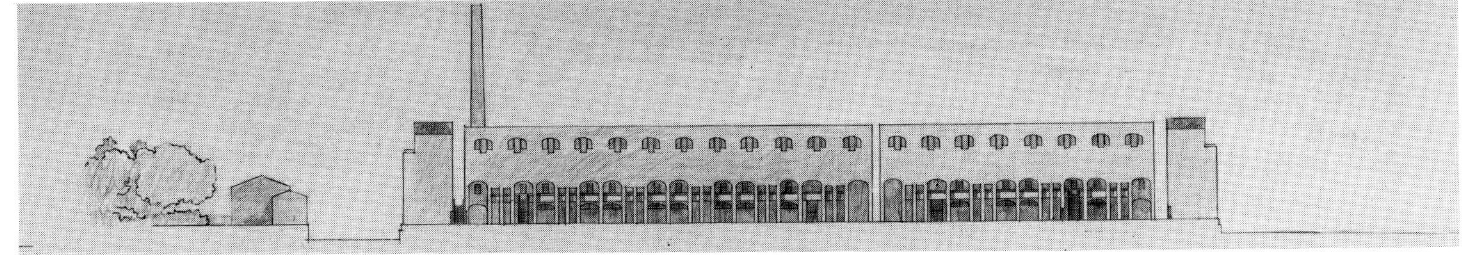

WEST PROFILE

SOUTH PROFILE

## "RENOVATIO URBIS"
Venezia nell'età di
Andrea Gritti (1523-1538)

# DEPARTMENT OF ARCHITECTURAL HISTORY

# PAOLO MORACHIELLO
## The Department of Architectural History
## A Detailed Description

**O**FTEN THE ARCHITECT HAS MADE THE LOFTY CLAIM **that he can give finished form to the world's requirements, resolving them into order or dissolving them into disorder.** He works with the seductions and illusions of the image. The historian is less fortunate. He cannot create illusions and for him seduction is at most the path to rigour, the one valid affirmation of his being. He must aspire to rigour in recounting what has happened and why it has happened. He must break down the construction, the sign, the text and the image and faithfully and tirelessly recover their causes, without idolising either the building or the drawing or still less the document. This is implicitly the historian's intent: his method, always supposing that one exists, depends upon his intent and the object of his study.

This presentation of the work of the Department of Architectural History must therefore be in the form of a detailed description rather than a projection of aims. However, this description can still offer explanations. Knowledge of ends and causes leads to knowledge of the things debated and, better still, to an awareness of the modes of their interpretation. Manfredo Tafuri directs the department's research work, which is divided into four main categories. In describing these, we shall follow a purely chronological sequence.

The first area concerns Venice during the 'long Renaissance'. Over this period there were tensions caused by renewal, as well as religious ferment, self-celebration by patrons, scientific debate and rivalry between individual architects. This was a central chapter in the history of the city, when the Republic emerged and was taken up as a field of historiographic experimentation. The areas which the department focuses on are: the architecture of the period; the interweaving of politics, science and architecture (using studies by Antonio Foscari and Manfredo Tafuri on the scientific tendencies in Venice in the second half of the sixteenth century); the structural and functional dynamics of a place assigned to the production of ships and machines and the interaction within that space between architecture, new techniques and science; the heated debate between institutions, architecture and the military on the making of the city (using Ennio Concina's analyses of the Arsenal from its founding up to the Napoleonic period and the planning of defence in Venice in the sixteenth century); the weight and constraints of tradition, landed interests and the aspiration to give shape to images of Venice as a mercantile city (using Donatella Calabi and Paolo Morachiello's study of the rebuilding of the Rialto market and bridge).

The myth of the classical and its dissolution is the subject of Georges Teyssot's work. Teyssot studies the example of the Soane Museum, which emerges as the place of the 'crisis of the classical object' *par excellence*; a heterotopia where the value of all historical models is questioned from one room to another. It offers a grand tour, within historical time and geographical space, through 'historical space', in short, through architecture. It negates all mimetic planning processes; it is a place of continual invention derived from Piranesi; it is a place which reaffirms the subjective need for play and, consequently, poetry, in the face of the rule of regularity.

The distribution of collective facilities and installations throughout the city and territory and the organisation of dwelling and working space are aspects of a single urban strategy which does not attempt to determine the whole but rather acts on the parts, the masses, the flow, promoting and stimulating needs and behaviour. The programme, however, underlies the strategies and techniques of intervention. It brings together practices and branches of knowledge to build up principles which then govern the project. Yet because of the programmes' excess of logic and theoretical absoluteness, they inevitably meet with resistance. In fact, the people who they are applied to, who are too often regarded as malleable masses to be educated, slum-cleared and put in order, appear positively intractable in face of them. This is the exact opposite of a linear history which investigates the origins of modern town planning at the same time as it enquires into the beginnings of its crisis. In this respect, the following studies should also be mentioned: Renzo Dubbini on prison building; Donatella Calabi and Georges Teyssot on domestic architecture in Great Britain and France in the nineteenth century; Paolo Morachiello and Georges Teyssot on Napoleonic cities of state; and Paolo Morachiello, Amergio Restucci and Gian Domenico Romanelli on institutional spaces, architecture and Italian cities in the nineteenth century.

The fourth group of departmental research explores the history of contemporary architecture. Francesco Dal Cò has carried out historical 'excavations' in Europe and the USA and has located archival material relating to the work of Mies van der Rohe; work has now begun on a complete collection of his manuscripts. Through research in the archives of Berlin, Dresden, Burg-Ludwigstein, Weimar and Vienna, Marco de Michelis has been able to form a picture of Heinrich Tessenow's personality and to catalogue his works. Other lines of research explore and critically reconstruct the work of Hugo Haring within the context of the harsh architectural climate of Germany during the twenties and fifties (see the studies by Sergio Polano), the transformation of the centre of Berlin in the twenties and thirties (see the studies by Ludovico Scarpa) and the development of the Hampstead Garden Suburb between 1905 and 1914 (see the analyses by Guido Zucconi). A research project by Giorgio Ciucci and Guido Zucconi aims to define the notion of style in the work of Gio Ponti between 1928 and 1941, when the two reviews *Domus* and *Stile* were founded. This phase seems to have been characterised by a sort of expressive uncertainty which many critics have hastily dubbed 'eclecticism', but Ciucci and Zucconi have put forward the hypothesis that the architect tended to sound out the expressive potential of the various architectural 'languages' over the range of themes of his planning. Giorgio Ciucci's studies on architecture and the city during Fascism include an examination of the figure of the 'total architect', as postulated by Gustavo Giovannoni, which was pivotal to the schools of architecture at that time. He has also analysed the relationship between architecture and politics; the work of Sandro Fonti draws together the previous research with an analysis of the complete works of Pier Luigi Nervi.

Francesco Dal Cò, along with scholars from other institutes, was involved in organising an exhibition of the work of Carlo Scarpa. The exhibition, which was held in the summer of 1984, was a review of original drawings, objects and sculptures examined in relation to the artistic and architectural experiments of the period.

Some research tangential to the previous subjects has been carried out on the production of machines (that is, on the *Vitruvian machinato*) as well as on the status of their builders. On one hand, we have the study by Luigi Spezzaferro of the research laboratory at Ferrara; on the other, we have the more general investigations of Paolo Morachiello and Antonio Manno into the image of the engineer between the fifteenth and eighteenth centuries. Both these studies contribute to an understanding of how the 'mechanical arts' were structured as 'practical sciences'.

However, the history of architecture is inseparable from the history of styles, aesthetics and representations, just as the work of the historian is indissociable from all kinds of written, drawn or built documents. For this reason research into the history of theoretical and aesthetic thought and the history of techniques and methods of representation are indispensable. From the history of theoretical and aesthetic thought emerge two substantial and ready-structured concerns: one aims to understand the re-emergence of myth in the literature of the modern age, the other attempts to further the knowledge of contemporary theories of representation and figuration.

Studies carried out by Franco Rella indicate that the revival of mythical themes is not as significant in those areas where it is most obvious (that is, in philosophy, poetry, writing and art), as it is in attempts to establish a 'knowledge of the possible' through images and narrative structure. The resurgence of myth in the work of D'Annunzio and other 'decadent' writers is interesting, but more interesting, if less obvious, is the attempt made by Kafka to explain the world 'through the events of the plot', or mythical peripetia. Research in this area implies new reflections or, rather, reconsiderations of the *mythos*; the narrative in which Aristotle recognised a knowledge of the possible, making it 'more philosophical' than the historic knowledge of *de facto* states.

The subject of the research by Massimo Cacciari (with the collaboration of Giorgio Frank) is not literary texts but the figure itself. Their work is not simply a matter of analysing the sign-meanings of the artistic expressions of the twentieth century (line, point, colour etc) but of defining their actual symbolic importance. This leads to a search for origins and these are clearly visible in eighteenth-century romantic experiments (the development of *Farbenlehre* can be followed from Goethe to Schopenhauer through Impressionism up to Kandinsky and Klee). The reconsideration of such theories has a double purpose: first, to free the analysis of the so-called avant-garde from semiological reductivism or, worse still, historicist-sociological patterns; second, to show how it is possible to establish clearly defined equivalencies and isomorphisms between theories of representation and key problems in contemporary epistemological research. Contemporary research tends to deal with the fragmentary and the ephemeral. There is a need to understand how the work of the avant-garde is also the work of the builders of cathedrals. Research into representation therefore assumes great importance.

Massimo Scolari has chosen to investigate the history of axonometrics with the aim of filling a gap that is all the more sharply felt because it is in contrast to the extensive literature on the method and technique of the perspective. His work is set out in more detail in the following essay.

Giorgio Ciucci's research examines the theme of representation of space in architecture with particular reference to France in the first half of the seventeenth century and to Girard Desargues. Desargues had a clear commitment to the definition of a universal technical language for architecture. He also examined the use of projective geometry to represent technical operations such as the cutting of a stone in a clear, legible manner; and a proposal for a 'universal method' to draw up a perspective without vanishing points off the sheet of paper.

Renzo Dubbini's research also touches upon representation in a certain sense. However, he is concerned not with techniques of image building but rather with a system that made constant use of images—the scientific theatre between the sixteenth and the nineteenth centuries. From Guido Camillo's 'theatre of memory' through the scientific theatres (optical, automata, etc) of the seventeenth century to the 'panoramas' of the nineteenth century, the theatre has been the privileged field where things and their representations have met. Dubbini's

study occupies a position between a world of built objects (models, stage sets, optical devices) and modes of vision and representation. The scientific theatre emerges as an experimental laboratory, a potential arena of knowledge where machines, automata, mirrors, painted surfaces, light and shade offer a reduced representation of nature.

The refinements in photogrammetric techniques and interpretation are the main areas of interest for the department's photogrammetry laboratory, with research by Clement Di Thiene, Roberto Masiero and Paolo Torsello. Their general aim is to free the architectural survey from its use as an explanatory support for *a priori* critical theses and give it instead a scientific structure of its own. The laboratory has tackled a series of works of an extremely diverse nature. New surveys have been made of Raphael's Palazzo Alberini, Palladio's Rotunda, Scamozzi's Rocca Pisani, various Venetian *palazzi*, the great staircase of the Scuola Grande di San Giovanni Evangelista, the Palazzo Balbi in Genoa and the Sforza castle in Vigevano.

This research also carries over to the courses. A sample syllabus, chosen from many similar ones, follows:
*Science, architecture and civic life in Venice in the second half of the sixteenth century (1556-1612).*
In 1556 Daniel Barbaro published his Vitruvian *Commentari*. In 1612 Venice was freed from the Interdict and the Senate rejected a Dutch offer which would have given her a new trading structure. Between the two dates the Republic was torn by an intense debate—triggered by the *renovatio* of Doge Andrea Gritti—over the delicate relationship between power and knowledge.

The patrician class harboured Romanist and curialist factions with clearly oligarchical tendencies, but Barbaro's *Commentari* (on which Palladio collaborated) was the manifesto of a *scire per causes* aiming to break the organisation of the traditional Venetian guilds—to reform institutions on the basis of a new scientific awareness. In this sense, the architecture championed by Barbaro had a degree of contact with the new scientific vision emerging from Vesalius' texts on anatomy, Agricola's texts on metallurgy, and Zabarella's work on logic. Palladio's work in Venice between 1560 and 1580 can be interpreted as emblematic of the difficulties which such 'scientific' projects encountered. It is certainly no coincidence that Jacopo Contarini, friend and patron of Palladio, turned out to be a supporter of Galileo's acceptance into the Paduan Studio.

In the meantime, the constitutional crisis of 1582-83 took place: as a result, the 'young men' assumed power and Doge Leonardo Donà—supported by the theological and juridical knowledge of Paolo Sarpi—later challenged the papacy. However, the political advances of the years of the Interdict were to be negated. In a last flicker of life, Venice was preparing to outlive herself.

This course will cover this series of events, building upon the historical points of contact where political, economic and artistic events came together: Palladio's activity in Venice and its territory will be interpreted in the light of the development of architecture as an 'absolute' discipline, while the link between science, art and institutions will be considered using as examples the actions of the Accademia della Fama, the relations between Barozzi, Barbaro and Contarini, and the relations between Galileo, Sagredo and Sarpi.

The course will also examine the conflict between the last phase of Jacopo Sansovino's activity in Venice and the work of Palladio, the plans of Alvise Cornaro for the drainage and restructuring of St Mark's basin, the discussions regarding the Rialto bridge and the fabric of the bridge itself, the early years of Vincenzo Scamozzi, Cristoforo Sabbadino's plan for Venice (1557), and the building of the Fondamenta Nuove.

We do not wish to be like Don Giovanni's stone commendatore who, when invited to dinner, gave the bold, impenitent and genial creativity of the libertine (or the architect) short shrift; but nonetheless, we too have been intentionally rigid and severe. For the architect, history and its innumerable articulations are bound to seem like the stone dinner-guest: neither punitive, nor generous, nor existing solely for their own ends, but simply necessary.

MASSIMO SCOLARI, 'BEYOND THE SKY' 1982

# REPRESENTATION

# MASSIMO SCOLARI
## Elements for a History of Axonometry

**F**OR OVER HALF A CENTURY, ERWIN PANOFSKY'S *Perspective as Symbolic Form*[1] **has dominated studies of representation. A vast literature has discussed the theses** it contains, contradicting them or amplifying them, but never shifting attention from the main theme: central projection, or the perspective. To some this might seem justified, given the extraordinary importance of the Italian Renaissance in the history of Western culture, but the hegemony of the perspective has prevented consideration of other equally important modes of representation. Even a summary examination of the history of representation in the West will show how parallel projection has alternated with central projection at least twice within the past two thousand years. It can be found in representations on classical Greek vases, on frescoes in Pompeii, on Byzantine mosaics and in the Italian Renaissance. And it can be found in the return of the axonometric in the historical avant-garde.[2] Usually only one point of this alternating system is investigated, that of the perspective as arbiter of the relationship between the eye and the projective plane.[3] This text is intended to be an initial contribution to a history of the axonometric, a style of drawing which studies of the perspective always consider to be incomplete in itself, a mere precursor to the central projection of the Renaissance.[4]

## The Figure in the Proof

The use of parallel projection by Leonardo da Vinci and the unknown author of the *Codex Coner* during the perspective-oriented Renaissance is significant, for it proves the continuity of a mode of representation other than the pictorial 'view'. Although Da Vinci knew the laws of perspective perfectly well (to the point of transgressing them with the aerial perspective), he seems to have given precedence to the older system of parallel projection in many of his sketches. Parallel projection appeared in Western culture as early as the fourth century BC, and is the predominant form of representation in China. In times of transition it is often found together with 'convergent' projection as, for example, in Giotto's work around the time of the fifteenth-century 'rediscovery' of perspective. Da Vinci obviously did not use parallel projection because he was uncertain of other techniques or because he wanted a method that was 'quick', but seems to have chosen it because it was better suited to representing the *actual space of the object* rather than the object in space.

Whatever the case may be, the drawings of Da Vinci, Kyeser and Taccola go beyond the pure view of presentation because of their accentuation of mechanical-functional elements. They tend to straighten out the conical nature of perspective by retaining the parallelism and measurability found in Vitruvian orthogonal projections and wooden models, but use the very old tradition in a new way—*as the three-dimensional proof of functioning and buildability*. This is an effect that could not be achieved with the perspective, and by the time construction had begun on the great sixteenth-century worksites, Vitruvian *iconographia* and *orthographia* had regained their primacy in architectural drawing.

Alberti and Piero della Francesca had already formulated the theoretical and technical code of the perspective by the beginning of the sixteenth century, but there is no explicit mention of parallel projection in any Renaissance text before the second half of the sixteenth century. However, Luca Pacioli[5] and Niccolò Tartaglia[6] used it widely for proofs in solid geometry. Oronce Finé went even further, reproducing on the edges of his oblique figures the *metrie* (measurements) from which *axonometrics* took its name three hundred years later.[7] It is almost as if it had been given by nature as the only way to work out geometric proofs exactly. In geometry, to the detriment of the perspective's 'realism', the plane and solid figures must remain object-like and retain as far as possible the quality of resemblance. The problem of using the perspective for geometrical proofs was summed up by Descartes: 'In following the rules of perspective, we often represent circles and squares with lozenges rather than with other squares... so that often, in the name of making more perfect images and better representing the object, we draw things that do not resemble them at all.[8] Only Desargues' invention of projective geometry was able to transport the oval back into the realm of pure geometry as the 'conic section'. But applied geometry still maintained its pre-perspectival status while the perspective grew in figurative and technical stature. In almost all the texts concerned with solids or their proofs, oblique parallel projections appear alongside the classical *iconographiae*.

At the end of the first half of the sixteenth century geometry was not the only field that demanded more accurate possibilities of representation. As a result of the need to give workmen clear instructions on the cutting of timber and stone, Philibert de l'Orme wrote a treatise and the literature of stereotomy was begun.[9] Cosmography once more

FRAGMENT OF A TARENTINO BOWL, 4TH CENTURY BC

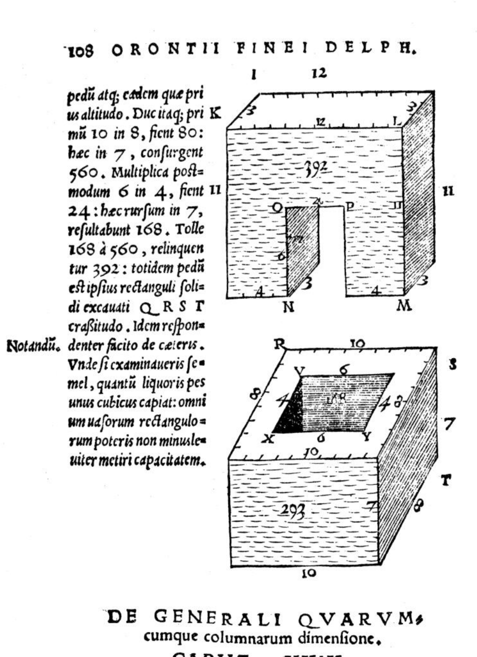
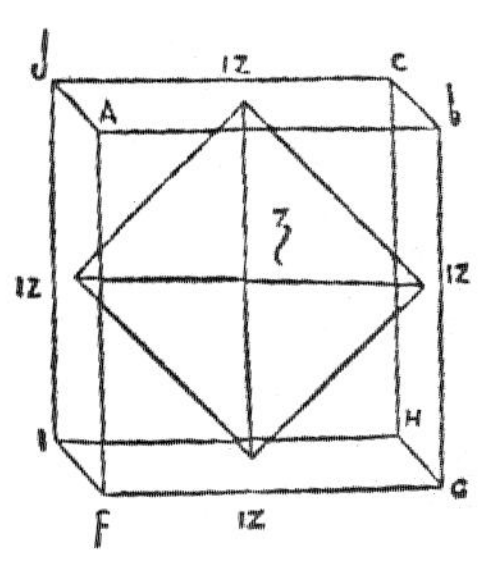
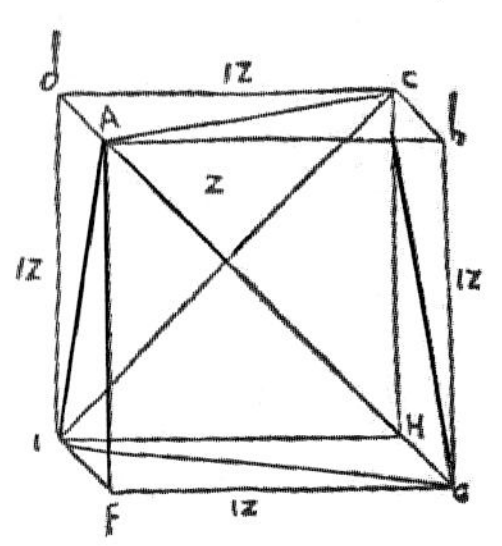
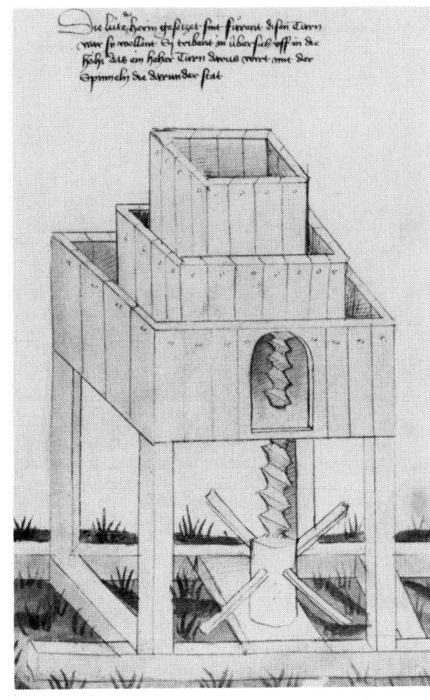

LEFT TO RIGHT: KYESER, BELLIFORTIS, 15TH CENTURY, LUCA PACIOLI, DIVINA PROPORTIONE, VENICE 1509, ORONCE FINE, FROM THE BOOK OF PRACTICAL GEOMETRY, PARIS 1567

adopted Ptolemy's applied geometry and produced the famous Mercator projection. And military architecture broke away from the tranquil Renaissance perspective, because it demanded a rapid measurability which the technique could not give.

**The Military Perspective**

After 1550, the theme of war was no longer a part of general treatises but a literature on its own. New techniques of war and the 'Turkish syndrome' stimulated the pursuit of impregnability. Dozens of treatises on fortifications offered the warring princes of Europe the secrets of an architecture whose only ornament was its geometric impenetrability. It was no longer a question of designing ideal fortresses, but of building efficient bulwarks in the defence of kingdoms and principalities. The nobleman Diego Gonzales de Medina Barba, for whom defence was *catolicamente permetida*, pointed out that the precision of the drawing was vital because 'an imperfection of a line could mean the loss of an army.'[10] Traditionally great architects had devoted themselves to these defensive works and now a new class of experts, the soldier-engineers, joined them. The soldiers contrasted the practice of war with theoretical projects, and saw no sense in seductive perspectives. The dogged march of death made rapid descriptions necessary. A bullet's lethal trajectory had to be measured with the same precision as the bulwarks built to deflect it. The *ars mechanica* of war, like applied geometry, used techniques other than the perspective.

In 1564 a work explicitly contrasting parallel projection with Renaissance central projection was published.[11] It was the result of a collaboration between the King of France's Superintendent of Fortresses, Jacomo Castriotto, who was killed at Cales shortly before the work's publication, and his friend Girolamo Maggi, who met the same fate ten years later at the hands of the Turks at Famagusta. They said: 'No one should expect to see in these works the methods or rules of the perspective; firstly, because it is not part of a soldier's profession to produce them, and secondly, because the foreshortening involved would remove too much from the plans, whereas the entirety of these works lies in such plans and outlines as shall be called *perspectiva soldatesca*.'[12] The woodcuts which accompany the text are perfect military axonometrics, despite the fact that they are improperly defined as perspectives: for almost three hundred years, all English and French works continued to call oblique parallel projection 'perspective',[13] flanking the word with adjectives stressing simplicity and practicality to differentiate it from the other method.[14]

Lorini called it the 'more common perspective,'[15] describing it in this way: 'Such perspectives have to show their own height from close-to; thus they are all formed of parallel lines both for the height and the width of any building whatsoever, though placed perpendicular to its plane...drawing the lines so that they fall perpendicular and remain parallel to infinity.' In his original proposal for a soldier's dagger-ruler[16] Bartolomeo Romano described a spherical perspective in which the 'measured parts shall give the right distances, which the oval form would not do because of the foreshortening its parts produce.' And Giovan Battista Delici, who was firmly convinced that 'speculation is part of the soldier's art,' used parallel representation because 'we need to see the thing whole, distinct, clear; one can find the truth precisely with compasses.'[17] He favoured the axonometric over the perspective because in war 'one single view does not serve, since the whole has to be shown.'

Treatises written over a fifty-year period attribute primacy in the actual design of fortresses to the military perspective. Jacques Perret de Chamberry wrote an elegant treatise (dedicated to King Henry IV of France, who entered Paris triumphantly in 1594) in which almost all of the 54 plates engraved by Thomas de Leu are military perspectives. By this time the procedure seems to have been taken so much for granted that Perret restricted himself to explaining how one could obtain all the measurements on the plane and in perspective by simply keeping the compass *sur l'echelette*.[18]

With the outbreak of the religious wars of the seventeenth century, writing on the military and perspective was dominated by the Minims and the Jesuits, great confessors to kings and princes, who sensed its political and cultural importance. Renaissance perspective survived in that bloody and colourful century by progressing from the mystery of the anamorphosis of Père Niceron, *La perspective curieuse...*(Paris 1638), to Padre Pozzo's solid treatise, *Perspectiva pictorum...*(Rome 1693-1700). At the same time it was seized by *l'esprit de géométrie* and incorporated into mathematics. This paved the way for the technical legitimisation of parallel projection, which became the accredited status of representation for engineering matters.

**Vision and the Fundamental Principle of Parallel Lines**

Although it is relatively easy to follow the application and perfection of parallel projection in the course of the sixteenth century and to speculate on its continuity from the vase-painting of Magna Graecia through Byzantine mosaic art to late-medieval painting and beyond, it is not so easy to locate its theoretical and technical beginnings. If we accept Panofsky's thesis, we can easily understand the birth of the

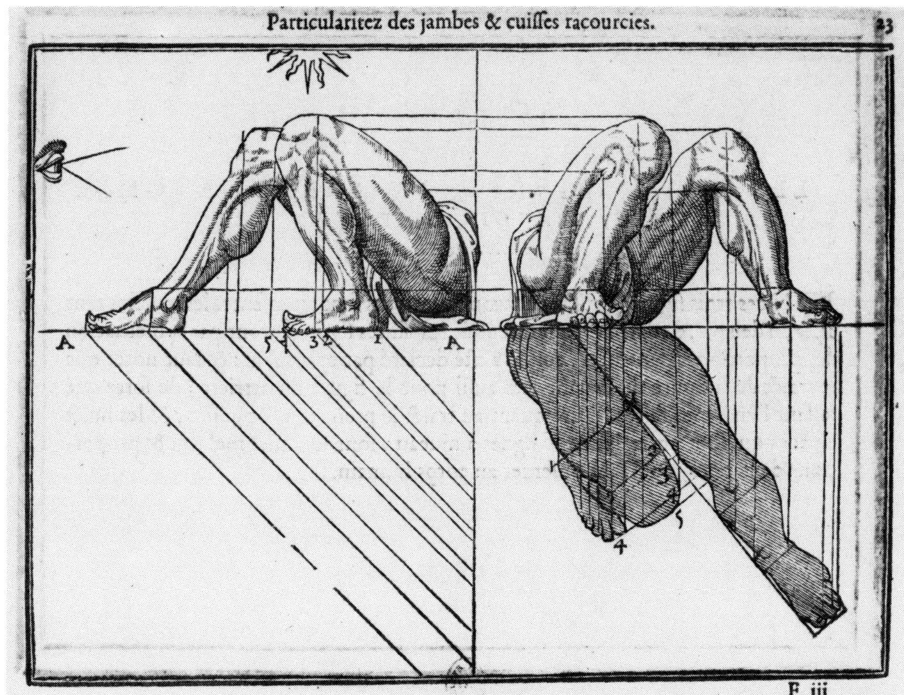


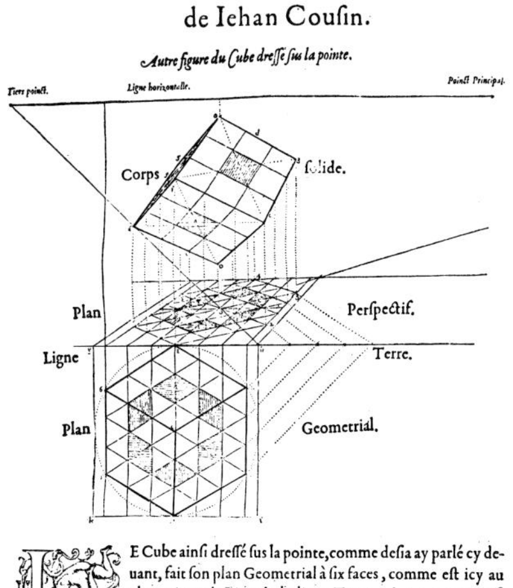


LE Cube ainsi dressé sus la pointe, comme desia ay parlé cy deuant, fait son plan Geometrial à six faces, comme est icy au
plan mis au dessouz de la ligne Terre, 1. 2. 3.4.5. 6: & aussi
party des sections Geometriques, comme pouez voir en ce
quarré Geometrial, merqué g.h.i. k, reduires le Perspectif en
la maniere cóme les reigles cy deuant mises le demonstrent,
& le corps solide du Cube, esleué sus la platte forme Perspectiue, merqué des
mesmes lettres & chiffres, cóme le Geometrial & Perspectif facillement & ayse-
ment vous le fera entendre, comme pouez voir par ces petites lignes punctees,
prenants leur origine du plan Perspectif, lesquelles estants si bien concatenees
peuuent parler, seullemét à les voir, encor' mesmes qu'il n'y eust aucune description & traité fait.

P iij

LEFT: JEAN COUSIN THE YOUNGER, BOOK OF PORTRAITURE, PARIS 1571. RIGHT: JEAN COUSIN THE ELDER, PARALLEL ORTHOGONAL PROJECTION OF THE CUBE, PARIS 1560

Renaissance perspective, but the problem is more complicated for parallel projection: its constant presence in the ancient world obliges us to go back many centruies with little hope of finding written sources to enlighten us. All we can do is start from the Renaissance perspective and see if its nucleus has any residual elements which can lead us backwards, any cold and obsolete remains of the stages it replaced.

If one frees perspective from all of its 'symbolic' aspects, all of its 'soft' parts, what remains immediately sends us back to Euclid's optical and geometrical formulations. Of particular interest are his theory of vision, which was contradicted by the School of Democritus (although it later played a very important part in Renaissance perspective), and the V-postulate of parallel lines, which D'Alembert called 'the scandal of geometry.'

Let us consider the theory of vision first. Euclid explained the mechanism of vision by saying that visual rays sent out by the eye form a 'visual pyramid'. This theory was not fully accepted by the Latin tradition until the end of the fourteenth century, when optics freed its body of disciplines from all metaphysical and physical intrusion. Significantly, Euclid's mechanism was unknown in the Chinese world, where oblique projection was the only form of representation.

Franco Alessio[19] showed that the application of geometry to optics in the Latin tradition took place within a period of two hundred years starting with the Oxford School of Robert of Lincoln at the beginning of the thirteenth century. The various works on perspectives which flourished at that time favoured the Arabic formulations of the tenth and eleventh centuries, especially those by Al-hazen and Al-kindi, over the optics of Euclid and Ptolemy. The works of Roger Bacon and Witelo concentrated on the psycho-physiological theories of the Arabic School and left aside the more abstract and geometrical Euclidean Greek School. Their interpretations gave a philosophical and gnoselogical significance to the Arabic texts, which were basically scientific in character. Perspective stopped being merely a *science* and became the *science which was the door and the key to all sciences*. In this way *lux* (light) became 'the original essence of the created being, the truth and the reason of the unity which produces space and time.' *Lux* 'summed up within itself the supreme condition of all physical events.'[20]

The theological consequences of this position are easy to deduce, and reference may be made to Alessio's essay for more on the subject. What concerns us is its influence on pre-Renaissance 'oblique' representations. Al-hazen maintains, in the second book of his *Thesaurus opticae*,[21] that knowledge of the world is not determined by Euclidean visual rays but by rays emanating from things and carrying the qualities of the *species* to the eye. In *De Multiplicatione specierum*, Roger Bacon claims that 'the universe from each of its points radiates influences in all directions, rays and *species*, so that each point is *per se* an active centre, a sort of eye sending *species* over the entire universe and receiving them from the entire universe.' No human eye orders this world, for it is composed of an infinity of radiant points where space, to use an expression of Proclus, is nothing more than 'thinner light'; it is not anthropomorphic, it has no privileged points but only *directions*. In this view of the world, neither convergent representation nor even the idea of a point of conjunction of the visual rays was possible. Biagio Pelacani da Parma removed any remaining doubts about the matter in *Quaestiones*, which he wrote around 1380. He explains that the system which Renaissance perspective replaced was not ordered by sight. Its visual rays did not concur at the same point and therefore remained parallel, like the rays of the sun.

The discovery of perspective brought the Euclidean visual pyramid once more into the centre of representation and blocked all theorising about parallel projection for almost a hundred years. But, as with the military perspective, it was the problem of measuring that caused parallel projection to be reconsidered in the middle of the sixteenth century. This time the subject was not the metaphysical *lux* of thirteenth-century perspectives but rather the 'physical' light of the sun created by God.

In 1551 Oronce Finé[22] once more took up the gnomonic tradition and linked shadow indissolubly to measurement. He observed that 'if the said shadow of the sun is precisely at 45°, then all shadowy bodies are equal to their shadows whether right-side round or reversed.' A few years later, Gemma Frizon explained how to 'find the height of anything by its shadow' and observed that when the sun is at its zenith 'the shadows of all objects are equal to those objects.'[23] Thus both the plan and the elevation could be measured by shadows, but for the measurement of the elevation, the projection of the sun's rays had to occur obliquely. This oblique shadow is nothing other than the oblique axonometric representation of the body which, at 45°, takes the form of isometry ('cavalier' axonometry).

Before these observations could be reflected in representation, two mathematicians—Guido Ubaldo del Monte and Francois d'Aguillon—had to sweep the field clear of all perspectival prejudice. Del Monte, in his commentary on Ioanne de Roja's *Planisphere*, pointed out how

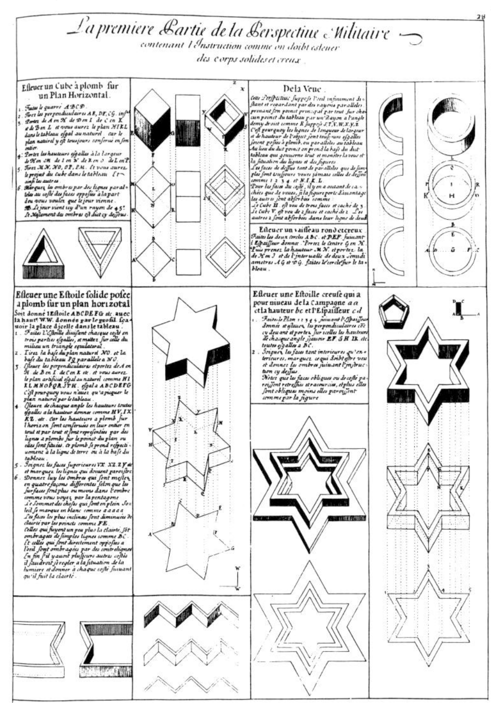

T LUDERS, MATHEMATICAL TREATISE, PARIS 1680

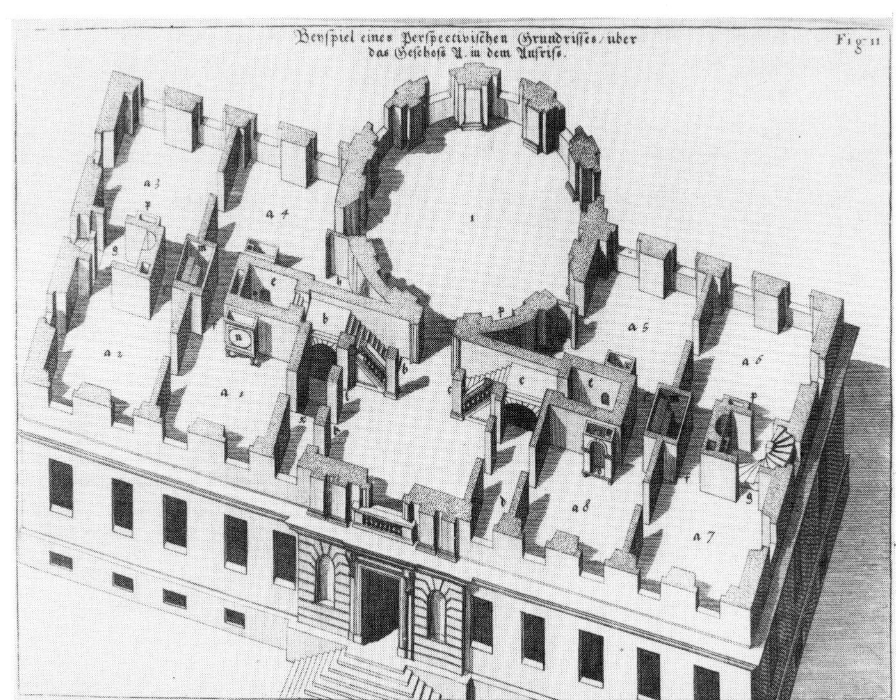

L CH STURM, CIVIL BUILDING, AMSTERDAM 1699

the author avoided explaining where the eye must be placed while at the same time deducing everything from the perspective; while his master, Gemma Frizon, claimed that '*oculos in infinitum (si fiera potest) abistat.*'

It is clear at this point that parallel projection has nothing to do with perspective even if the eye, at an infinite distance, remains the causal centre of representation. In perfectly describing the isometric projection of the cube in a hexagon (which Cousin had already drawn in 1560)[25] d'Aguillon talks of '*Orthonograficae proiectiones*' as being that method '*in quo oculos a re infinitae abesse supponitur*' and which can be applied not only to the celestial sphere '*sed etiam aedificia quaecumque libuerit describenda occurrunt.*' But he also claims that '*in orthograficis proiecturis radios ducere convenit parallelos*' and since they '*numquan concurrunt... ac proinde in orthograficis proiectionibus radii paralleli ducendi sunt, nulla habita oculi ratione.*'[26]

Thus the way was definitively opened to the reaffirmation of parallel projection as conceptually different from conical projection. In 1625 Pietro Accolti wrote a book with the significant title *Lo inganno degli occhi* (The Deception of the Eyes) in which he applied parallel projection to the problem of shadow. The theory of shadow was resolved by casting light on a shadow and discovering that it was a representation. Accolti was concerned with the practices of painting and claimed that '...the evidence of the visual sense (to which painting alone is subject) teaches us that shadows are sent parallel to the plane...with the infinite distance of what is luminous from what is opaque...thus we are able to draw representations of any given body exposed to the 'eye' of the Sun exactly as the Sun sees it; whence we understand that the Sun never sees any shadow, and the surface that he looks at and shines upon and all those things that come into his sight are lit up, and conversely all other things hidden from him remain in shadow...Thus we see that the above-mentioned drawing, which represents the Sun's view, should be completed with lines and parallel sides and does not need perspective at any point.'

After almost two hundred years the circle was coming full round. Anti-Euclidean parallel projection was returning, not as an all-embracing metaphysical force, but as a means to measure the world and represent it. Indeed, in Desargues' projective geometry, all symbolic connotations were removed from the 'eye of the Sun' and parallel projection became the instrument of exact representation.

The second pointer, the question of parallel lines, must now be examined. In Renaissance central projection, the straight lines parallel to the plane of projection remained parallel by convention, as did the lines perpendicular to the ground plane. This maintenance of parallelism is what we might call the Achilles' heel of Euclid's *Elements*: it makes the opposite of the V-postulate a provable theorem. Proclus, who was the last director of the Platonic Academy in Athens,[28] was perfectly aware of this, and in his very fine *Commentary upon the First Book of Euclid's Elements* he wrote 'Even if the straight lines of the V-postulate get closer and closer the further into the distance they run, there is no sign of their meeting.' He still retained faith in Euclid's postulate, but not everyone shared it. Panofsky said, 'According to Kem and Wolf there must have been a controversy in Antiquity and the Middle Ages over the problem of whether parallel lines which run off into the distance coverge at some point or not.' Witelo's *Optica* in particular argued against the theory of the vanishing point, and Panofsky claimed that the concept of the vanishing point could not be fully expressed since the concept of limit was absent and was in fact not formulated until the beginning of the seventeenth century by Desargues. In reality, Witelo was against Euclid's theory of vision, but was not opposed to Euclid's geometry, which had nothing to do with the problems of representation. However, it is significant that Proclus' confirmation was followed by half a millenium of parallel projection while the confirmation *per absurdum* made by the Jesuit Girolamo Saccheri at the beginning of the eighteenth century led, unintentionally of course, to the non-Euclidean formulations of Gauss, Lobacevskii and Bolyai. And these theories were in turn taken up by El Lissitsky as a theoretical explanation of his pictorial conception, which was in fact perfectly Euclidean.[29]

As can be seen, the geometrical question of parallel lines penetrated deeply into the mechanism of representation and often affected its figuration. Parallel projection was used to detach earthly images from the human eye during the first thousand years of the Christian era, when the dawning spirituality of the religion was deeply imbued with neoplatonism. In Byzantine art, the glittering light of the gold background which projected the 'oblique' figures was cast onto the plane of the mosaic. However, these representations were used not only for their optical and geometrical effect, but also because they made it possible to interpret the opposition to Romano-Greek realism. This opposition had its roots in the thinking of the neoplatonist philosopher Plotinus (203-270 AD), but was also alive to the mystical and spiritual stimuli which united paganism and early Christianity.

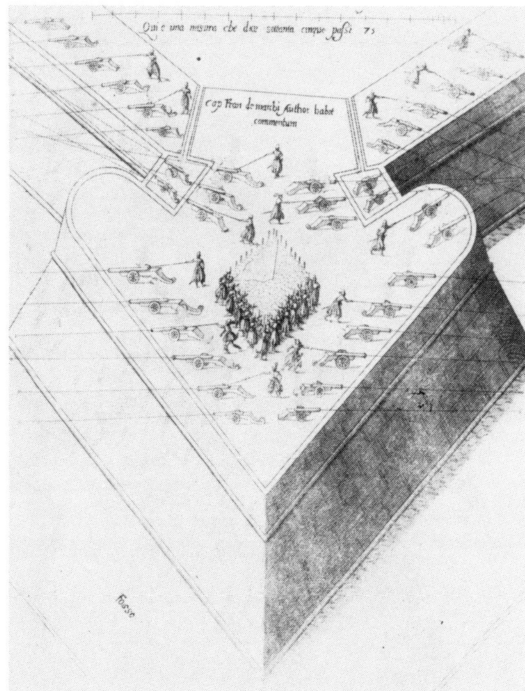

F DE MARCHI, ON MILITARY ARCHITECTURE... BRESCIA 1599

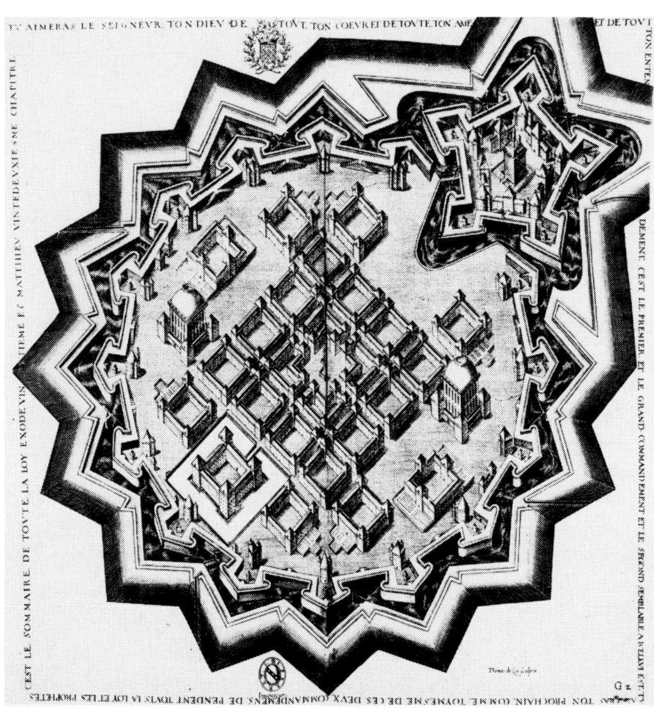

J PERRET DE CHAMBERRY, DES FORTIFICATIONS... PARIS 1601

## Plotinus and the Problem of Depth

The works of Plotinus were collected in fifty-four treatises and arranged in six *Enneads*, of which the first and the fifth deal with aesthetic problems.[30] For Plotinus the image was the reflection of the thing which, in accordance with the Stoic principle of universal sympathy, shared the same nature as its model. The purpose of the image was not merely to reproduce the appearance of the object but rather, on a grander scale, to allow man to know through it the Universal Soul, the *nous*, the Intellect. Yet the necessarily abstract images of art had neither to provoke mere aesthetic pleasure nor imitate the appearance of reality nor provide moral teachings. Plotinus therefore found it necessary to establish the conventions that today we call the statutes of representation. They stated that to achieve knowledge of the *nous*, the observer had to be acquainted with the physical nature of vision: only in this way was it possible to perceive the message of the work correctly. In considering the problems of vision, in particular the reduction of distant dimensions and the weakening of colour in distant objects, Plotinus claimed that the only view faithful to the true sizes and tones of colour was the one very close to the eye, which represented the object in its completeness. Only this view made it possible to see things in detail and correctly assess measurements and overall size. Distant objects were indeterminate and thus imperfect; all objects had therefore to be represented in the foreground, in the very fullness of light, with exact colours, in all their details and without shadows. This meant avoiding depth, since depth entailed shadow or obscurity and thus empty matter. According to Plotinus, the eye had to become 'equal and similar to the object in order to contemplate it...one can never see the sun without becoming similar to it, and a soul can never contemplate beauty without being beautiful itself.' This form of interpenetration was not possible with the 'eye of the body' but only with the 'inner eye'. The importance of this claim is obvious: when seventeenth-century optics correctly resolved the geometrical problem of vision, it found that the 'eye of the body' was only a channel of vision and that perception really began from the retina—*the inner eye*.

Similar arguments were put forward by mystics before Plotinus and by Christian theologians after him, but his claims are important because they were applied to the problem of representation. They implied the annulment of the space between the observer and the object, and thus the nullification of the point of view. Plotinus said that 'there is no point at which one can fix one's own limits and say: this is as far as I am going.' He claimed that perception 'clearly takes place where the object is...to see, it is necessary to lose consciousness of one's own being, it is necessary in some way to stop seeing.'

Plotinus' ideas did not have a direct influence on the painting of his day, but they certainly affected representation up until the Middle Ages. Their anti-perspectival characteristics, together with their breadth of philosophical conception, allow us to extend the symbolic scope of the limits which fourteenth-century optics put on fifteenth-century painting. At the same time it is worth pointing out that parallel projection should have avoided the formation of depth by avoiding convergence, leaving the Euclidean 'eye of the body' out of consideration. It would have then been possible to 'see' the geometry of real measurements and understand how the 'eye of the sun' was bound to represent it without shadows. Is the outside view not perhaps that 'becoming equal and similar to the object' which Plotinus described? From the fifteenth century onwards the *inner eye*, freed of its fixed mysticism and the symbolic insularity of painting moved to become the place of exact knowledge where measurement shatters the seduction of the gaze.

## NOTES

1 Erwin Panofsky, *Die Perspektive als symbolische Form*, Vortraĝe der Bibl. Warburg, Hamburg 1924-25.

2 In this connection, see the recent essays by Reichlin and Bois: B Reichlin, *Preface to Alberto Sartoris*, Zurich and Lausanne 1978; Yve-Alain Bois, 'Metamorphosis of Axonometry', *Daidalos*, No 1 1981, pages 41-58. The arguments that the two authors put forward on 'axonometry as a symbolic form' in connection with the historical avant-garde seem highly debatable to us. The use of the 'axonometric method' (Doesburg) is simply the signal for a different methodology and certainly not a new systematics. It should be remembered that although perspective was emerging as a symbolic form at the same time as it was being codified during the Renaissance, the axonometry that was 'rediscovered' in the 1920s had already concluded its course of scientific codification at least half a century previously. Apart from the studies by W Farish, T Sopwith, J Jopling, G Codazza and Q Sella, see the fundamental work by L J Weisbach, 'Die monodimetrische und axono-

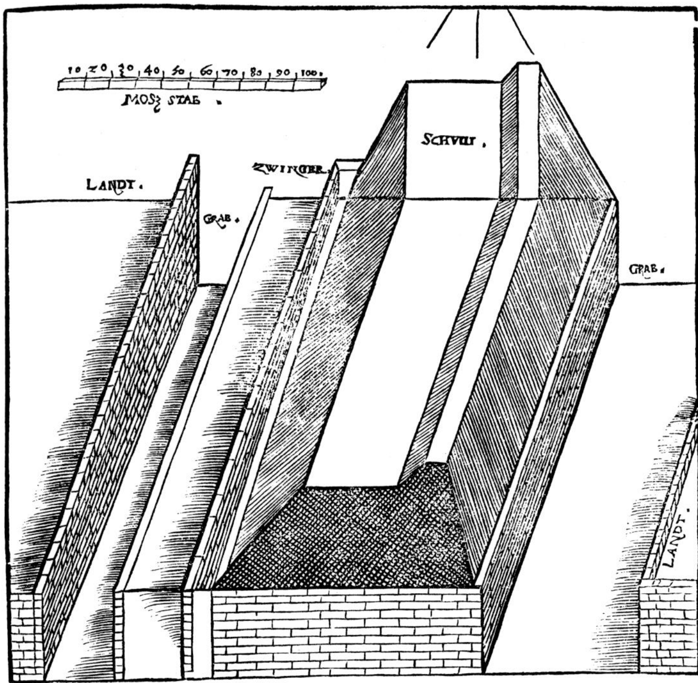

G MAGGI, J CASTRIOTTO, ON THE FORTIFICATIONS OF THE CITY, VENICE 1564

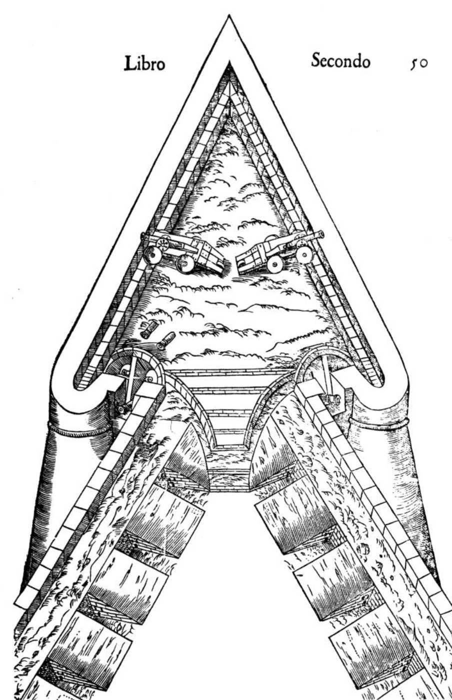



WALTER HERMANN RYFF, NEW PERSPECTIVE, NUREMBERG 1547

metrische Projectionsmethode', L Volz und Karmarsch, *Polytechnische Mitteilungen*, 1, Tübingen 1844. For oblique geometry see the definitive account given by K Pohlke, *Darstellende Geometrie*, Berlin 1860. The essay by Bois attributes the first geometrical explanation of axonometry to C Rieger's *Perspectiva militaris*, 1756, and does not take into account sixteenth-century treatises or the works of d'Aguillon (*op cit* note 26), J Du Breuil (*La perspective pratique*, Paris 1651, especially the chapter 'De la perspective militaire ou élevations geometrales', pages 161-171) or A Bosse, (*Traité des pratiques géométrales et perspectives*, Paris 1665, pages 65-87).

3  On the Euclidean character of visual space see the interesting essay by Mario Zanetti, 'La Géométrie du champ de regard et le postulat des parallèles', *Revue d'optique theórique et instrumentale*, 1, 1986.

4  This contribution constitutes the first summing up of the research on axonometry and the shadow directed by the present writer at the Department of Architectural History at the School of Venice. The publication of a text on the history of the axonometric is anticipated.

5  Luca Pacioli, *Divina Proportione*, Venetia 1509.

6  Niccolò Tartaglia, *Questiti et inventioni di...*, Venetia 1546.

7  Oronce Finé (Orontius Fineus), *Liber de Geometria pratica*, Argentorati, 1544.

8  R Descartes, *Dioptrique*, Leyden 1637, page 113.

9  Philibert de l'Orme, *Le premier tome de l'architecture*, Paris 1567. For a concise exposition of stereotomy up to the time of Guarini see W Müller, 'The Authenticity of Guarini's Stereotomy in his Architettura Civile', *Journal of the Society of Architectural Historians*, 1, March 1968.

10  Diego Gonzales de Medina Barba, *Examen de Fortificacion...*, Madrid 1599, page 5.

11  G Maggi and J Castriotto, *Della Fortificazione delle Città*, Venice 1564.

12  *Ibid*, Book II, page 43.

13  W Farish uses the term 'isometrical perspective' in presenting his 'invention which is none other than an isometrical orthogonal projection of the classic cube along the diagonal leading from opposite corners'. See: On isometrical perspective, *Transactions of the Cambridge Philosophical Society*, 1, 1822, pages 4-9. After Meyer called this type of projection 'axonometry' we find the same imprecision in successive treatises; J A Aldhemar, *Traité des ombres: théorie des teintes, des points brillants et de la perspective cavalière*, Paris 1874-75 and N Brithof, *Traité de perspective cavalière*, Paris 1881.

14  The term 'cavalier perspective' must almost certainly derive from the word 'cavalier' as L Marini defined it: 'a circular or polygonal elevation...which dominates the other parts of the fortress...like a man on a horse, a cavalier, who by virtue of his elevated height can survey all that surrounds him, *L' architettura militare di F Marchi*, Rome 1810, page 41.

15  B Lorini, *Delle fortificazioni*, Venice 1597, pages 32-34.

16  B Romano, *Proteo Militaire*, Naples 1595, page 104.

17  G B Belici, *Nuova invention di fabbricar fortezze...*, Venice 1598, pages 1-6.

18  J Perret de Chamberry, *Des Fortifications et artifices de architecture et perspective*, Paris 1601.

19  Franco Alessio, 'Per uno studio sull'Ottica del Trecento', *Studi Medievali*, vol 2, December 1961, pages 445-504.

20  Alessio, *op cit*, page 467.

21  Al-hazen's *Optics* was known in the Christian West long before the translation by Gherardo da Cremona in 1175. Neoplatonist in derivation, it took up the theory of Democritus' *scorze* in contrast to the Euclidean theory.

22  O Finé, *Le sphère du monde proprement dit cosmographie...*, Paris 1551, page 43.

23  Gemma Frizon, *Les principes d' astronomie*, Paris 1556, chapter 13, page 89.

24  Guido Ubaldo del Monte, *Planispherium Universalium theorica*, Pesaro (Pissauri) 1579, Book II, page 57.

25  J Cousin, *Livre de perspective*, Paris 1560. Page Piij. As far as we know, this orthogonal projection must be considered the first 'isometric axonometric' of the cube. The opinion of Loria is therefore important; he attributed this primacy to Kepler in the imperfect figure on pages 58 and 180 of Book V, chapter 1 of the *Harmonices Mundi*, Lincii 1619 (from G Loria, *Storia della geometria descrittiva*, Milan 1921, page 412).

26  Francois d'Aguillon, *Opticorum libri sex*, Antwerp 1613, page 503.

27  P Accolti, *Lo inganno degli occhi*, Florence 1625, page 143.

28  The Academy was closed down by Justinian in 529 AD.

29  El Lissitzky, 'Art und Pangeometrie' in *Europa Almanach*, Potsdam 1925.

30  Even from a necessarily different point of view, the considerations made here are broadly based on the interpretation made by A Grabar in his fundamental essay, 'Plotin et les origines de l'esthétique médiévalè', *Cahiers Archéologiques*, 1, 1945.

# MASSIMO SCOLARI
## Suggestions for an Exercise on Palladio
## Analysis of the Four Books of Architecture

**1 DRAWING IN FREEHAND, IN PENCIL, showing the twelve villas to a uniform scale of 1:500. The student should** proceed by copying the various complete villas one underneath the other, placing the paper vertically and leaving all the remaining free space to the right side free for annotations and sketches.

The twelve villas are described in the *Four Books of Architecture* and can definitely be attributed to Palladio. In the chronological order given by L Puppi, they are:

Villa Godi, Lonedo di Lugo Vicentino, 1537
Villa Pisani, Bagnolo di Lonigo, 1542-45
Villa Saraceno, Finale di Agugliaro, 1545
Villa Thiene, Quinto Vicentino, 1545-46 (partially built)
Villa Poiana, Poiana Maggiore, 1548-49
Villa Pisani, Montagnana, 1552
Villa Badoer, Fratta Polesine, 1556
Villa Cornaro, Piombino Dese, 1558
Villa Barbaro, Maser, 1557-58
Villa Foscari, Gambarare di Mira, 1559-60
Villa Emo, Fanzolo di Vedelago, 1564
Villa Zeno, Donegal di Cessalto, 1565

The first five villas were commissioned by clients from Vicenza, the remaining seven were built for Venetian noblemen. It is also necessary to know the other villas in the *Four Books of Architecture*, as well as the Rotunda and Villa Mocenigo, described as 'suburban' villas.

When copying from the *Four Books*, the student should point out any discordances graphically in the plan and elevation. The shading and cross-hatching

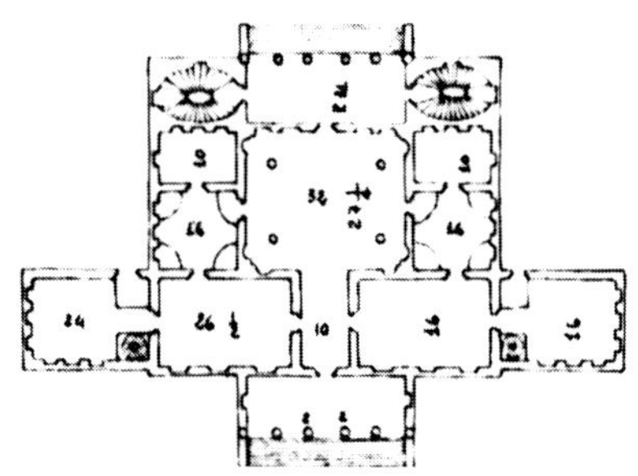

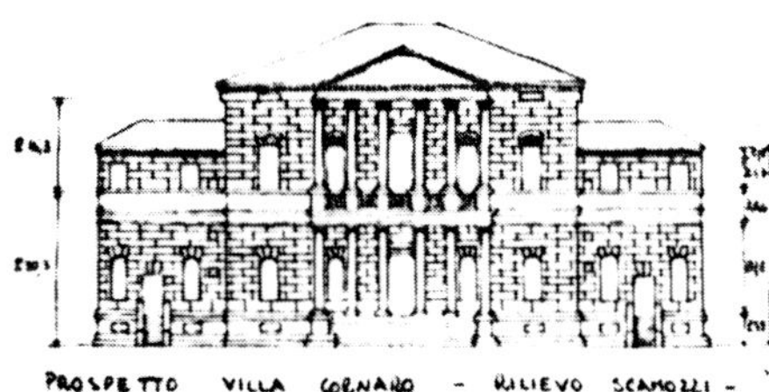


VILLA CORNARO, PLAN AND ELEVATION COPIED FROM THE FOUR BOOKS OF ARCHITECTURE COMPARED WITH AN ELEVATION BY SCAMOZZI

should be removed to make the plan and elevation 'clean', and the parts in section should be graphically stressed.

There are several possible ways to group the villas: chronologically, by patron, type etc, but the student should respect chronological order unless there are other carefully considered grounds.

**2** Comparative analysis of Palladio's drawings of Roman antiquities and studies for villas (cf Zorzi) with the copies made from the *Four Books*. This part of the exercise may be completed by finding and copying the typological precedents of the Palladian villa: the pre-Palladian mainland villas of the Veneto and the Venetian *palazzi* (here, the copies do not necessarily have to be 'clean' or to the scale 1:500, but may be done with sketches on comparable scales).

**3** a) Marginal annotations of the drawings in connection with the distributive and functional suggestions made by Palladio in the *Four Books*, in particular at the beginning of Books I and II. b) Copying of the proportional schemes described by Palladio for determining the height of rooms. c) Graphic comparison with Pythagorean-Platonic ideas of harmony (cf Wittkower). d) Examination of proportional schemes in Palladian projects with the help of surveys done by O Bertotti Scamozzi (1796).

**4** Study of the sources of architectural treatise-writing (these notes, in sketch or diagram form, must be placed in logical relation to the copies in the right-hand margin).

**5** Copying of Scamozzi's neoclassical survey and comparative analysis between it and the drawings

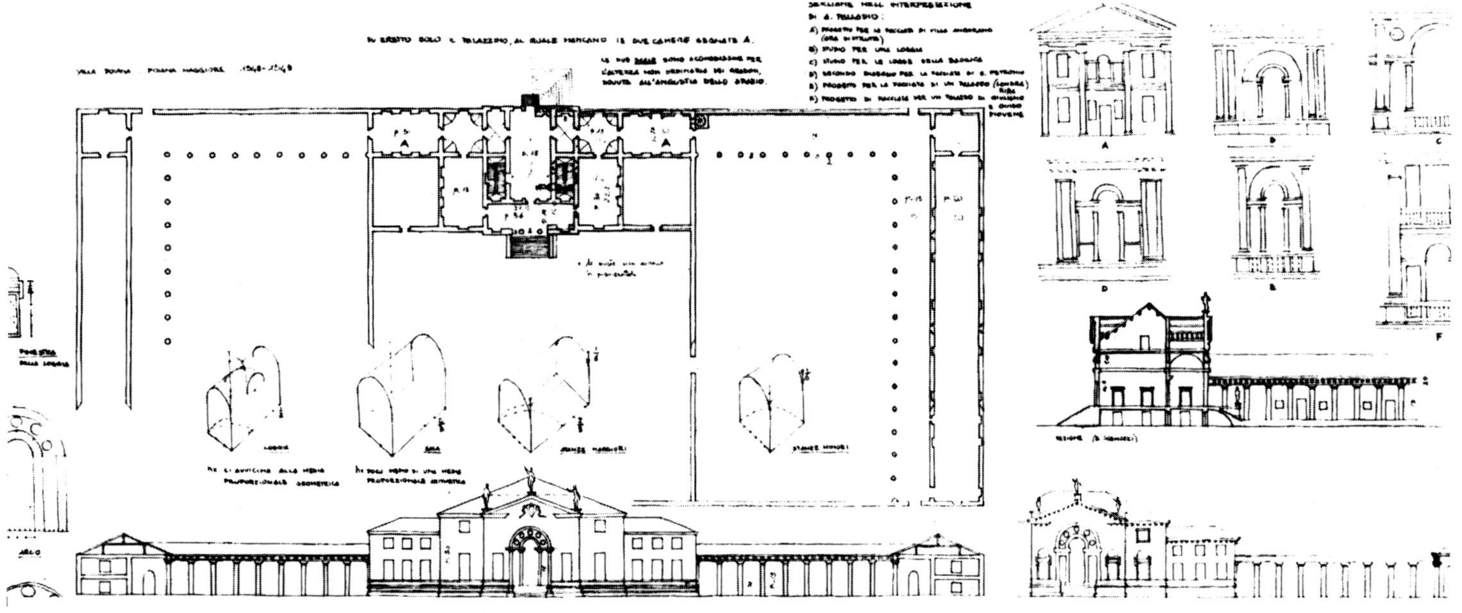

VILLA POIANA, EXAMPLES DRAWN FROM THE FOUR BOOKS TO ILLUSTRATE DIFFERENT SERLIAN 'TYPES'

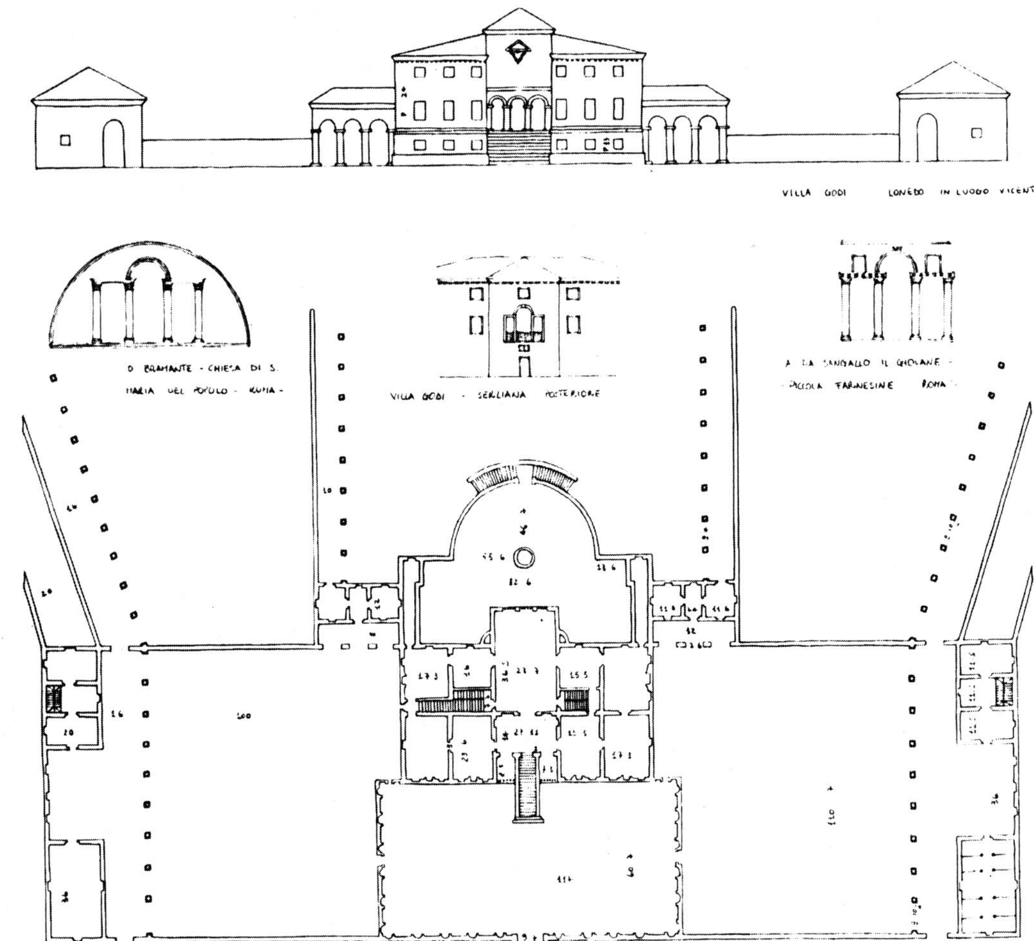

VILLA GODI, PLAN AND ELEVATION WITH COMPARISONS OF THE SERLIAN MOTIF

for the villas in the *Four Books*. In addition to allowing a comparison between Palladio's project and Scamozzi's survey, this analysis also leads to an initial understanding of the neoclassical interpretation of Palladio.

**6** Survey on site of one of the twelve villas and examination of all data gathered. A direct visit to the site of one of the twelve villas will enable the student to compare all the graphic material he has gathered and classified with elements taken from an examination of the villa as it appears today. The suggestions provided for the previous points may be developed in more detail for the particular villa under examination.

**Working Suggestions**

Each piece of work shall be carried out individually by the student. All the drawings must be in freehand, in pencil and 'clean', except where there is an indication to the contrary. The drawing paper is to be fine-grained and matt, with a precise format of 50 x 70 cm. It should be used vertically and on one side only. For exercises in the lecture hall the format is 50 x 35 cm. The use of ordinary wooden F- or H-type pencils is advised. The drawings of the villas should be done axonometrically, all on the scale 1:500 and details and references should be drawn on comparable scales. For the breakdown of the volume of the villas, axonometry, but no shading, should be used.

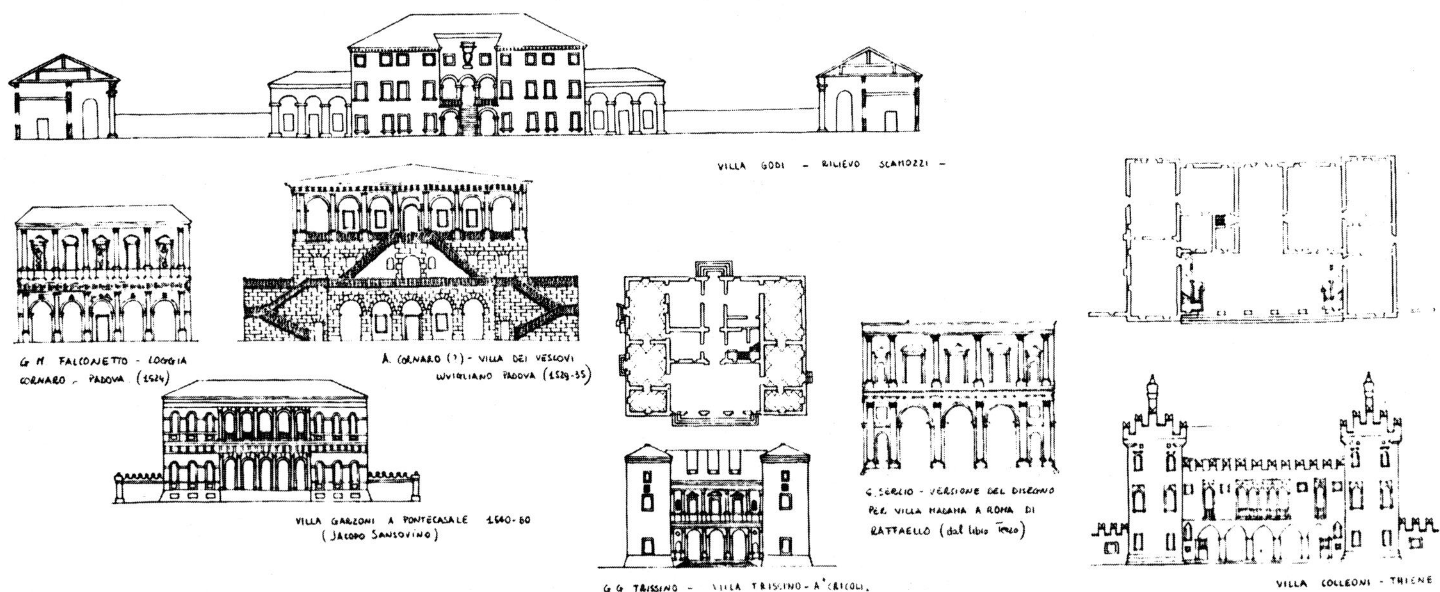

VILLA GODI, COPY OF A RELIEF BY SCAMOZZI, WITH COMPARATIVE STUDIES OF THE CENTRAL SECTION